Encyclopedia of the Dog

Encyclopedia
of the
Dog

General Editor
Richard Marples

American consultant
John Mandeville
Director of Public Communications
American Kennel Club

First published in Great Britain 1981
by Octopus Books Limited
59 Grosvenor Street, London W1.

This edition published by Crescent Books

© Octopus Books Limited, MCMLXXXI

Library of Congress Cataloging in Publication Data

Main entry under title:

The Encyclopedia of the dog.

1. Dogs. 1. Marples, Richard.
SF426.E56   636.7   79·23054
ISBN 0·517·30820·7

Produced by Mandarin Publishers Limited
22a Westlands Road, Quarry Bay, Hong Kong.

Printed in Hong Kong

Endpapers: Four fully grown Basset Hounds. Half-title: The soft expression and attractive coat and features of this Spaniel are some of the characteristics which make these very popular breeds. Title: The Finnish Spitz puppies are playing inside a cardboard box. This page: A lone sportsman and his dog move off over marshy land and water.

Contents

Foreword
by Walter Fletcher
New York Times
Correspondent on Dogs

At long last we have an all-inclusive volume that belongs on the book shelf of every philotherian. For here is a scholarly work that covers every aspect of the dog and will prove invaluable to the serious breeder and exhibitor as well as those millions who just own and enjoy a pet.

In my 50 years on The New York Times, the question I most frequently had to answer was 'What kind of a dog should I buy?' Had *The Encyclopedia of the Dog* been published at the time, it would have made life much easier for me, since I could have directed the would-be owner to this volume.

There is a thumbnail sketch of not only the dogs being shown in the United States and Britain but many others from around the world. To make it easy for the reader, the breeds are in alphabetical order – Affenpinscher to Whippet. Given the history and characteristics of a breed, along with its picture, in color, the prospective buyer should be far more knowledgeable, when it comes to actually making a choice of an animal.

Too many dog books have been poorly researched but the 11 renowned contributors to this opus have done their homework. We learn about the evolution of the *Canis familiaris*, how the earliest fossil finds of domestic dogs go back 12,000 years in what now are Iraq and Israel. Then there are studies in canine behavior, anatomy, genetics and an excellent chapter on ailments affecting the dog.

There's sage advice on how to choose a pup and once this is done, some good practical hints on housebreaking, grooming and feeding. Since Mr. Dog is strictly a pragmatist, whose main interest is getting the most out of life with the least effort, the reader learns how to train the animal to take its place as part of the family.

In baseball phraseology, this Encyclopedia touches all the bases. Whether it is hunting, coursing, field trials or obedience competition, it is all to be found in this indispensible guide, with in-depth coverage.

A dog is a great companion. Indeed, no other animal has such a strong devotion for man. In its loving, the dog doesn't care about age, beauty or wealth. It is unquestioning in both giving and returning affection. As Samuel Butler, the 19th century British novelist, wrote 'The great pleasure of a dog is that you make a fool of yourself with him and not only will he not scold you, but he will make a fool of himself too.'

In its 192 pages, with over 290 dazzling color photos and artworks, the Encyclopedia makes a real contribution to a more enjoyable and knowledgeable relationship between man and his best friend.

Contributors

Mr Douglas Appleton
Author and international championship
show judge.

Mr Stanley Dangerfield
Author and international championship
show judge.

Mr Bernard Hall
Author, breeder and kennel owner.

Mr Frank Jackson
Author, international championship show judge,
breeder and exhibitor.

Dr Peter Larkin, MRCVS
Veterinarian and author.

Mr Richard Marples
Publisher of Our Dogs magazine.

Mr Peter R Messent, MA, D.Phil
Animal behaviourist, researcher and author.

Mrs Pamela Cross Stern
Kennel and quarantine kennel owner,
international championship show judge,
breeder, exhibitor, and author.

Mr Michael Stockman, MRCVS
Veterinarian, past President of the British
Veterinary Association, member of the General
Committee and Breed Standards Committee of the
Kennel Club.

Mr Alan Walker, BSc, ARCS, PhD
Consultant on animal diet, Scientific Fellow of the
Zoological Society.

Lt. Cdr. John Williams
Past Secretary of the Kennel Club.

Introduction
by Richard Marples

The dog, *Canis familiaris*, the friend above all other animals of man, extolled in legend and depicted in art, has been a constant companion of human beings for thousands of years. Fossils suggest that *Miacis*, a small carnivorous animal, was numerous some 40 million years ago and that he was the ancestor from whom, some 30 million years later, emerged the forefathers of the present dog, although archaeological and scientific evidence has yet to prove with certainty the exact source. Certain it is, however, and sufficient for our purposes, that whilst a relationship with man has probably existed for a million years any form of selective breeding has been practised for but ten thousand.

Equally as uncertain as the ancestry of the dog is his exact historical relationship with man. Theories abound, but it is more than probable that his uses as hunter, guard and, not least, companion were swiftly recognised and developed. The exact processes of domestication will never be known but what more poignant reminder of the early association is needed than that of the recent discovery in Israel of the 12,000-year-old fossilised skeleton of a man with his hand on the head of his dog, which lies by his side.

It is from these early beginnings then that man has developed what we now regard as the pedigree dog – the result of man's selective breeding, from the genetic source of the dog's wild ancestry, generation after generation developing the most valuable traits for a particular purpose. Such was man's skill that eventually dogs were no longer bred entirely for utilitarian purposes. And so the evolution continues until today, when more than 200 breeds are recognised throughout the world, all of which originated for a particular purpose. Most of these very breeds, the distillation of countless centuries and all the relevant facts associated with them, are encompassed within this *Encyclopedia of the Dog*.

The number of pedigree dogs and the interest shown in them is ever increasing, and it is not only confined to their owners, in a wider search for knowledge and information, but equally to the prospective dog owner that this encyclopedia will appeal. The foremost authorities in their specialised fields, acknowledged as such throughout the world of pedigree dogs, have contributed to this work in a manner immediately comprehensible and practical to novice and established owner alike.

Every possible aspect of the dog – from its origins and evolution to its domestication and social history; from management and training to anatomy and breeding; from shows and trials to work and sport – are comprehensively covered. All this, profusely illustrated in colour, together with a description and photograph of each of 150 breeds, combines to give a greater insight into the nature of the dog.

1 | Evolution and Social History

The evolution of the dog as a species and the manner in which it became both a servant and friend of man took place over millions of years in response to environmental changes and the growth of human civilization.

Below: Children and puppies playing together.

Fossil evolution suggests that about 40 million years ago, during the late Eocene and early Oligocene periods, there flourished a small carnivorous mammal called *Miacis*. This small mammal, an offshoot of the stock which gave rise to all carnivores, is similar to the ancestors from which bears, raccoons, weasels, civets, hyenas, cats and dogs are all descended. During the mid-Oligocene period, *Miacis* gave rise to *Cynodictis* which, during the late Miocene epoch, over 10 million years ago, in turn gave rise to *Cynodesmus* and *Tomoritus*, forerunners of present-day canids. The evolution of the canid line then continued through the Pliocene and Pleistocene epochs culminating in the appearance of wolves, foxes, jackals and coyotes as they are today. While the evolution of the domestic dog is only very recent in fossil terms, the seeds of the association that exists between dogs and man may have been sown as man emerged in his present form, about 1 million years ago.

During the many years which it took the dog to evolve from a wild animal to one which lived in the closest relationship with man, adaptations occurred which altered its physical characteristics to changing needs in many ways. But man probably only began to develop any selective breeding of dogs at some time between 20,000 and 10,000 years ago.

At present the earliest fossil finds of domestic dogs date from about 12,000 years ago. One find from this period was in the Palegawra cave in Iraq, and another in northern Israel. There are several other dog fossil finds dating from about 8,000 to 10,500 years ago from such widespread sites as Idaho in the United States; Turkey; Staw Cave in Yorkshire, England; Maglemosian deposits in Denmark and at like settlements in Switzerland.

In spite of a growing body of archaeological evidence, it is not possible to say with certainty from which wild ancestor domestic dogs have evolved. Many scientists have made the attempt, but no-one has yet been able to support their theories with any real weight of scientific evidence. The great zoologist Charles Darwin suggested that two species – the wolf (*Canis lupus*) and the golden jackal (*Canis aureus*) – might have given rise to the domestic dog, with some degree of cross-breeding. Konrad Lorenz at one time supported this idea, and considered that certain breeds, such as the Chow Chow and Husky, displayed a high degree of wolf ancestry. The others displayed mainly jackal ancestry. Lorenz has subsequently altered his opinion on behavioural grounds, and now considers the wolf to be the ancestor for all domestic dogs.

R. I. Pocock, writing in 1935, suggested that four types of wolf contained the genetic information necessary to develop all modern breeds of dog. The fact that the modern dog is able to produce fertile offspring when mated to wolves adds weight to the belief that we need look no further for the ancestor of domestic dogs. The four types cited by Pocock were the Northern grey wolf (*Canis lupus*), the pale-footed Asian wolf (*Canis lupus pallipes*), the small desert wolf of Arabia (*Canis lupus arabs*) and the woolly coated wolf of Tibet and north India (*Canis lupus laniger*).

The more recent work of Richard and Alice Fiennes has tended to confirm this view and to mirror doubt on the work of those who seek to involve other ancestors on the

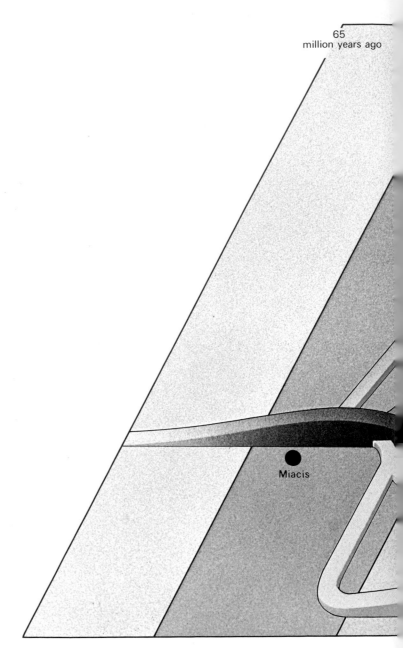

65 million years ago

Above: Dogs, like the other canids such as wolves, jackals and foxes, are carnivores, a group of meat-eating animals evolved from primitive mammals like *Miacis*. *Miacis* possessed the well-developed canine teeth and modified molars or carnassials for slicing flesh that typify carnivores today. Other primitive carnivores died out during the Eocene and Oligocene epochs and are not shown in this diagram, which traces the evolution of living carnivores. The origin of the domestic dog is still a matter for debate, obscured by the lack of archaeological evidence and confused by man's creation of many dog breeds, both in the past and today. However, it is widely accepted that the wolf (right) is the ancestor of the dog.

dubious evidence of a cingulum or an alleged difference in dentition. It is also possible that domestication from certain breeds of wolf might have happened in various geographical sites at around the same time, for example in North America, China and Africa as well as in the Middle East. This could also help explain some of the variations seen between today's breeds of dogs. It is likely that a desire to find an ancestor for our favourite companion other than the despised wolf is, in fact, based on nothing more than a lack of understanding of the nature of wolves.

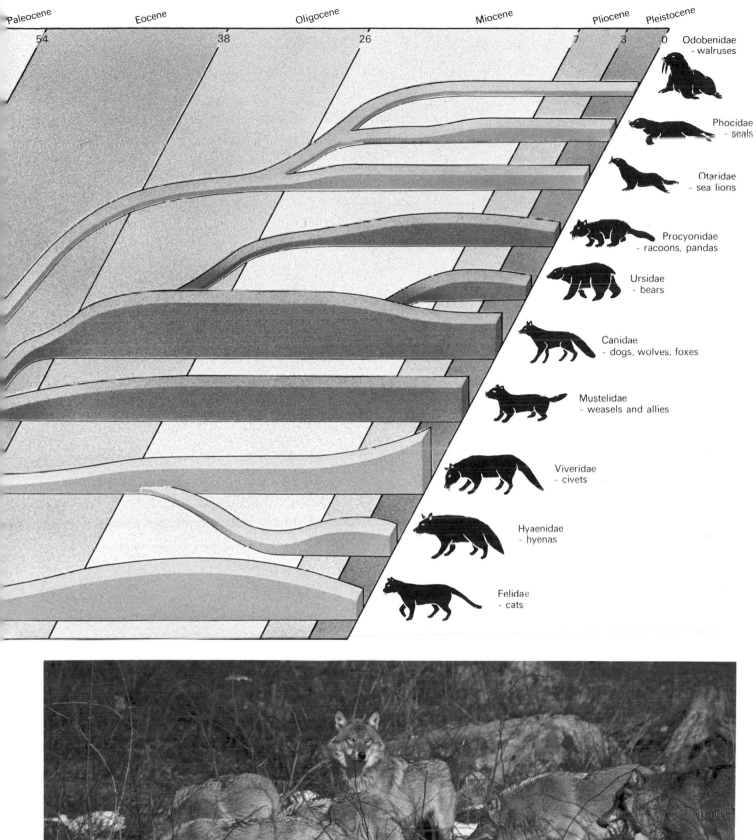

Paleocene   Eocene   Oligocene   Miocene   Pliocene   Pleistocene

54   38   26   7   3   0

Odobenidae
- walruses

Phocidae
- seals

Otaridae
- sea lions

Procyonidae
- racoons, pandas

Ursidae
- bears

Canidae
- dogs, wolves, foxes

Mustelidae
- weasels and allies

Viveridae
- civets

Hyaenidae
- hyenas

Felidae
- cats

Just as the exact ancestry of the domestic dog is uncertain, so too is the nature of the relationship between man and dog at the start of domestication. There are several theories for this, and it is possible to describe hypothetical scenarios to illustrate them.

A first theory is that dogs were originally used by man to help with hunting. At close quarters, man was physically no match for many of the animals with which he had to compete for food, and was no match for them as a hunter either. However, by throwing sticks and stones from a distance he was fully able to drive other animals from their kills, and thereby to enjoy the benefits of their skills and hunting prowess. Often the animals on which he might scavenge for food would be wolves, which deprived of their hard-won dinner might remain close until man had satisfied his hunger. Perhaps by the training of orphaned wolf cubs man might have employed the hunting skill of wolves more directly.

From that beginning a much closer relationship might have developed. Wolf and man had in common with one another a social system based on the family, as adult wolves retained contact with their offspring long after the cubs were fully grown and able to live independent lives. This social system made a degree of organization necessary. Leaders emerged and the rest of the family responded to this leader. Sharing a common social organization gave man and wolves the ability to recognize in one another abilities which could be used to mutual advantage, and meant that wolves would respond to man's leadership.

A second possible theory behind the original domestication of the wolf is that man might at first have hunted wolves for food. This theory is not by itself very likely, since the wolf would have been a relatively scarce species compared with various herbivores such as deer. However, the killing of adult wolves would sometimes have left helpless young which in times of plenty might have been taken back as playthings for young children, much as today's children will bring up the young of wild species such as fox and badger from time to time.

A third theory for the domestication of the dog is that dogs were, right from the start, pets or companions rather than working animals. It is easy to see how children might have brought up wolf cubs as pets. It is perhaps more difficult to see why man should have apparently given hard-won food to support another species. Yet recent support for this theory was provided by a fossil find in Israel of the skeleton of a puppy with the hand of a man's skeleton resting upon it. This configuration was highly suggestive of a companionship relationship between man and dog 12,000 years ago. Thus perhaps the working uses of the dog followed from an understanding developed between young children and pet dogs that grew up with them in or close to their homes.

A fourth theory is that the benefit of early domestic dogs was for guarding rather than hunting. Their superior senses of sound and smell might have alerted man to danger threatening his campsite which he had not noticed, whether from wild animals or other humans. Perhaps this is why barking is a common behaviour in the domestic dog, but not in the wolf. This guarding could then have been extended to use with flocks of sheep and cattle since man soon domesticated these as well.

A fifth theory is that perhaps man did not actively domesticate the dog, but that a relationship developed on a mutual basis. It has already been described as to how man and wolf probably existed side by side since they were both hunters of similar prey. Perhaps the initiative was not just taken by man, but the wolf too learned to exploit food discarded by man, as well as hunting the rats and other species that might have lived on grain stored by man. Tamer individuals that were thought useful in keeping down vermin might have been tolerated and then befriended by man. The friendship would then have developed from this initial mutual understanding, leading to the dog as the worker and companion of today.

It is certain that the exact process of domestication will never be known. Probably the relationship built up through a combination of reasons, and it may have started in different geographical areas in slightly different ways. As time went on, the wolf offspring would live and grow in the closest possible association with man. They would learn to respond to his moods, and to obey his commands, while man too might have learnt from the inherent hunting skills of these partially domesticated wolves.

Right: The Assiniboin hunter with his two wolf-like pack dogs were photographed by Edward S. Curtis in 1926, and they show the relationship which is thought to be the basis for the domestication of the dog. **Below:** The map of the world shows the site of the first known domestication. Domestic dog then spread to Australia via Indonesia, to Africa via Egypt, to Europe via Turkey and to North America via the Bering Straits, an isthmus of land no longer present. These geographical wanderings may explain the different dog types.

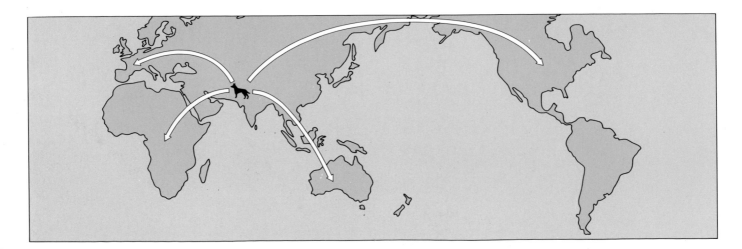

After the archaeological remains testifying to the close association which existed between dog and man, the next evidence of such a relationship is from Palaeolithic cave paintings in the Pyrenees, which show bowmen and dogs co-operating in a hunt. These dogs are invariably lightly built, long-legged with pointed muzzles and prick ears, very similar indeed to the wolves which then inhabited southern Europe but possibly possessing some differences which demonstrate that already man was beginning to select the dogs which best suited his purpose and that the favoured type differed slightly from wild stock.

In Britain the discovery in 1928 of the Windmill Hill dog in excavations at a Neolithic settlement near Avebury showed that the process of domestication and the effects of selective breeding were already well advanced in Britain as elsewhere in Europe about 5,000 years ago. At this time man was less of a nomadic hunter but was beginning to make permanent settlements and to farm the land. The development of this new way of life placed new demands on dogs which lived with him. No longer were they used exclusively as hunters, to track, hold and kill animals for man. Now dogs had to learn not to kill the cattle which man kept but to protect them from attacks by the wild relatives of these early dogs. Man now had possessions to be protected, a home, a stock of food, farm animals; and he expected his dogs to help him to protect this new life style. In return he gave them the means of a meagre existence to be supplemented as best they may by independent hunting trips.

As man became more prosperous he was able to afford the luxury of keeping dogs which were not able to hunt, to protect his flocks or his home. He began to keep dogs simply because their appearance or their temperament pleased him. Man had become a dog breeder and was able henceforth to produce dogs able to accomplish a wide variety of tasks. This was seen in the periods of some of the great civilizations.

During the zenith of the great Babylonian empire about 5,000 years ago huge Mastiff-like dogs began to be represented in the art of the period. These dogs were massive creatures with heavy wrinkled heads and curled tails. The massive quality of these dogs, probably used as guards or in war, is in contrast to the small, long-legged, short-backed and small-headed Windmill Hill dog just as they also contrast with the hunting dogs of the Assyrians some 2,000 years later. These fleet-footed Assyrian hounds are very similar to the ones found in Egypt and most often associated with that country, but they are quite unlike the short-legged, long-backed dog found on the Beni-Hassam carvings and dating from about 4,000 years ago. It can therefore be conclusively demonstrated that several thousand years ago dogs had diverged into a number of very different breeds which exhibited none of the more obvious characteristics of their wild ancestors. Despite this marked degree of physical adaptability the extent of mental adaptation which dogs had to achieve was much more impressive.

From this stage the way was open for man to use his growing skill at, and interest in, breeding animals, using the scope offered by the genetic pool available in the dog's wild ancestors to develop types of dogs which suited his particular purposes. As civilization developed man learned to appreciate appearance for its own sake. He also had the leisure to indulge in sporting activities. No longer therefore were dogs bred purely for utilitarian purposes. Some were bred for the novelty or beauty of their appearance or to provide companionship in the home, and so the breeds of toy dogs slowly began to evolve. Others were bred to chase game or to fight, either one another or other animals. Both of these were developments of existing valuable traits but the desire for sport produced types of hounds and terriers which had not previously existed. Then man, ever an aggressive animal,

realized that he could utilize the dog's loyalty and its desire to protect him to breed large and ferocious dogs which could be used in conjunction with his own armies, to harass his enemies as well as to protect his own army encampments and their supplies. From this source developed many of the massive guard dogs.

Then too a dog's incredible degree of adaptiveness and desire to please its master encouraged man to use the animal for many uses which arose as a result of changes brought about by a developing civilization. Such develop-

ment has continued to this day when many of the traditional uses to which dogs have been put have declined while some, thankfully, have become illegal. There is now no need for Comforters to attract the lice and fleas which would otherwise infest their owners. The need for Turnspits to turn meat cooking over an open fire has disappeared. The use of dogs as carriage animals is replaced by mechanical transport and civilized man no longer enjoys seeing dogs fight among themselves or with other animals. Nevertheless, our civilization has also introduced other needs which dogs willingly seek to satisfy. Their acute sense of smell, developed by selective breeding, is used in the investigation of crime and they have gone into space to test the survival of mammals in that alien world. Dogs are bred to guide blind people, and they can bring comfort and help to those whose mental state deprives them of the ability to make contact with their fellow beings. In very many ways they continue to contribute to the quality of our lives.

Left: The Bayeux Tapestry is just one of many illustrated pieces of evidence to show that man has bred dogs to suit his purposes for many hundreds of years. Dogs in World War I were used as Red Cross dogs, trained to find the wounded and carry medical supplies. Below left: By the eighteenth century in Britain breeding had reached a fine degree of excellence. The painting by George Romney shows the Countess of Albemarle with her son and two gun dogs. The ownership of such dogs would, at that time, be part of the accoutrements of wealth and social position. Below: Some of the many and varied breeds which exist today.

2 | Aspects of the Dog

It is essential to know as much as possible about your dog, from the way its body works, its patterns of behaviour, how to cope with illness or accident, to how much to feed a puppy and rear it successfully.

Below: A fine example of a healthy Beagle.

The dog's behaviour is well adapted to the needs of man. As a pet it has become man's friend and companion, and as a working animal it can be trained to perform a wide range of useful tasks. Unlike the cat, which seems to choose when to give companionship, the dog is unquestioning and reliable in both giving and returning affection.

The dog, like its ancestor the wolf, is essentially a pack animal. Pack behaviour can be seen if a group of dogs live together or come together for a period. They will stay close to each other and do the same type of things at the same time. Some individuals are dominant and an order of 'rank' is formed.

For owners the most important consequence is that the human family becomes the dog's pack. It is essential that the owner and not the dog is the one that dominates, otherwise the dog will give problems. If the dog is submissive to its owner it will give respect and affection and will learn, with training, to respond to commands. The dog is content in such a relationship, since to live in a pack is natural to it, and no disadvantage attaches to the fact that the dog is not the leader.

Since a dog is highly social it needs to learn how to live with others. Research in the United States suggests that this learning is confined to a brief period at puppy stage. It was found that the best time to remove a puppy from its mother and litter mates seems to be about six to eight weeks of age. The puppy will then become used to people and will still mix well with other dogs. If a puppy is removed any earlier it may become too close towards humans and be overly dependent. If puppies were left with their mother and litter mates and did not have their first human contact until they were about 13 weeks old or more, they could never adjust well to people. They stayed fearful, withdrawn and almost incapable of being trained.

The most important stage in the development of normal behaviour in dogs is the one just described. Before then the newborn pup shows only the most basic of behaviours. These have to do with feeding, keeping warm and sleeping, the last taking up about 90 per cent of its time. While awake the pup either searches for a teat, using swimming-like movements of its front legs to pull itself along on its stomach, or else it is busy suckling. Young pups will make a mewing call if in distress for any reason

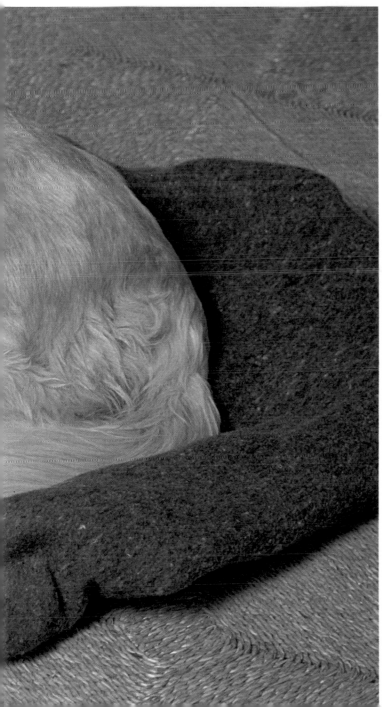

Dogs, like their close relatives wolves (top), adopt a pack leader, but for dogs man has replaced one of their own species in this role (above). Left: Puppies have to learn between the ages of 6 to 8 weeks to live with their human companions in order to complete their social education.

such as cold. Surprisingly, if the mother can hear but not see a mewing pup she will not usually respond to the call. She will, however, retrieve a pup if she sees it moving around some way from her nest.

In the first four weeks of life a pup's development is rapid. The eyes open at the earliest after 10 to 15 days and the senses of hearing and smell also improve about the same time. From about four weeks a pup becomes much more active and will start to play with its litter mates. This marks the start of the process when the pup learns to live with others. From the end of this phase, at about 13 weeks, behaviour changes little except that the puppy matures and becomes more responsive to being trained. The coming of adulthood is marked by a range of courtship and sexual behaviour.

The way in which a dog interprets the world is very different from that of a human being. A dog's sense of smell is far superior to man's and is evident in the way a dog uses its nose while on a walk or when investigating an object it has found. It is thought that its sense of smell is at least 100 times better than man's, and possibly more for certain smells.

The hearing of a dog is also superior to that of a person. Dogs seem to be more sensitive to some sounds, especially those at high frequencies. Hence the use of 'silent' dog whistles, audible to the dog but not to humans. This probably explains the ability of a dog to detect the arrival of a particular car, or the footsteps of its owner, well before these sounds can be humanly recognized. The moveable ears help localize the source of a sound since they can be directed towards it.

In vision the dog is inferior to man. There is some controversy as to whether dogs are colour-blind or not. They probably have some colour vision but it is not very good. Compared with a person, a dog has much less visual acuity and sees only moving objects well. At night, however, a dog sees better than a human being. The way a dog's eyes light up in the glare of car headlights is an indication of this. Light is reflected from a layer at the back of the animal's eye and passes twice through the light-sensitive retina, thus doubling sensitivity. They have better peripheral vision giving a larger visual field.

Communication between dogs is impressive. Sounds, body signals and chemical smells are all employed. Facial and body expressions indicate feelings. The eyes are also important. The stare, for example, is a threat signal usually given only by a dominant dog to a submissive one. If a person stares at a dog it will usually look away and become submissive, sometimes rolling on its side. Occasionally a dominant dog will respond aggressively to a stare. The way the ears are held is an important indicator of expression. Ears held back against the head show submission or fear. Erect ears indicate alertness. These expressions will almost always be combined with some from the mouth and lips as well as the body. A tail held high usually indicates alertness. A wagging tail probably indicates

Below: Although the German Shepherd Dog remains lying down, it has obviously sensed a welcome presence. The ears are pricked and have moved round in the direction of a sound and the nose has picked up a scent.

excitement, and a tail held low may mean fear or a position of submission.

Communication by body language is complex and confusion can arise since fear and submission, or excitement and aggression, both have components in common. Some breeds, by virtue of ear shape or lack of tail, are unable to communicate visually as well as others can.

The use of smell is very important. When two dogs first meet they usually smell each other's face and then their inguinal regions. Scent plays a significant part in territory. A male dog cocks its leg to mark prominent objects while out on a walk in order to mask the smell of dogs that have recently passed by. Scratching with the back feet, seen mainly in male dogs after defaecation, leaves a chemical

signal, known as a pheromone, from special glands between the toes. Faeces may be used as scent markers, and a dog has anal glands that secrete a mixture of chemicals. Dogs may sometimes roll in strong-smelling substances. The strong odour may give extra social status. A bitch in heat gives off special smells from the vagina, also present in the urine, which indicate her sexual status.

Sounds used include barking, whining and howling. Barking is usually done to gain attention and was probably originally encouraged for watch-dogs during domestication. Whining, often given when a dog is left alone, is a distress call aimed at the owner, hardly ever at another dog. Howling is probably a warning sound used to protect a territory.

Left: The graph illustrates the increased acuity of the dog's hearing compared to man's. A dog can hear sounds that are very much quieter than those to which man is sensitive.
Below: The dog has heightened senses of smell and sight compared with man. The nose contains complex bones, called turbinates, which provide a large surface area for the scent sensitive tissue that covers them. The Jacobson's Organ, which lies in the roof of the mouth, is an extension of this sensitive tissue or olefactory epithelium, and is used for analysing food in the mouth in a similar way.

Light falling on the back of the eye excites the sensitive cells of the retina causing nerve impulses to be sent to the brain. Light not absorbed on its first passage across the retina is reflected back by the tapetum, a structure not present in man. On this second journey more light is absorbed by the retina thus enabling the dog to make best use of available light and to see well in dim conditions.

The dog's senses of sight and smell

A dog is exceptionally playful, even once it has grown up. It uses a classic pose to start play, often called the 'play bow.' The head and front quarters drop to the ground, the hind legs remain upright and the tail is held high. This indicates that what follows will be play. It is important to communicate this because during play the normal relationships between dominant and submissive dogs will be temporarily abandoned. A dominant individual may sometimes fall on its side in a submissive gesture to a smaller dog in order to encourage play.

Play is first seen in young puppies of about a month, when play fights act as a rehearsal for adult behaviour. The exact function of play in adults is unknown. The continuation of this behaviour is probably because it has been encouraged by the dog's human companions during the period of domestication.

Some dogs may be called aggressive, but aggression is not a single type of behaviour. There are probably about eight varieties that may be exhibited by dogs, and all have different causes that can be isolated.

Predatory aggression or the catching of prey is seen when a dog chases a bird, a rabbit or even a cat. This type of aggression is never normally directed at humans. If a dog is taught to attack a person, as police dogs are, it is trained aggression and will not occur without a spoken command.

Territorial aggression is more commonly directed at humans, usually in the form of a threatening posture. A dog may defend its territory against its own species as well as people. This behaviour is usually seen in dominant dogs, or if the owner is absent for a period, when the dog may assume territorial dominance. Postmen may especially notice this. If they wear a distinctive uniform and retreat, the dog will be encouraged to threaten again next time in defence of its territory.

Fear-induced aggression probably accounts for many of the dog bites suffered by children. Some dogs, for example, are easily frightened by a child rushing up with outstretched hands. What is intended as a friendly gesture can easily be interpreted otherwise by the animal. Pain-induced aggression is similar, except that the dog reacts to a genuinely painful stimulus. Dogs that have been injured may therefore snap unexpectedly.

Some male dogs are especially prone to get into fights with other male dogs. This seems to have something to do with the male sex hormones. A mother protecting her puppies may sometimes be aggressive. This is comparable, if only because she is in a special hormonal state at this time.

The final type of aggression results from competition for something desirable, such as food or even affection from the owner. In the wild most competitive fights would soon be resolved by signals, such as threats followed by submission. With pet dogs, however, the protection offered by an owner to an underdog may interfere with the natural resolution of such conflicts.

Play and aggression have both been encouraged by the dog's human companions. Below: A classic 'play bow' which is used to start a game with a human or another dog. Below centre: The submissive roll is often used to indicate a desire for play. Below left: The sparring or play fighting by the Great Dane on the right is obviously not being taken seriously by its partner on the left. Right: There can be no mistaking this expression of aggression. Man has used this fierceness plus the dog's loyalty to its owner as a means of protection.

The male dog is always ready for mating once it is sexually mature. Bitches show cyclical sexual activity and average two cycles each year, although it varies. Males are usually sexually indifferent to a bitch, but they will be attracted to her when her body releases pheromones. She will refuse the advances of males for several days until she reaches the sexually receptive stage or a period of heat. The eggs are generally shed about the third day of true heat, but she will often continue to accept a male for a week or more after that most fertile time.

Dogs go through a courtship ritual before mating. It includes sniffing each other and play fighting. Finally the bitch will adopt a characteristic standing posture with tail held to one side, signifying acceptance of the male. After mating, the pair remain joined in the genital lock or tie with the dogs facing away from each other. This can last from a few minutes up to an hour or more.

The mating process takes longer for an inexperienced pair, and dogs that have had little contact with other dogs may have difficulties. The bitch is usually brought to the male. Since he takes the dominant role, he performs better in his own territory. Noise or disturbance can often distract a pair while mating. There is evidence of individual preferences, especially with the bitch, which may refuse some males.

The behaviour of the bitch undergoes considerable change in the course of pregnancy and lactation. Near the end of pregnancy she will often become restless and may roam around the house. This probably indicates her search for a nest site. She may also make digging movements, even at a solid floor, or may tear up paper or other material. She may also cease obeying commands.

Behaviour patterns associated with sex are many and vary from that of the male in search of an oestrous female to the instinctive maternal behaviour of the bitch when giving birth or looking after her puppies. Right: A casual meeting between two dogs will always result in a great deal of sniffing so that each can discover a great deal about the other. Although sniffing is a part of the sexual ritual not all such meetings result in mating. Above: The mother continues to care for her pup's hygiene long after birth, although the puppy has been weaned and is making exploratory journeys into the world.

Most bitches have relatively few problems at whelping and instinctively perform the necessary tasks. A bitch will lie on her side during labour and pups are born at irregular intervals with either head or breach presentation, generally about 20 to 60 minutes apart. Disturbance may interrupt the normal process of labour. After the birth of a pup, the bitch removes the sack enclosing it and then vigorously licks it. She then bites through the umbilical cord and eats the after-birth. She may even continue to lick still-born pups until they get cold.

After the birth of the pups, most mothers stay in the nest with them, leaving only for brief intervals such as to feed. By the time the puppies are two weeks old, the mother may leave the nest area for periods of two or three hours. Lactation usually declines at about four to five weeks. At this time an unusual form of behaviour may be seen as the mother regurgitates food in the nest for her young. Such action is inherited from the dog's wild ancestors, when the mother used this method to bring back food she had caught away from the nest.

The skeleton of the dog is in two parts, known as the axial skeleton and the appendicular skeleton. The axial skeleton consists of the skull and the vertebrae that form the spinal column. The size and shape of individual bones may vary from breed to breed but the essentials do not. The skull of the Bulldog, for example, is thick and solid while that of the Borzoi is long and much less massive.

The neck contains seven vertebrae which are known as cervical vertebrae. The first (the Atlas) allows the head to nod up and down and the second permits the Atlas and the head to rotate. This second cervical vertebra (the Axis) allows the dog to turn its head on one side. The remainder of the neck vertebrae permit the dog to bend its neck and look behind much more efficiently than a person can.

Behind the neck are 13 thoracic vertebrae. They protect the spinal cord and support the ribs, which enclose the chest cavity or thorax. The seven lumbar vertebrae support the abdomen. They lead to the sacrum, which usually consists of three vertebrae fused together. The sacrum supports the pelvic girdle and the hind limbs. The

number of tail bones varies greatly according to breed.

There are 13 pairs of ribs. Those at the front of the chest are joined at their lower ends to the sternum or breast bone, but the final pair are not. The thoracic vertebrae, the ribs and the sternum form what is commonly known as the rib-cage, which encloses the heart and the two lungs. The rib-cage allows a significant amount of movement between the ribs themselves so that the lungs can expand and contract to permit breathing.

The appendicular skeleton consists of the two pairs of limbs, the front and hind legs. At its upper end the front leg has a triangular-shaped bone called the scapula or shoulder blade. This is attached to the chest by muscles that allow the greatest freedom of movement backwards and forwards but very little in a sideways direction. The lower end of the scapula is fitted with a cup or socket that allows the top end of the next bone, the humerus, to form a highly mobile shoulder joint.

The lower end of the humerus forms a joint with the radius and ulna bones. These three together form the elbow. The radius and ulna are twin bones, like the forearm in humans; the elbow joint has a similar 'hinge' action. They end in the wrist or carpal joint, made up of several small bones arranged in two rows. Most movement of the carpal joint is by flexion and extension but

The points of a dog are the terms used to describe the external physical features of the dog's body and to enable judges, breeders and pet owners to have a common language to describe the breeds' standards and generally to discuss dogs.

The points of the dog

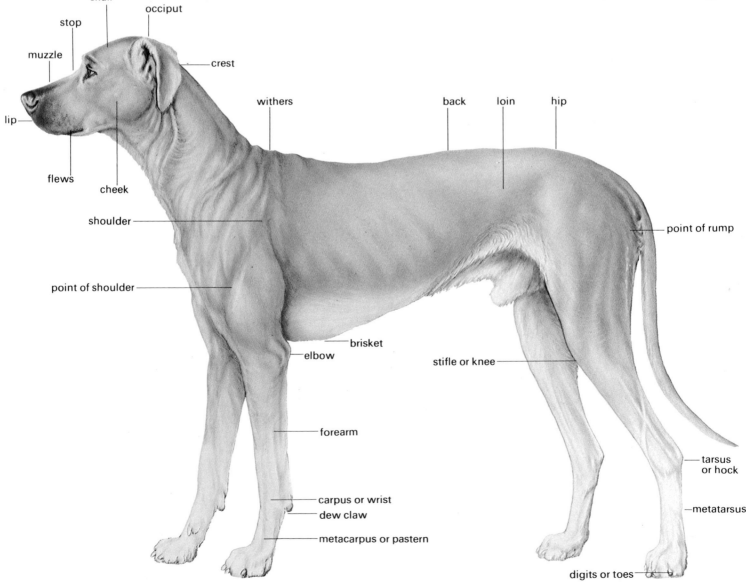

some rotation is possible. The carpal bones form a joint with the foot, which is a series of five metacarpal bones side by side; the inside ones are the smallest. Each metacarpal has a corresponding 'finger' or digit consisting of three phalangeal bones, the third of which is covered by the dog's claw. The inside digit is the smallest and is known as the dew-claw; it is often absent.

The hind leg is attached to the axial skeleton by means of the bony pelvic girdle, three paired bones fused together to form a ring. On either side of this girdle is a small depression called the acetabulum which forms the cup for the femur or thigh bone. This is the hip joint. The femur forms the knee or stifle joint with the tibia and its smaller partner, the fibula. There is also the patella or knee-cap. The tibia articulates at its lower end with the tarsal or hock joint, equivalent to the carpus in the front leg. The hind foot has the same bone structure as the front one, but the dew-claw is an even rarer occurrence.

Left: The Borzoi illustrates the extreme flexibility of the dog's neck. Below: The skeleton comprises two parts. The axial skeleton is the skull and spinal column, and the appendicular skeleton is the shoulders, pelvic girdle and limbs.

The skeleton

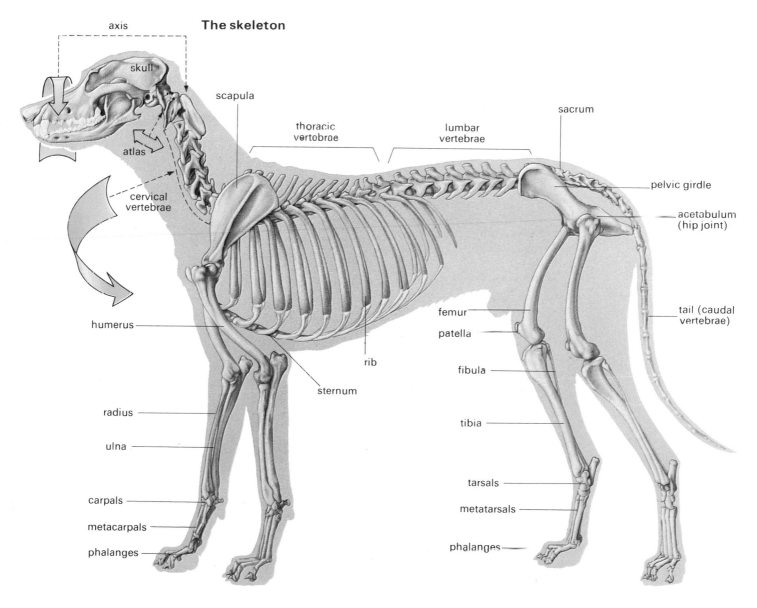

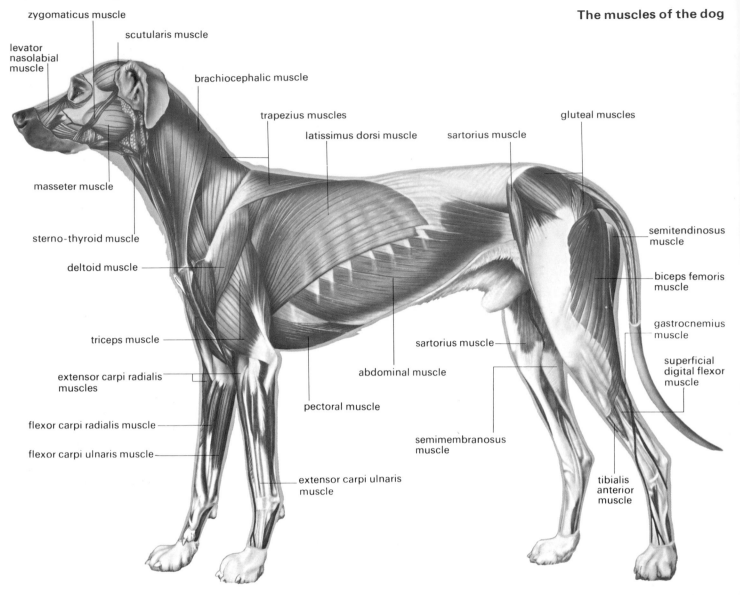

zygomaticus muscle

scutularis muscle

levator nasolabial muscle

brachiocephalic muscle

trapezius muscles

latissimus dorsi muscle

gluteal muscles

sartorius muscle

masseter muscle

sterno-thyroid muscle

deltoid muscle

triceps muscle

extensor carpi radialis muscles

flexor carpi radialis muscle

flexor carpi ulnaris muscle

extensor carpi ulnaris muscle

pectoral muscle

abdominal muscle

sartorius muscle

semimembranosus muscle

semitendinosus muscle

biceps femoris muscle

gastrocnemius muscle

superficial digital flexor muscle

tibialis anterior muscle

Ligaments and muscles control the working of the joints and nerve-cells carry impulses from the dog's brain to the muscles and body organs. Different muscles have very different functions. It depends on whether they are part of the system controlling the limbs or whether they form the muscular walls of the chest and abdomen. All, however, act in the same manner by contracting or relaxing. The heart beats because its muscles regularly contract and relax. In the same way the muscles of the chest constantly work to expand the rib cage, drawing fresh air into the lungs, and to release it, pushing spent air out.

Special tissues line the chest and the abdomen. The chest lining is known as the pleura and in the abdomen it is called the peritoneum. These are highly sensitive tissues and help prevent infection entering the body cavities. If infection does occur it can lead to inflammation. If the chest is affected it is called pleurisy; if the abdomen is affected then it is known as peritonitis.

The locomotor muscles, which provide the means by which a dog moves its limbs, are attached to the various bones. As the individual muscles contract so they draw together the bones to which they are attached. Similarly, as they relax they allow the bones to move apart. In such a way the joints are flexed or extended. By this means the limbs are moved and progress in any direction is achieved. Muscles with different bone attachments can modify or

cancel the effects of others. By using these opposing actions different positions and gaits can be controlled.

Every part of the body of a dog, and every bodily function, is controlled by the brain, which contains the majority of the nerve cells in the body. From these cells messages are transmitted to the tissues throughout the body. These communication links are located first in the spinal cord. At various points along the length of the spinal cord, bundles of nerve processes leave the cord, pass through the spinal column between the vertebrae and travel on to muscles and organs.

These nerve bundles carry messages in both directions. Some messages are from the brain and control functions, instructing a muscle, for example, to contract, or a gland to discharge its contents. Others 'report back' to the brain, keeping it informed of what is happening all over the body. If, for example, a dog's skin is inflamed a message indicating pain will be transmitted to the animal's brain, which may then 'instruct' a leg to scratch the area concerned. If a nerve is seriously damaged the message will not get through. The result of this will be loss of feeling and motor paralysis.

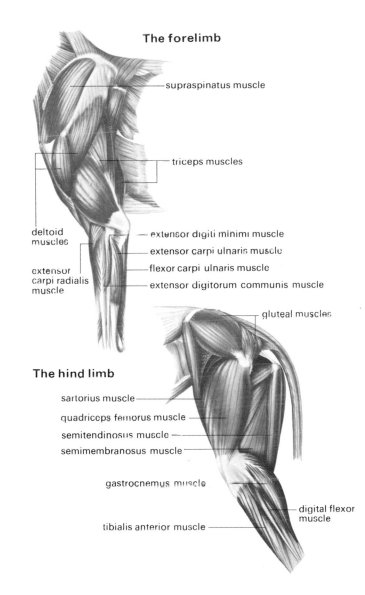

The forelimb

— supraspinatus muscle

— triceps muscles

deltoid muscles

extensor carpi radialis muscle

— extensor digiti minimi muscle
— extensor carpi ulnaris muscle
— flexor carpi ulnaris muscle
— extensor digitorum communis muscle

— gluteal muscles

The hind limb

sartorius muscle —
quadriceps femorus muscle —
semitendinosus muscle —
semimembranosus muscle —

gastrocnemus muscle —

— digital flexor muscle

tibialis anterior muscle —

Far left: The dog's skeleton is covered by layers of muscles, and these provide the complex system necessary to precisely control movement. Muscles always act in pairs or groups in which some contract to bend a joint while others contract to straighten the joint. Contraction of the muscles causes them to swell as can be seen in the insets (left) of the forelimb and hind limb tensed. Muscles are richly supplied with blood vessels and nerves. The nerves carry messages to and from the brain and spine causing voluntary and involuntary action and reaction. The energy needed to power the muscles' contraction is produced when the oxygen in the blood combines with sugar. **Below:** The Greyhound is the fastest breed of dog and the effect of contraction and extension of the muscles can easily be seen in the limbs of the two visible dogs.

The alimentary canal

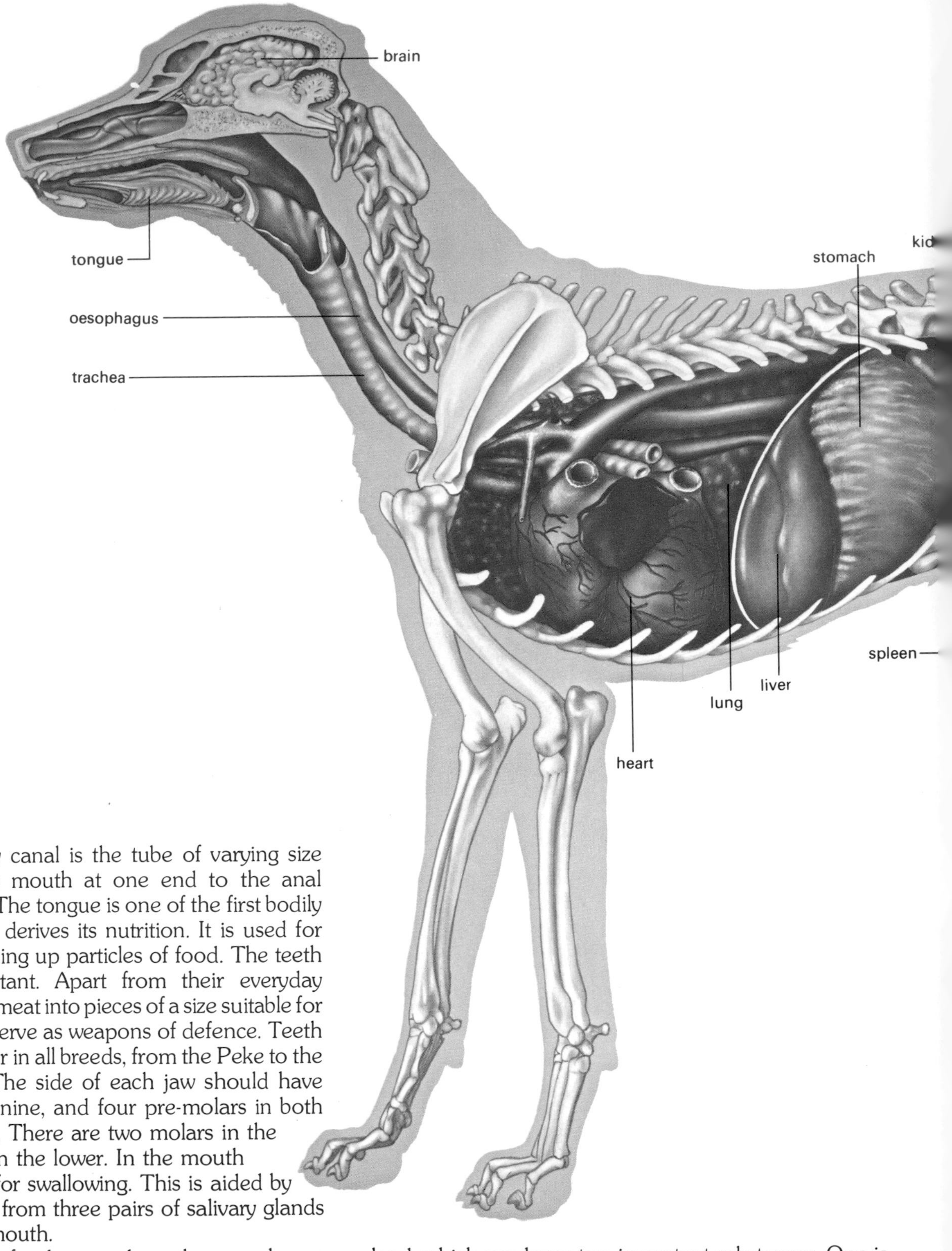

brain

tongue

oesophagus

trachea

stomach

kid

spleen —

liver

lung

heart

The entire alimentary canal is the tube of varying size which runs from the mouth at one end to the anal opening at the other. The tongue is one of the first bodily parts by which a dog derives its nutrition. It is used for lapping fluids and licking up particles of food. The teeth are extremely important. Apart from their everyday function of cutting up meat into pieces of a size suitable for swallowing they also serve as weapons of defence. Teeth are identical in number in all breeds, from the Peke to the German Shepherd. The side of each jaw should have three incisors, one canine, and four pre-molars in both upper and lower sets. There are two molars in the upper jaw but three in the lower. In the mouth the food is softened for swallowing. This is aided by the addition of saliva from three pairs of salivary glands that empty into the mouth.

From the mouth the food passes down the oesophagus which passes down the neck and the chest into the abdomen and the stomach. There, acids and enzymes work on the food, preparing it for passage through the pylorus, a ring-shaped muscle around the hind end of the stomach, and into the small intestine where the useful parts of the diet are absorbed into the bloodstream. After everything of value has been extracted from the contents of the small intestine the rest moves on into the large intestine, where excess fluid is removed. What is left after that passes into the rectum and finally out through the anus as faeces.

Near the first part of the small intestine is the pancreas gland, which produces two important substances. One is insulin, a deficiency of which causes sugar diabetes; the other is trypsin which, if not produced in sufficient quantity, will lead to chronically soft faecal excretion.

The liver has a great number of functions. It sits in the front of the abdomen and its main task is to aid the digestion of food that is taken from the stomach and the small intestine. It also produces bile, which assists in the digestive process and is stored in the gall-bladder.

The urinary tract provides the means by which most of the liquid waste is voided by the dog. The starting point are the two kidneys, which receive all the blood that has been carried to other parts of the body. The kidneys act as

Food taken in through the dog's mouth is roughly chopped by the teeth. It passes down the oesophagus, or food pipe, into the stomach where the chemical breakdown of the food, begun in the mouth with saliva, continues. The food then passes into the small intestine where nutrients are extracted. The small intestine, although smaller than the large intestine in diameter, is of very great length, and this is coiled within the abdomen. Fluids in the food are extracted in the large intestine where faeces are formed before elimination through the rectum. Waste fluid is passed through the kidneys and the bladder and out through the penis.

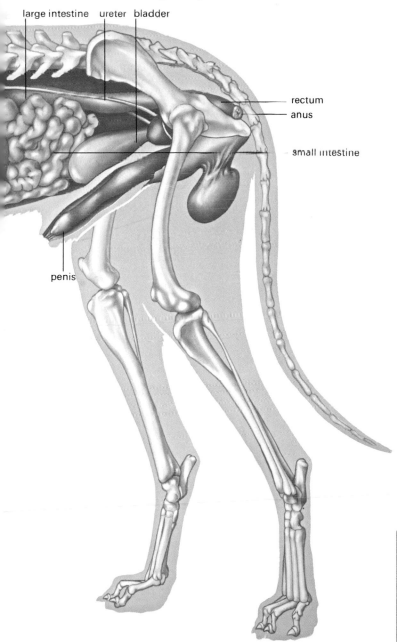

Dentition

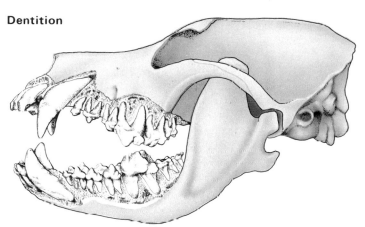

The adult dog's skull showing upper and lower jaws and teeth

The last premolar of the upper jaw and the first molar of the lower jaw are modified into carnassial teeth, a type found only in carnivores. The sharp edges of these teeth slide over each other like scissor blades. These teeth can best be seen in action when a dog gnaws meat from a bone using the side of its mouth.

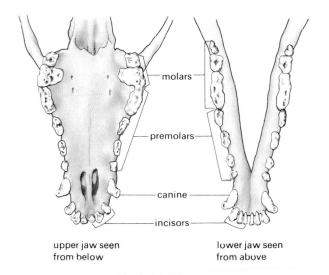

upper jaw seen from below   lower jaw seen from above

a sophisticated filter. The waste matter they remove, which is now in the form of urine, passes down the ureters to the bladder. Here the urine is temporarily stored. Periodically a sphincter muscle at the hind end of the bladder is relaxed and the urine flows out through the urethra. In the dog it passes through the penis directly outside. In the bitch the urethra empties into the hind part of the vagina and urine is then passed out of the body through the vulva.

The skin and the lungs also play an important role in expelling waste products from the body, the first by direct transmission into the atmosphere and the second by the breathing out of waste gases via the trachea.

At birth no teeth show above the puppy's gums, but between three to five weeks later the milk teeth appear: canines, incisors and three premolars. At about four months of age the first adult teeth appear, pushing out the milk teeth. The back molars of the lower jaw are the last to appear at about eight months after birth.

Anatomy: Respiration and circulation

In order to stay alive a dog needs to have an effective means of drawing oxygen into its body and ridding itself of waste gases. Air is drawn into the two lungs via the nostrils and the area at the back of the mouth (the pharynx), through the larynx, to the trachea or wind-pipe. The trachea passes down the neck and consists of a series of cartilaginous rings. It then enters the chest. Once inside the chest the trachea divides into two bronchi, one to each lung. Each bronchus in turn splits into a series of smaller air passages called bronchioles. Through this system air is drawn into the functioning cells of the lungs, where the oxygen is diffused into the dog's bloodstream. Waste gases such as nitrogen and carbon dioxide are transported in the bloodstream back from the body to be exhaled into the atmosphere.

The nostrils take air through the nasal cavities and thus over the highly specialised cells that register the sensation of smell. A dog is an efficient user of the power of scent. There are two main reasons for this. A dog has a greater length of nasal passage than most other animals, and it also has bones within the nose that are shaped something like a scroll; these are known as turbinates. This extra bone area means the dog has a greater number of scent cells than man.

The respiration and circulation systems

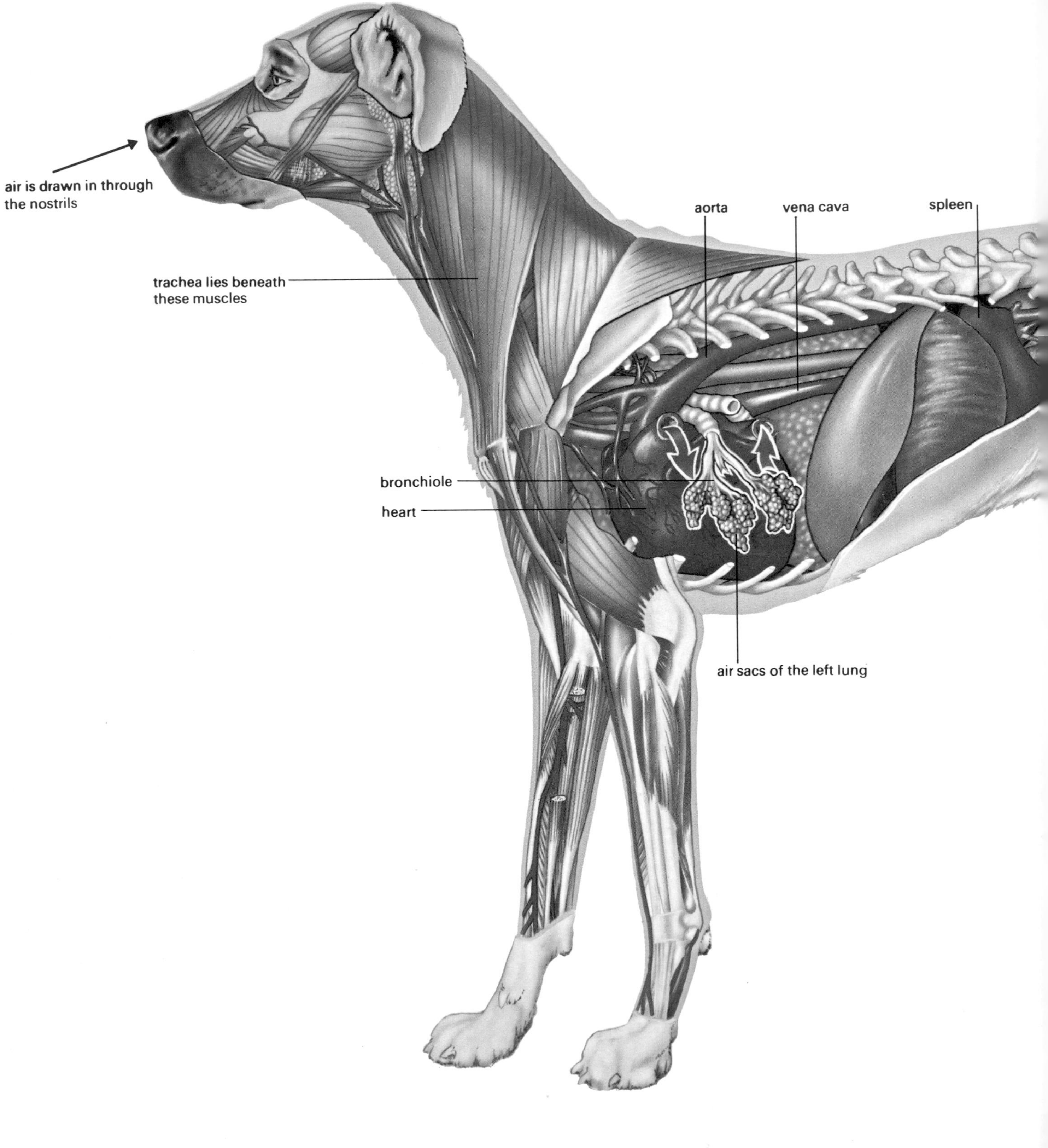
air is drawn in through the nostrils
trachea lies beneath these muscles
aorta
vena cava
spleen
bronchiole
heart
air sacs of the left lung

Right: The Deerhound is not only increasing the supply of oxygen to its blood by panting, but aiding perspiration. Perspiration mainly takes place through the pads on the paws, but by panting the dog causes evaporation and therefore loss of heat. Below: In the illustration most of the left lung (the blue, sponge-like area) has been omitted, leaving only a diagramatic representation of some of the bronchioles and air sacs of which the lung is composed. Air, rich in oxygen, is drawn in through the nose and down the trachea, or wind-pipe. From the trachea the air passes through the bronchi and bronchioles, which are extensions of the trachea and which gradually reduce in diameter, and finally into the air sacs in the lungs. These sacs have a rich supply of tiny blood vessels called capillaries which absorb the oxygen from the air and release waste carbon dioxide from the blood into the air sacs. This waste gas is then expelled when the dog breathes out. The oxygenated blood, shown in red, enters the heart and is pumped into the aorta and the arterial system for distribution around the dog's body.

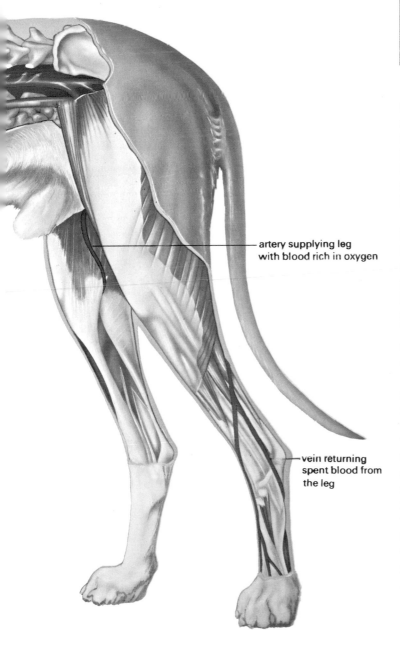

artery supplying leg with blood rich in oxygen

vein returning spent blood from the leg

Within the larynx are situated the vocal cords. A dog with a sore throat can become just as hoarse as a human, and the sound of its bark is noticeably altered. The technique of panting is another function connected with the respiratory system. Panting serves a useful purpose. Cold air is drawn in over the tongue and passed out again, taking with it moisture. It thus reduces the dog's body-heat by evaporation.

The circulatory system consists of the heart and the blood vessels that take blood from the heart to the organs and muscles. These particular blood vessels are the arteries. They lead away from the heart having received a rich supply of oxygen from the lungs. The further from the heart an artery is, the smaller it becomes. The smaller arteries are called arterioles and the tiniest are capillaries. The blood in the arteries is pumped along by the beat of the heart. In most arteries it is possible to feel the effect of each heart-beat in the form of a pulse.

Arterial blood is usually redder than that which does not contain a useful supply of oxygen. This darker, more maroon-coloured blood is venous blood. It is returned to the heart via the venules and veins and finds its way back to the lungs, where it is re-oxygenated. The venules and veins are generally wider than arteries, have thinner walls and do not pulsate. The function of the blood is to carry nourishment to every cell in the animal's body and to remove waste products. So every cell of tissue, bone, muscle, organ or skin has an arteriole bringing a constant supply of oxygenated blood, as well as a corresponding venule carrying waste-bearing blood back to the lungs for regeneration. The spleen, which lies alongside the stomach, helps filter out old blood cells and produces new ones, but in older dogs most of these functions are carried out by other tissues such as bone marrow.

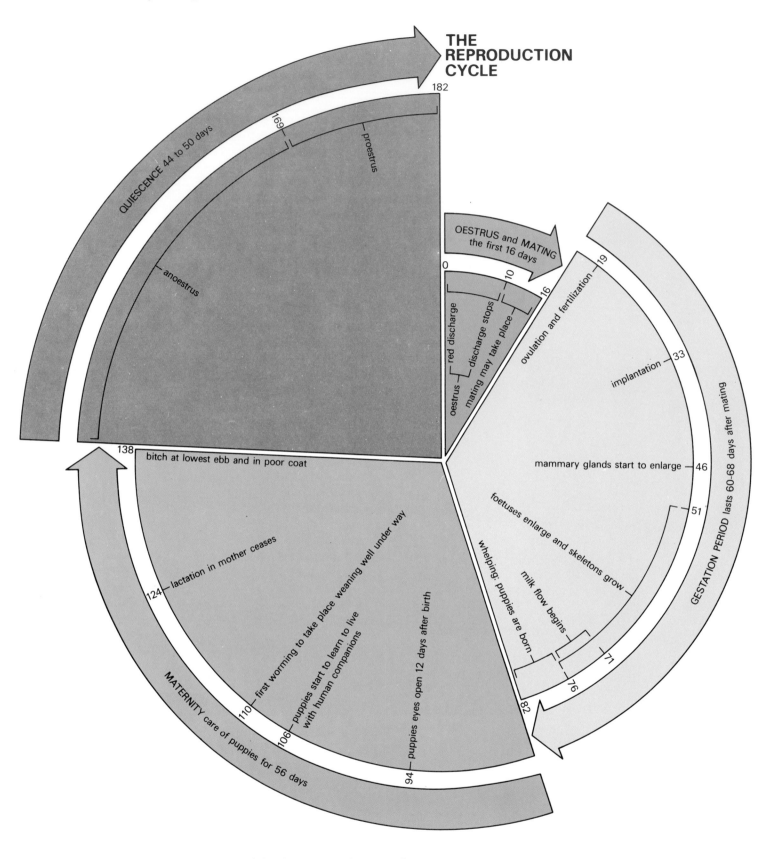

THE
**REPRODUCTION
CYCLE**

QUIESCENCE 44 to 50 days

169

proestrus

anoestrus

182

OESTRUS and MATING
the first 16 days

0

10

16

red discharge

discharge stops

mating may take place

oestrus

ovulation and fertilization

19

implantation — 33

mammary glands start to enlarge — 46

GESTATION PERIOD lasts 60-68 days after mating

51

foetuses enlarge and skeletons grow

138

bitch at lowest ebb and in poor coat

lactation in mother ceases

124

first worming to take place weaning well under way

110

puppies start to learn to live
with human companions

106

MATERNITY care of puppies for 56 days

puppies eyes open 12 days after birth

94

whelping: puppies are born

milk flow begins

71

76

82

A bitch comes on heat usually twice a year, which gives
a cycle lasting roughly 182 days when successful mating
has taken place. For the purpose of this diagram, mating
takes place on the 16th day of the cycle, the last day
of the possible mating period.

The male reproductive organs

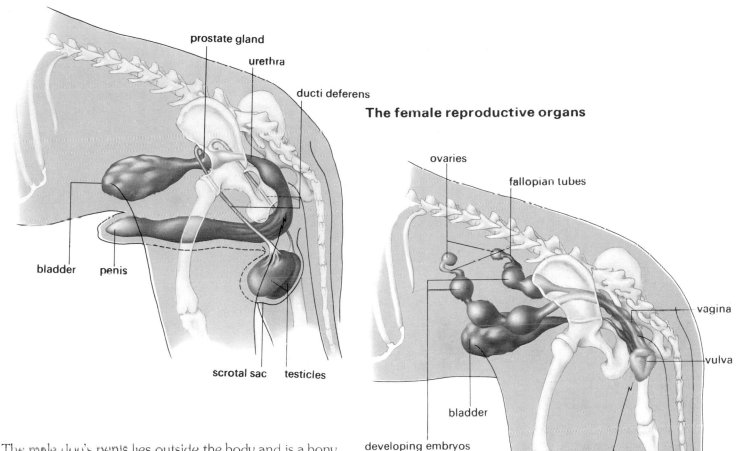

The female reproductive organs

The male dog's penis lies outside the body and is a bony structure that envelops the urethra, a channel through which urine or seminal fluid passes. Two testes or testicles lie in the scrotal sac, a pouch between the thighs. The testes produce spermatozoa or sperm, as well as male hormones. The upper surface of each is overlaid by the epididymis, where sperm is stored. Most of the seminal fluid ejaculated at mating is produced by the prostate gland, which is located in the abdomen. During copulation sperms and hormones pass from the epididymis along the *ductus deferens*, a tube that leads to the urethra, where they meet the fluid from the prostate. This seminal fluid emerges through the penis.

Of the bitch's reproductive organs, only the slit of the vulva, the end of the genital canal, is visible. The other organs of the reproductive system are the vagina (into which the penis is inserted and from which the puppy emerges), the cervix (a valve-like constriction between the vagina and the uterus), and the uterus itself, which has two 'arms' or horns that each lead to a fallopian tube and an ovary. Each ovary produces female hormones and eggs.

A bitch comes into season or heat twice a year usually, but some breeds (the Basenji, for example) do so only once a year. Puberty is usually attained between 6 and 14 months of age, the time being determined by such considerations as breed, feeding, health and environmental factors. A season lasts about 21 days and may be divided into two periods of roughly equal length. The first period is when the vulva becomes enlarged and discharges a fluid that is opaque at first but later becomes stained with blood. This occurs when the walls of the uterus prepare to receive fertilized eggs. After 10 to 14 days the discharge loses its colour. From then until the end of heat a bitch is most likely to be receptive to mating.

The illustrations above show the male and female reproductive organs which enable puppies to be conceived, carried and born after a dog and bitch have mated successfully. The horns of the uterus in the female show the bulges of developing embryos.

It is the period when the eggs produced by the ovaries are liberated and flow into the fallopian tubes to await fertilization and eventual implantation.

To indicate that she is ready to accept a dog, a bitch will stand with her tail held out to one side. The dog then mounts her from the rear, holds her flanks with his forelegs and inserts his penis into her vagina. The vagina closes firmly around the penis and this is known as the copulatory tie or lock. Although it is not essential to mating, the tie does help prevent the sperm-bearing fluid from escaping. The animals may hold the tie for up to 30 minutes or even longer. They should not be forcibly separated, as this will cause them pain. Let them uncouple when they are ready to do so.

Seminal fluid is released via the penis into the vagina. The sperms in the fluid propel themselves towards the cervix, which opens to allow it to pass into the uterus and thence to the fallopian tubes where the eggs are stored. Mating will only succeed if male sperms fertilize the eggs. If this is done the fertilized eggs travel into the uterus and attach themselves to its walls. The embryos that form will develop into puppies which will be expelled through the vagina after about 63 days.

Genetics is the science of heredity, which means the transmission to offspring of the characteristics that are in-built in previous generations of animals and plants. Inherited characteristics may be both physical or mental. They may be greatly modified by the environment, even to the extent that an inherited tendency may never manifest itself because of over-riding factors during growth.

The sum total of an animal's make-up is a combination of inherited and acquired characteristics, the latter result-ing from environmental factors and such things as accidental or deliberately imposed features of its rearing from conception. There is an important distinction be-tween truly inherited features and congenital abnor-malities. A congenital disease or abnormality arises when the foetus in the womb is developing. The animal may be born with the defect already apparent, but it is not necessarily an inherited problem. It may be acquired by accident prior to birth.

Genes are the hereditary material in reproductive cells. They are carried in thread-like chromosomes. Each species has a specific number of chromosomes, which occur in pairs. The dog has 39 chromosome pairs. The total gene content of an individual is called its genotype. In contrast, the sum of all the animal's characteristics, including those determined by its genetic make-up and its environment, is known as its phenotype.

Chromosome pairs are alike in gene content, and genes are also carried in pairs. While it is often possible to correlate one pair of genes with one inherited charac-teristic, most characteristics depend on the interaction of genes. One pair of genes may also affect more than one characteristic. The pairing of genes is responsible for the phenomenon of dominance and recessiveness.

Each individual has only two genes of each kind. One is derived from the father and one from the mother. Each gene may be either dominant or recessive to its pair. A simplified example is the genes for eye-colour. The gene for brown eyes is dominant, the gene for blue eyes is recessive. If an animal receives genes for blue eyes and for brown eyes from its parents it will have brown eyes because of the dominance of that gene. It will have blue eyes if this gene is passed on from both parents.

This leads to further conclusions. A blue-eyed animal has genes for blue eye-colour alone and it is known as

Mendelism

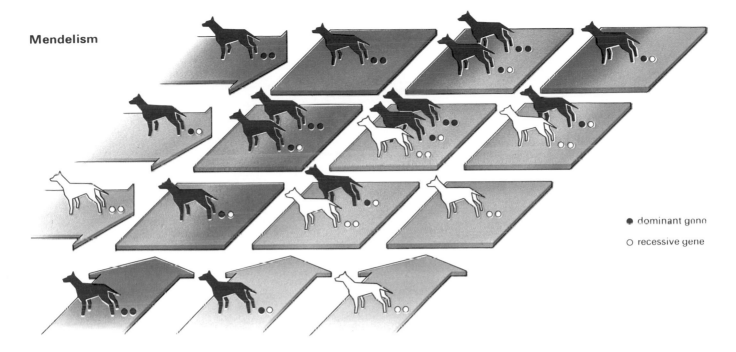

● dominant gene

○ recessive gene

Above: This simple chart demonstrates the pairing of genes and the domination of one gene over another. Each pair of genes can comprise two dominant genes, or one dominant and one recessive gene, or two recessive genes. To discover the effect of mating on genetic inheritance for, say, eye colour, follow the arrows of one dog on the left-hand side and of one dog from the bottom row until the lines meet on a common square. For example, when the dog on the left-hand green arrow mates with the dog on the bottom row red arrow the lines meet on a half-red, half-green square and the offspring have inherited either all dominant genes (one from each parent) or one recessive and one dominant gene (again one gene from each parent). Left: The litter of puppies illustrates the different genetic inheritance between siblings.

homozygous for that characteristic. If a brown-eyed individual has one gene for blue eyes and one for brown it will be known as heterozygous for eye-colour. It is impossible to tell the difference by physical examination between a heterozygous and a homozygous brown-eyed individual.

The population of dogs available for breeding may be regarded as a population of genes – the gene pool. The long-term objective of a breeder is to alter, by selection, the frequency with which genes occur. He gambles on breeding an outstanding individual but calculates on improving the overall standard of the breed and particularly his line of dogs. Individuals with undesirable characteristics should be eliminated from the breeding programme and individuals carrying desirable traits should be selected.

An animal's appearance alone may be a poor guide to its ability to reproduce its own characteristics. A knowledge of the animal's ancestry can help. Line-breeding and family breeding are diluted forms of in-breeding, or the breeding of closely related individuals. And the more closely related the animals of a particular line are the more reliably will they reproduce their characteristics (whether good or bad). For this reason close in-breeding demands the greatest of care.

Healthy dogs are not difficult to feed if they have been sensibly reared. Possibly because of their long association with humans, dogs thrive on similar food to man's own. They need a little more protein and do not require fruit or green vegetables because they can make vitamin C in their own bodies. Nearly all foods of animal origin, cereals, root, vegetables and fats are well digested but may require cooking. Water is essential to life and therefore plays an important part in feeding.

The secret of correct feeding is, then, to give a balanced diet. This is a diet which supplies all essential nutrients in adequate amounts and in the proper proportions to one another for the purpose intended – work, breeding, growth or healthy adulthood.

The essential nutrients are an energy source (protein of high quality), fat as a source of essential fatty acids, about 20 mineral elements and a dozen vitamins. Energy is supplied by the digestion of fat, protein and carbohydrate at the rates of 265, 120 and 120 kcal per ounce respectively. Carbohydrate in the form of cooked cereal starch or sugar can supply up to 70 per cent by weight of a dog's food (after deducting any water present) or about two-thirds of the calories. Biscuits, bread and cooked potatoes are three useful energy foods for dogs.

Protein varies greatly in its usefulness to the animal. Plant protein is generally inferior to animal protein, though a mixture is satisfactory. The dry matter of a dog's diet should contain at least 15 per cent protein, of which at least half should come from animal foods (meat, fish, poultry, offals and dairy products) or high quality vegetable protein such as soya. Fat adds to palatability but otherwise is needed only as a source of essential fatty acids, sometimes called polyunsaturates.

The most important minerals are calcium, phosphorus and sodium chloride (common salt). Combined calcium and phosphorus make up most of the mineral matter of bone and should be supplied at the rate of about 3 per cent calcium phosphate in the dry diet. A small amount, 0·5 per cent, of iodised table salt in the diet is sufficient. Further minerals occur naturally in meat, cereals and other ingredients of the balanced diet. Vitamin B_1 is supplied by cereals while meat, fish and dairy products provide other B vitamins. Liver is the most readily available source of all vitamins, including A, D and E. Alternatively, vitamins can be provided as a concentrate or in specially supplemented manufactured foods.

Traditionally, dogs have been fed on meat mixed with household scraps such as stale bread, trimmings and so on. This can be satisfactory if the proportion of scraps is restricted to a quarter. All types of fresh meat and offals are suitable, as are fish and dairy products. Liver is rather laxative but highly nutritious; 5 per cent is an appropriate amount. Fresh meats should be lightly cooked for reasons of hygiene. Large bones, such as pieces of ox shank bone, provide the calcium and phosphorus lacking in meat. Gnawing bones also keeps the teeth clean. Chicken, fish and rabbit bones should not be given as they may lodge in the throat or puncture the intestines. Excessive gnawing of bones may cause a block of mineral matter in the bowels.

There are four main types of manufactured dog food.

Biscuits and meals are based on wheaten flour and prepared as either whole biscuits or a broken meal. Most are supplemented with vitamins and minerals. Fat and protein meals may be added to improve palatability.

Tinned foods are based on meat, offal, poultry or fish and supplemented with vitamins and minerals. Some use minced meats and contain cereals; in others the meats are cubed or diced and set in gravy or jelly.

Complete dry meals are a mixture of cereals, protein meals and other ingredients to make a balanced diet. They are made as loose mixtures (usually with pre-cooked cereals), compressed pellets or 'expanded' meals – pellets of open texture, coated with fat to improve palatability.

Below: The puppy chewing the bone is gaining many nutrients including the calcium and phosphorous lacking in meat. Gnawing is also beneficial to teeth.

Intermediate moisture foods consist of cooked meats mixed with sugar and other preservatives plus other ingredients to make a balanced diet.

The amount of food needed depends mostly on a dog's size but is also affected by its activeness, its individual nature and the temperature of its surroundings. Be careful not to overfeed. Many dogs will overeat until obese and this will have serious effects on their health and life expectancy. Young dogs and those being worked may need a great deal more food (calories) than shown in the panel (right), whereas an inactive, old dog will need less. If possible, weigh a dog regularly and watch its condition.

Using the information in the tables (below) and in the panel, it is possible to devise many satisfactory diets. Here are some useful examples:

7kg (15lb) Shetland Sheepdog: 113g ($\frac{1}{4}$lb) minced beef, 113g ($\frac{1}{4}$lb) wholemeal bread, one saucer of milk a day

11kg (25lb) Cocker Spaniel: 225g ($\frac{1}{2}$lb) tripe, 170g (6oz) biscuits a day

25·5kg (65lb) Labrador Retriever: 1 tin cereal dog meat, 312g (11oz) biscuit meal a day

45kg (100lb) Bloodhound: 680g (1$\frac{1}{2}$lb) expanded meal a day

Healthy adult dogs need only one meal a day for they are adapted to take in large meals of concentrated food. Very small dogs and breeds prone to digestive problems may be fed two or three times a day. Working dogs are fed in the evening after the day's work but may also be given a light morning meal. A common pattern with pet dogs is to give the main meal in the morning and a few biscuits in the evening. Variety in either the food or the dietary regime should be avoided. Dogs do not become bored with a consistent diet of palatable, wholesome food and their digestions benefit from the regularity. They should not be given snacks between meals.

Traditional food	Protein	Energy value	
	%	kcal/lb	kcal/kg
Minced beef	20	1250	2750
Ox liver	21	750	1650
Ox lung (lights)	18	500	1100
Ox spleen (melts)	17	500	1100
Ox tripe	15	450	990
Shank bone	10	250	550
Whole egg	12	650	1430
Whole milk	3$\frac{1}{2}$	300	660
Potato	2	100	220
Wholemeal bread	9	1000	2200

Manufactured food	Protein	Energy value	
	%	kcal/lb	kcal/kg
Biscuits/meals	11	1600	3520
Tinned, jelly type	11	400	880
Tinned, cereal type	8	500	1100
Expanded meal	24	1500	3300
Intermediate moisture	25	1400	3080

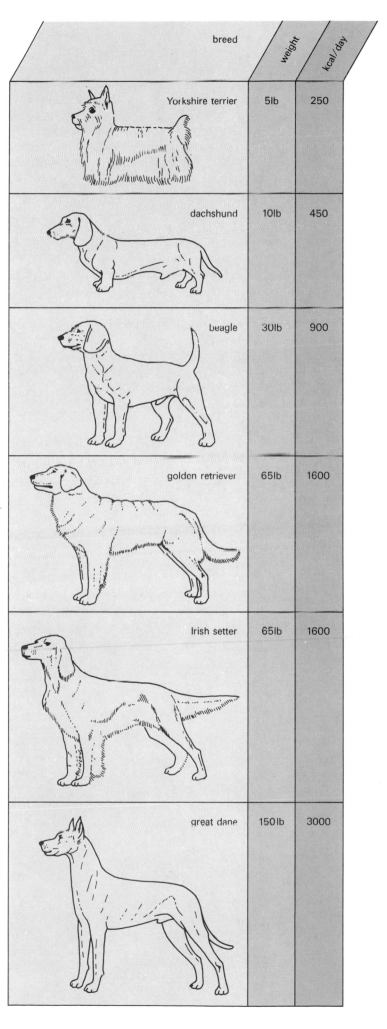

breed	weight	kcal/day
Yorkshire terrier	5lb	250
dachshund	10lb	450
beagle	30lb	900
golden retriever	65lb	1600
Irish setter	65lb	1600
great dane	150lb	3000

If dogs are fed a balanced diet of adequate quality and maintained in lean, hard condition there is no need to adjust the diet before mating or during the first four weeks of pregnancy. In the fifth week appetite should increase if the bitch has pups. Increase the food gradually and divide the total amount about equally between two meals. By the ninth week a medium-sized bitch carrying an average litter of five or six should be eating about two-thirds more food than for daily maintenance. A small bitch may need twice as much food. The extra food may be mostly meat, although this is not essential with a balanced diet. Shortly before whelping a bitch will lose her appetite and may vomit her last meal. During whelping provide only water or a little milk at intervals.

Within a day of a normal whelping the bitch should regain her appetite as the puppies begin to suckle. During lactation, assuming a litter of average number, she will need about three times as much food as usual, divided between three meals. The third meal should be rich in protein, vitamins and minerals. Calcium is particularly important, to protect the bitch from eclampsia or milk tetany. This dangerous condition is caused by a lowering of the blood calcium level brought about by the bitch's production of milk. Cows' milk is a useful supplementary food in lactation, but is laxative if given too freely.

Lactation usually continues for at least three weeks. Each puppy should be weighed every day for the first two weeks. Puppies of small breeds should gain about 28g (1oz) a day, those of medium-size breeds 56g (2oz) and of large breeds about 112g (4oz). Continue to weigh at least twice a week. The bitch is 'dried-off' during the next two or three weeks as the litter is weaned. Her food is gradually decreased, first by reducing and eliminating the third meal and then by bringing the other meals back to their normal level. When weaning is complete the bitch should be at her normal weight and in healthy condition. If she appears thin, give a little extra meaty food until condition is restored; if overweight cut down her carbohydrate intake.

Sometimes a bitch is lost during whelping or fails to nurse the litter. The puppies must then be reared entirely by hand. More frequently, and nearly always in the case of a large litter, some supplementary feeding is necessary. If the pups are weakened, consult your vet. Orphan puppies should be given a little glucose solution (28g to 0·5 litres or 1oz to 1 pint of boiled water) via a dropper or a premature baby's feeding bottle. Newborn puppies must be kept warm and massaged to promote excretion. After one or two glucose feeds, milk feeds should be begun at two-hourly intervals, lengthening to three-hourly after a day or two and then to six a day within a week. Four feeds a day should be sufficient from then to weaning.

Cows' milk should be fortified with extra protein and calories. Evaporated or condensed milk tends to be too laxative. Instead, casein (milk protein) and vegetable oil should be blended into Guernsey or Jersey milk at the rates of 28g and 14g per 0·5 litres (1oz and ½oz per pint). Use a kitchen homogeniser for efficient dispersion and warm to blood heat before use. Give as much as the puppy wants at each feed. This preparation is also suitable for supplementary feeding of backward puppies. Begin weaning orphan puppies as soon as they can stand to lap, or will take solid food from your fingers.

Changing the puppy's diet from its mothers' milk to the more solid diet of adult dogs can usually start at three weeks of age, but a backward litter may be a little older. In nature the mother starts to regurgitate her own partly digested food as her milk begins to dry up. Breeders attempt to simulate this diet either by scraping meat to a fine paste or by soaking pre-cooked cereals in cows' milk. The second method is, on the whole, less trouble and means that the dog will not become reliant on an expensive meat diet.

Begin by teaching the puppies to lap warm milk from a saucer. If necessary wet your finger in the milk, or dampen their muzzles with it to encourage them. Offer a fresh saucer of milk three times a day, in the early morning, at noon and in the early evening. As the litter begins to lap start to reduce the mother's food and keep her away from the litter for periods of two or three hours. Continue to weigh each puppy at least twice a week, or even daily, to check progress.

When the puppies are lapping freely introduce solid food. Soak a little baby cereal or specially prepared puppy meal in an equal volume of hot milk and allow the mixture to cool to blood heat. Offer this food two or three times a day at what you intend to be regular meal-times. At first the pups will attempt to suck out the milk but in about a week they should be eating the solid food. The texture should not be sticky but consist of separate, soft, moist pieces. Continue to reduce the bitch's food. Remove her from the pups except at night, and for one or two brief periods during the day.

After five to six weeks the puppies should be fully weaned and the bitch separated. If she is in discomfort consult a veterinary surgeon. It is now important to increase the quantity of food rapidly to keep pace with growth. The midday meal is kept small while the quantity

Below: The Retriever puppies go on feeding from their mother for several weeks after they have begun to eat solid food. Although they no longer need mother's milk, they will continue to enjoy it.

Above: an orphaned puppy can be raised without its mother. Special feeding bottles are available, although the puppy's weight should be checked regularly (right). An accurate set of kitchen scales can be used.

of solid food, but not of milk, is increased at the morning and evening meals. Water must now be freely available. A little warm milk can also be offered in the late evening. The total amount of milk each day should range from about 0·15 litres ($\frac{1}{4}$pt) for very small breeds to 0·5 litres (1 pint) for giants. It is wise to feed puppies from individual bowls to ensure that each gets its share.

As soon as the pups are satisfactorily weaned, meat can be introduced gradually if it has not already been given. Nearly all types, including tinned foods, are suitable but liver should be given only in very small amounts. All meat should be cooked and minced. Start by mixing the meat with the milk and cereal feeds morning and evening. If neither meat nor cereal contains added vitamins and minerals provide a reputable proprietary supplement. Increase the two main meals to meet appetite. From the age of about 10 weeks a puppy eats more than it will when fully grown. The milk can be given separately, as a dry mixture is beneficial for the puppy's teeth. The midday

small feed and optional late milk can be omitted from the age of three months, if not before.

Variation in size and the rate of growth makes it impossible to prescribe precise quantities of food. Continue to weigh the dog regularly and chart the results. When it is clear that growth is slowing down, stop the milk and begin to reduce one of the two meals. With miniature breeds this may be as early as five months while giant breeds continue to grow rapidly to at least eight months. It is wiser to underfeed slightly rather than risk producing an obese young dog, but with experience it is possible to adjust the food so that the dog remains in prime condition. From the age of about nine months feed as for an adult dog but observe its condition carefully and adjust the food intake if necessary.

Arthritis

Inflammatory disorders of the joints are common in dogs, particularly in the heavier breeds. Although usually associated with older animals, this disease may occur in dogs less than one year old when they are afflicted with such problems as hip dysplasia and Legge-Perthe's disease (a disorder of the hip bone). The cause of arthritis is not completely understood, but it frequently follows physical injury. Obesity tends to aggravate the condition. Signs are usually insidious, with slowly developing pain and lameness, often noticeable as stiffness in the morning which wears off with exercise. Diagnosis may require X-ray examination. Treatment is palliative, but weight reduction of obese dogs should be attempted, and making certain the dog's bed is warm and dry.

Bad breath

An offensive smell from a dog's mouth may result from infection in the mouth itself, either a specific bacterial infection or ulcers, from decaying teeth and associated gum disease, or from generalized disease such as chronic nephritis. It may also occur when the dog appears otherwise to be in perfect health. There is no first aid treatment for bad breath caused by disease; it will be necessary to have the dog seen by a veterinary surgeon. Foul stomach-smells, if temporary, may respond to a dose of milk of magnesia. The dog with chronic bad breath, which is not caused by apparent disease, will probably respond only temporarily to veterinary treatment but a complete change of diet may succeed. This change may need to be drastic, such as to rice and rabbit from beef and biscuits.

Canker *see* Ear diseases

Cannibalism

Bitches at whelping, even normally placid ones, may become sufficiently psychologically disturbed to attack, kill and even occasionally eat their offspring. There is no treatment, but it is essential to have as undisturbed and peaceful a situation as possible at whelping time, and to allow the bitch to whelp in surroundings with which she has become familiar, preferably over weeks rather than days. Quiet vigilance is needed rather than over-anxious 'help.'

Car sickness

Some dogs have this trouble and others don't. There is no certain way of preventing it, but if a dog starts to be travel sick it is important to treat it before it becomes a habit. Depending on the puppy's size, up to half an anti-travel sickness tablet may be effective, otherwise a veterinary surgeon can prescribe something. Tablets may take a long time to work, so the dose should be given about an hour before the journey. Much of the sickness suffered by older puppies and grown dogs is due to nervousness from remembered previous occasions. A few trips protected by tablets may overcome the problem.

Constipation

Simple constipation occurs fairly often as a result of eating bones or indigestible matter. It may also arise from the dog's refusal to defecate because of pain from infected anal glands, or even matted hair around the anus. There are other, more fundamental causes and chronic constipation, particularly if it is associated with alternating bouts of diarrhoea, needs veterinary attention. Constipation is accompanied by frequent attempts to defecate. A dog which makes no attempt to pass faeces for several days is not necessarily constipated. The best first aid is probably liquid paraffin by mouth, about a dessertspoonful for small dogs and four or five times that amount for larger dogs.

Coprophagy

This is the term for eating faeces. It is almost invariably simply a bad habit which is likely to have arisen out of boredom and close confinement, although it can occur for no discernible reason. There is no deficiency or disease condition which makes a dog eat faeces, and it will not be cured by providing additional vitamins or other supplement. The habit has to be cured by discouragement, and avoidance of the situation by removing faeces quickly. Some dogs will eat horse manure if they get the chance. It is so common that it has come to be regarded as normal behaviour, but it should be firmly discouraged.

Cough

Coughing is simply a sign of irritation in the dog's throat or bronchial tubes. It must be considered with other symptoms in determining the cause. Only rarely is a foreign body such as a bone involved, but an apparent attempt to clear the throat of something is often a sign of tonsilitis or kennel cough, a highly infectious although usually not serious disease. There is now a vaccination against kennel cough. It can be given as part of the standard distemper, hepatitis and leptospirosis shot. Any persistent cough requires veterinary attention. If the cough is accompanied by distress, or refusal of food, the attention should be prompt.

Deafness

This is not common in dogs, but it can occur as a congenital condition and be noticed by an observant owner while puppies are still in the nest. A simple hand-clap will usually show whether or not the puppy is reacting to noise, but hearing which is simply less acute than normal may be extremely difficult to determine. Deafness frequently accompanies old age. There is not usually any treatment available. Cleansing the ears of wax is unlikely ever to be more than of marginal benefit.

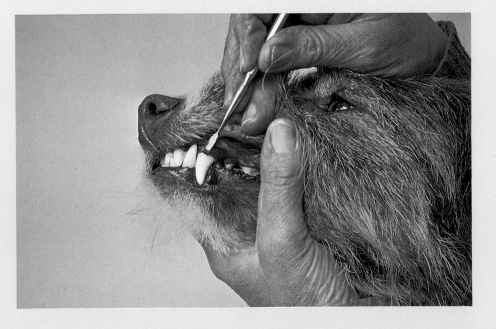

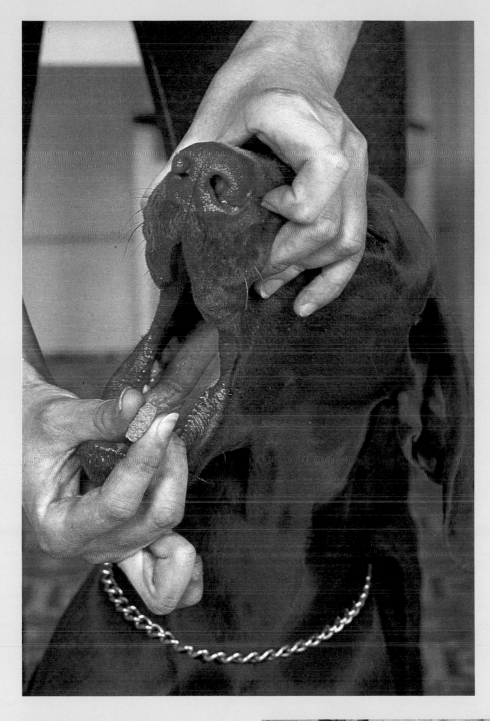

or diarrhoea; the whites of the eyes are usually inflamed. If infection progresses it will eventually affect the nervous system leading to intractable fits. The hard pad symptom occurs when the virus affects the horny layers of the pads, causing enlargement and leathery feel to the feet. Modern veterinary treatment, through the use of antibiotics, has tended to obscure the classical signs of pneumonia and enteritis in distemper. Little progress has been made in controlling the nervous involvement from which a high proportion of affected dogs die. **NB** Vaccination is highly effective in preventing the disease.

Ear diseases

Head shaking, ear scratching and an unpleasant smell are usually the first signs of ear disease, and when this is noticed the ears should be examined. Healthy ears are pale pink inside, shiny and free from discharge or wax. If the ear looks sore the dog needs veterinary attention. If the ears are simply dirty or contain a little clean-looking wax, clean them with liquid paraffin. Pour a small amount into the ear, work it gently from the outside and mop it with cotton wool. It is not safe to push pledgets of cotton wool into the ear unless you know there is nothing further down causing trouble. Acute inflammation, particularly in Spaniels, is often caused by a grass seed. More chronic infections frequently start off with ear mite infestations. Veterinary treatment depends on the cause, and in some cases may even require surgery to expose the inflamed area. Diseases of the ear are sometimes loosely referred to as 'canker' although it is a term that veterinary surgeons rarely use.

Above: To give a dog a tablet, hold the dog's mouth open gently, place the tablet towards the back on the tongue, hold its mouth closed and stroke its throat to encourage swallowing. Left: Removing plaque from the teeth can cure bad breath. Right: Flop-eared dogs should have their ears cleaned regularly.

Diarrhoea *see* **Enteritis and Diarrhoea**

Distemper and Hard pad

Both terms refer to a disease caused by a single virus that may show some variation in symptoms. The first sign of either form of the disease is a high body temperature, about 102°F (39°C). The dog refuses food and may have a cough

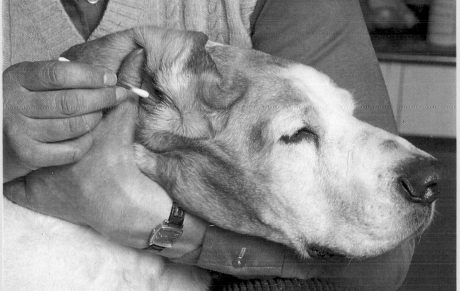

Eczema

Most skin conditions in the dog have a considerable element of self-infliction, and a dog can turn an itchy spot into a large patch of severe moist eczema in less than an hour. The first steps in preventing eczema are to stop the animal scratching or biting itself and then trying to find out what is causing the irritation. In more than seven cases out of 10 the cause will be parasitic, probably fleas. Most other cases will be diagnosed as allergic. Treatment of parasitic skin disease, while usually straightforward, demands far longer and more determined attack than it frequently receives.

Enteritis and Diarrhoea

Although most attacks of simple diarrhoea probably have a nutritional cause, specific diagnosis and treatment is necessary if an attack progresses to enteritis, or persists for longer than 48 hours. Parvovirus Enteritis, closely related to Feline Enteritis, is a highly infectious and frequently fatal virus disease. First signs are likely to be serious vomiting and often blood-stained diarrhoea. Veterinary help should be sought immediately. First-aid treatment for simple diarrhoea consists of removing all sources of food and drink and giving the dog a little plain boiled rice (possibly flavoured with chicken stock or something similar). Allow small amounts of glucose and water, given frequently. If the dog refuses rice, give it no food for 24 hours.

Eye troubles

Eye infections are common in the dog, usually as conjunctivitis, and prompt treatment with antibiotic usually effects a cure. Ulcerated corneas may be more serious and any indication of blueing, or damage to the surface of the eye, should be attended to without delay. An acute eye problem is usually signalled by watering of the eye and closing, partially or completely, of the eyelids. Gentle examination may reveal the cause. If it is a foreign body, such as a piece of grass and it can be removed by the fingers or the corner of a handkerchief, do so. But greater interference than that should not be attempted.

Fits

The presence of intestinal worms may occasionally cause fits in young puppies. The remedy is to give a regular worm dose to puppies under six months old. Epilepsy is a common cause of repeated

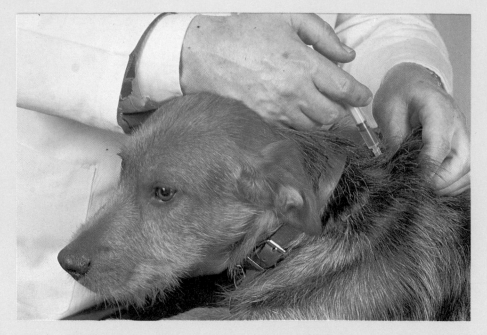

fits in adult dogs, often starting when the dog is between 12 months and three years old, but loss of consciousness (usually without the typical nervous spasms of a fit) also occurs during the course of a heart attack. The best treatment is to remove any object that might injure the dog and do not attempt to put anything into the animal's mouth 'to stop it choking.' This won't help and you may get bitten. Then take the dog to a vet.

Fleas *see* **Parasites**

Fractures

Suspected broken bones can only be confirmed and treated at a veterinary surgery. Despite a widespread belief to the contrary, sensible movement of the dog is unlikely to make the injury worse. The animal should be carried, if necessary on a blanket, and taken as soon as possible for treatment.

Gastric distension

Bloat, gastric torsion, or gastric distension, is a well-recognized problem in larger breeds of dog. Two to four hours after feeding the dog may show signs of obvious distress and pain. The abdomen will be distended and hard. This is a surgical emergency and must be treated immediately by a veterinary surgeon.

Gastritis

Vomiting is the most likely indication that a dog has an inflamed stomach, or gastritis, but grass-eating without vomiting may occasionally be a sign. Gastritis is often associated with simple diarrhoea, as in 'diarrhoea and vomiting' and in the more serious disease of gastro-enteritis.

Above: A dog is given an injection into the loose skin at the back of its neck. Right: If a dog has eye troubles it is essential not to attempt any more than gentle examination, and perhaps gentle bathing, until the dog can be taken to a veterinarian and treated accordingly.

Both of these may have mechanical origins, possibly a swallowed rubber band or undigested bone, or be caused by bacterial or virus infection. *See also* **Enteritis and Diarrhoea**

Grass-eating

This may be a simple habit of no significance whatsoever, or it may indicate irritation in the stomach (*see* **Gastritis**). It is generally believed that a dog instinctively takes grass to induce vomiting. Grass is most effective in wrapping itself around jagged foreign bodies in the stomach, so helping to prevent damage to the bowel.

Haemorrhage

Heavy bleeding is immediately obvious if the haemorrhage is external. The appropriate immediate action is to pad the wound with cotton wool or other material and bandage firmly with anything to hand. Severe haemorrhage is a real emergency demanding instant action. Surgery is the sole means of checking internal bleeding. The obvious signs of internal haemorrhage are blanching of the membranes of the mouth and eyes, and collapse of the dog. It may be necessary to muzzle a dog that is injured severely, since the dog might panic and bite even its owner. A strip of fabric may be gently wrapped around the dog's muzzle.

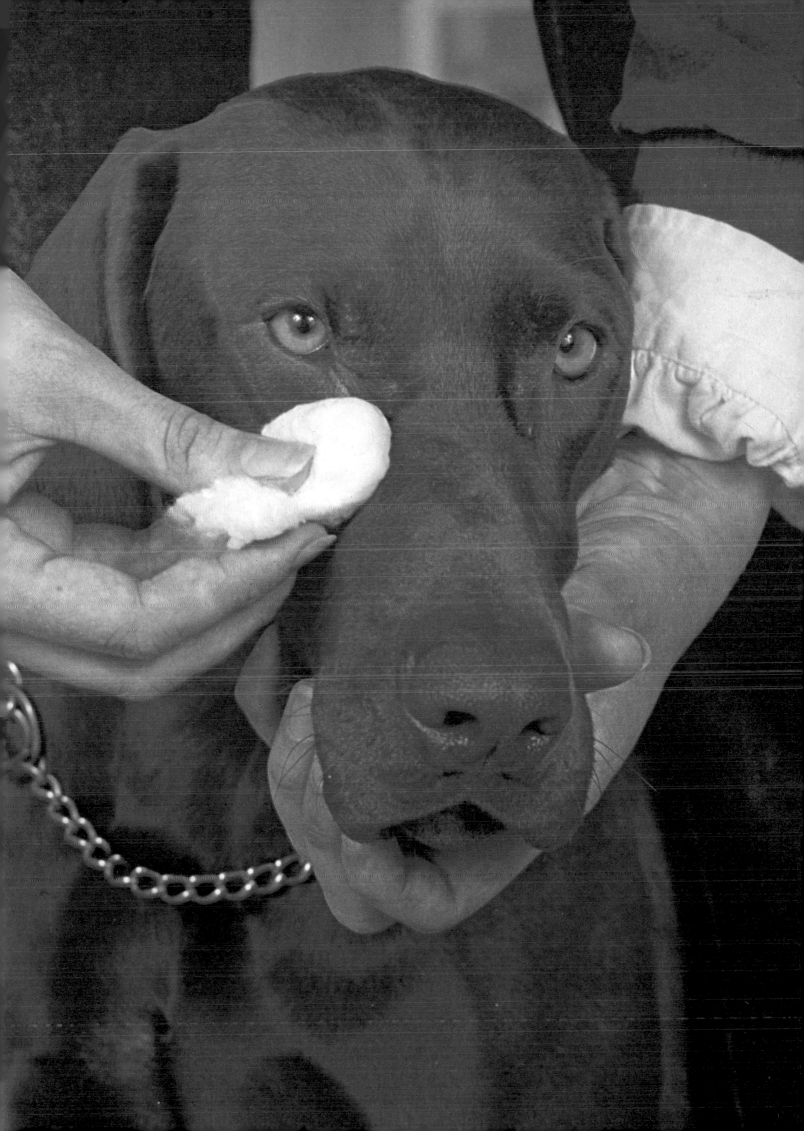

Hair loss

Shedding of hair in a seasonal pattern is normal in most breeds, other than those with a Poodle-like coat, but central heating seems to have interfered grossly with the pattern in many dogs. Hair loss occurs after whelping or at the same time in an unbred bitch's cycle, again normally as part of her annual cycle. No regular treatment can reduce or avoid coat-shedding; but regular grooming is essential at these times to prevent matting and itchiness from the dead coat. On occasions the loss may be so heavy that skin irritation becomes sufficiently severe to require veterinary treatment.

Hard pad *see* Distemper and Hard pad

Heart disease

Heart disease is almost as common in dogs as it is in humans, and often has similar causes. The obese Labrador, for instance, is particularly at risk. Congenital heart conditions can receive effective attention. The canine 'blue baby' syndrome is recognized and can be treated by surgery, but most cases of myocardial or valvular disease are treated by drugs rather than surgery. Proper management of cardiac patients is important. Weight loss is frequently required and moderate but not excessive exercise usually desirable. Many dogs will indicate their own exercise tolerance limits quite obviously.

Hepatitis

Viral hepatitis is infectious among dogs. Adult animals may develop fever, with temperatures of up to 105°F (41°C), lose appetite and show blood-stained diarrhoea and vomit. Intensive veterinary care is required, but death can result. Vaccination is a preventive measure against hepatitis, and is 99 per cent effective.

Hernia

Externally noticeable hernias in the dog are almost always congenital, and may occur at the umbilicas or in the scrotal or inguinal areas. Small hernias are not significant and are composed of fat trapped in a sac of tissue. If the bulge varies in size veterinary attention is necessary to advise on possible surgery. The rare, serious sequel to a hernia is 'strangulation' when intestines or some other vital organs become trapped in the sac. Prompt surgical treatment is required.

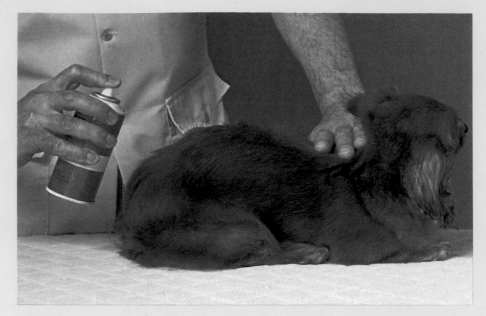

Hip dysplasia

This is a deformity of the hip joint caused when the joint is too shallow and the head of the femur is malformed. It occurs more often than usual in some breeds, such as Saint Bernards and German Shepherds. It manifests itself by pain in the area of the hip and by a swinging gait and a 'hopping' run. X-ray is needed for accurate diagnosis although there is no cure. Pain can be alleviated by drugs or through surgery. This deformity is generally considered to be hereditary, although the extent of this is unknown; in any case, no dysplastic dog should be allowed to breed.

Jaundice

Obvious jaundice with yellowing of the skin and membranes is comparatively uncommon in dogs, but the underlying causes – blood breakdown or liver disease – are regularly seen. The jaundice itself is a minor symptom but should never be ignored. Leptospirosis and virus hepatitis may both cause jaundicing of the tissues. These diseases are extremely serious. Effective vaccines are available for both and are usually included in the routine vaccinations administered to puppies.

Kidney diseases

Nephritis, inflammation of the kidneys, results from infections, including leptospirosis in particular. Affected dogs are acutely ill, and the disease commonly leads to chronic nephritis, from which many old dogs eventually succumb. There is no cure for chronic nephritis, although veterinary maintenance techniques may manage the problem effectively for varying periods, depending on

Above: External parasites can be controlled by baths, powders or spray insecticide.

the amount of kidney damage. Low protein diets may help. Leptospirosis can be prevented by vaccination, but annual re-vaccination is essential, even for older dogs.

Lameness

The precise location can be extremely difficult to pinpoint; it is hard to tell sometimes which leg is affected. It is useful to remember that the dog nods its head downwards as the sound leg touches the ground; similarly its rump will drop as the sound hind leg is put to the ground. It will help diagnosis at the veterinary surgeon's if you notice whether, for instance, the lameness is worse first thing in the morning, or if it is intermittent. Careful observation will help. Pain on slight pressure, indicated by tensing of muscles and withdrawal of the leg, may guide you to the site of the lameness. Any lameness that is not obviously improving in 24 hours needs veterinary attention, but young puppies will often be crippled with lameness at one moment and virtually sound in half an hour.

Leptospirosis

This is a common but serious bacterial infection of dogs. Although one type of the infection can be caused by contact with rats, the most frequent transmission is by carrier dogs' urine. For this reason the infection is considered to be more common in male dogs, which are more prone to lamp-post sniffing than bitches and consequently more likely to be contaminated by infected urine. In country districts carrier foxes may transmit the disease. It causes fever, marked depression, sometimes diarrhoea with yellow faeces, and often bright yellow urine. Visible jaundice is rarer, but both liver and kidneys are affected. Treatment is by antibiotics and effective nursing care. The disease can be prevented by annual re-vaccination.

Lice see Parasites

Mites see Parasites

Nephritis see Kidney diseases

Paralysis

Hind-limb paralysis is frequently seen in the long-backed breeds of dog because of pressure on spinal nerves including injury caused by the protrusion of intervertebral discs. Treatment may be prolonged, but should be continued while the dog has muscular tone in its hind limbs. Conscientious breeders have managed to control hind-limb paralysis in the most affected breeds such as the Dachshund. Weight control and exercise also help to prevent spinal and associated problems. Generalized muscular paralysis is sometimes a sequel to distemper, but is otherwise uncommon in dogs. Sudden paralysis of the back legs occasionally occurs through pressure caused by simple constipation. It will disappear when the constipation is treated.

Parasites

Common external parasites include fleas, which are light or dark brown, very mobile and readily visible when numerous. They are often passed back and forth between dogs and cats. Lice tend to be present in large numbers. The lice or their egg cases are quite firmly attached, often around the ears; they are white in colour and can be mistaken for skin scales or dandruff if not examined closely.

Sarcoptic mange is very serious and is caused by a smaller parasite that is not easily seen. It causes intense itching and skin sores.

Harvest mites are visible on careful examination. They occur usually in comparatively small numbers on the legs and lower parts of the body. They are not mobile, and cause intense local irritation.

Ticks are rarely important in Europe although they are carriers of serious diseases in Africa and parts of the United States. The sheep tick, *Ixodes*, is the common one to affect dogs in temperate climates. It looks like a small grey bladder when mature and is very firmly attached. It should either be left to fall off itself after a few days, or be removed very carefully by hand after anaesthetization with spirit. The sheep tick has long mouth-parts that are difficult to remove from the skin and cause localized infection if left in place.

Tropical ticks are easily removed, but may carry the blood parasite *Babesia*, which causes tick fever.

All these parasites may be controlled by baths, powder or spray insecticides.

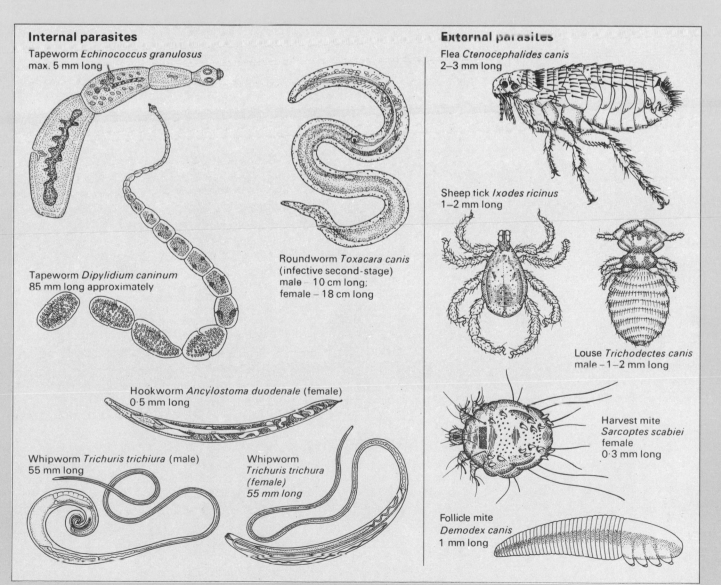

Internal parasites

Tapeworm *Echinococcus granulosus*
max. 5 mm long

Tapeworm *Dipylidium caninum*
85 mm long approximately

Roundworm *Toxacara canis*
(infective second-stage)
male – 10 cm long;
female – 18 cm long

Hookworm *Ancylostoma duodenale* (female)
0·5 mm long

Whipworm *Trichuris trichiura* (male)
55 mm long

Whipworm
Trichuris trichura
(female)
55 mm long

External parasites

Flea *Ctenocephalides canis*
2–3 mm long

Sheep tick *Ixodes ricinus*
1–2 mm long

Louse *Trichodectes canis*
male – 1–2 mm long

Harvest mite
Sarcoptes scabiei
female
0·3 mm long

Follicle mite
Demodex canis
1 mm long

Determined application over weeks or months may be necessary to eliminate them altogether.

'Fly Strike' occurs in untreated wounds of dogs. Certain flies lay their eggs in the dog's coat, attracted by the decaying flesh, and small white larvae hatch in a day or two. Treatment of the wound and insecticidal attack on the larvae is essential. Fly egg deposits in faecal matter caught around the anus of hairy breeds such as Old English Sheepdogs can be a serious problem also.

Internal parasites include the common intestinal worms. Round worms infest almost all young puppies and are passed on from the dam. The worms are responsible for the extremely rare condition in humans, *visceral larva migrans*. Because of this and their adverse affect on puppies, all litters should be dosed from about three weeks of age, and every three weeks thereafter until they are six months old. Residual worms in the adult are activated during pregnancy; the bitch should be dosed before she gives birth.

Tapeworms are common. All have a life cycle that includes a secondary host. The commonest dog tapeworm is one that has the dog flea as its secondary host. Other tapeworms have a life cycle involving sheep and are a great nuisance in sheep-farming countries. New Zealand, for example, has a compulsory treatment programme for dogs.

Hookworms and whipworms are less common, but they both cause intermittent diarrhoea and other symptoms.

Different drugs are effective individually against each of these worms. Some newer ones are able to combat most worms. It is worth discussing a routine with your veterinary surgeon.

Peritonitis
Acute peritonitis is uncommon in dogs despite the variety of apparently dangerous objects many of them swallow. Signs include high temperature and a tense, painful abdomen. More chronic inflammation can occur with remarkably few symptoms. Take the dog to a veterinary surgeon if you suspect peritonitis.

Pneumonia
Although bacterial pneumonia is no longer the scourge it once was it is still a serious disease. If suspected it needs prompt attention. The signs include difficult or distressed breathing and general malaise. A deep cough is usually apparent and the dog's temperature is

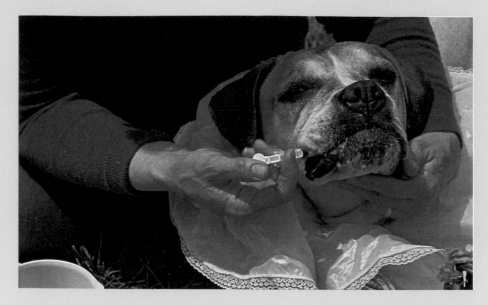

raised. Virus infections are also involved. Apart from conventional treatment with antibiotics and nursing, the use of oxygen may be helpful.

Poisons
Poisoning in dogs is uncommon. Signs fall into two general groups. There is nervous involvement with either heightened reactions ranging from muscular twitching to convulsions, or reduced reactions leading to coma. Modern insecticides are prominent in the poisons involving the nervous system. There is also the 'euteric' group causing acute symptoms of gastro-enteritis, with vomiting and diarrhoea. Caustic poisons result in an inflamed ulcerated mouth and tongue, and the 'Warfarin' (Coumarin) type of rat poison may cause severe blood disorders in dogs. In cases of suspected poisoning do not treat the dog without reference to a veterinary surgeon. Take any suspected container or material with you when the dog goes for treatment.

Prolapse
Rectal prolapse can sometimes occur through straining during defecation, more especially in old dogs with weak muscles. Vaginal prolapse is an even less common sequel to whelping, but prolapse of vaginal polyps, giving the appearance at first sight of vaginal tissue itself, is more often encountered. The prolapsed tissue should be kept as clean as possible and the dog prevented from licking or biting the lesion. Veterinary attention should be sought.

Rabies
Rabies is one of the most feared of all animal diseases. It can be transmitted to

Above: A dog that is weakened from illness or injury and that finds it difficult to eat or drink, can be fed glucose through the side of its mouth with a syringe-like applicator. Right: Rabies posters advertise the dire results of this terrible disease.

man and other mammals, has horrible consequences and invariably kills. An infected dog may suffer convulsions and snap and bite any object and refuse to drink. Dehydration later sets in, then total paralysis and death. But first signs are unlikely to be specific. The most commonly reported symptom is a complete change in the dog's nature, often involving apparent fear of its owner. Quarantine regulations are aimed at preventing the disease entering a country. If rabies is suspected a veterinary surgeon must be told without delay and the dog kept in total isolation.

Rheumatism
Muscular rheumatism is common in dogs, usually, but not invariably, after six or seven years old. The signs include intermittent pain, which may be localized or in various limbs. The condition is not usually serious but demands treatment nevertheless. Drugs are usually successful in alleviating the pain. A warm and comfortable bed may help.

Rickets
Rickets is a disease of growing animals, caused by an imbalance of Vitamin D, or calcium or phosphorous. There may be lameness, but the most obvious signs are enlarged limb joints, even enlarged bone-cartilage junctions down the length of the ribs. Giant breeds are particularly prone to the disease. A well-balanced diet is the best means of prevention.

Road accidents

The place to treat a dog injured in a road accident is at the veterinary surgery. Telephone first to make sure a surgeon is available, and transport the dog on a blanket or something similar, moving it as little as possible. The possibility of further injury through transportation is slight compared with the risk of complications caused by delay. If the dog is attempting to bite because it is in pain, tie a cord or belt around its muzzle and behind its neck.

Sex play

Male or female puppies will mount each other, or humans, in apparent sex play. In the young this is considered more as 'dominance play' than an act of overt sexual implication and should be regarded in that light. The sometimes aggressive sexual behaviour of mature male dogs to their owner may have the same origins, but it becomes actively sexual and antisocial if not curbed. It can sometimes be cured only by castration.

Shock

Shock occurs readily in dogs exposed to typical situations involving trauma, such as road accidents. The symptoms, which may include apparent fright, or dullness and blanched membranes, can mask signs of more serious injury. The dog should be kept quiet and calmed until veterinary assistance is obtained.

Shyness

This term tends to be used to cover any untoward behaviour of a dog, from disinclination to leap joyfully into a stranger's lap to attacking everyone it sees on sight. The first step to overcoming it is to decide what the problem really is. If the dog is just genuinely shy, give it a chance to meet new people on its own terms. If the dog is vicious, acknowledge the fact and decide whether you can handle the problem. It may be that the animal is hopelessly anti-social. There is an undoubted inherited tendency to shyness and similar behavioural problems, but many of them can be overcome with patience and advice on training.

Temperature

The normal rectal temperature of a dog is about 101·5°F (38·5°C), varying by half a degree up or down. Temperatures should be taken using a snub-nosed clinical thermometer. First shake the mercury to below 95°F (35°C), lubricate the thermometer and insert it for half its length into the dog's rectum. Hold it and exert slight sideways pressure to keep it in contact with the walls of the rectum. Virtually every thermometer gives an accurate reading in 30 seconds but it is usual to keep it in place for about one minute.

Ticks *see* Parasites

Vomiting

The usual cause of vomiting is some degree of gastritis but other causes include digestive upsets, bacterial infection and the presence of foreign bodies or indigestible bones. Vomiting is a symptom, not an illness in itself. Dogs can voluntarily vomit. If your dog does vomit, and this happens more than a few times in a short period, if blood is present or the dog appears to be in pain, seek veterinary help. *See also* Gastritis.

Warts

Older dogs of most breeds suffer from warts, but they are particularly common in Spaniels and Poodles. Surgical removal may be necessary, particularly if the warts become infected as often happens. A vaccine may be effective in preventing their re-appearance. Young puppies occasionally suffer from a crop of warts, but treatment to prevent soreness until they disappear is usually all that is necessary.

Worms *see* Parasites

Many owners have an almost instinctive recognition of something being not quite right with their dogs, but not every sick dog is recognized quickly enough. The ability to decide whether a dog is healthy or sick comes from a combination of experience and observation, both of which should be consciously developed by the concerned owner. Normal behaviour is an important indicator of a healthy animal and should be carefully noted by the owner. All dogs sleep a great deal, but should be alert and lively when they are awake. Sluggishness may result from a variety of causes, from old age or obesity to such serious diseases as acute anaemia.

Disease may be acute or chronic; the former develops rapidly, accompanied by signs of obvious illness, while the latter is insidious and consequently often unnoticed until the illness is far advanced. Appetite and bodily conditions are helpful guides in both forms of disease. Healthy dogs usually have a good appetite, but that of a sick dog may be reduced or vary from normal. Excessive thirst for instance is often an important sign of certain diseases, sometimes indeed the only obvious sign. Acute disease is often accompanied by a complete refusal to eat, but equally important is the slight, possibly inapparent loss of appetite which may accompany chronic disease. Prolonged, gradual weight loss should never be neglected; normal weight for its age is an essential sign of a healthy animal.

Chance observation is the usual way of noticing something amiss with a dog, but a straightforward methodical check over the animal's body will often help confirm the suspicion that the dog is not well, and can be a considerable help to the veterinary surgeon.
Starting from the head:
Do the eyes appear normal? They should be bright, no sores or ulcers, the whites of the eyes clear looking, with no signs of being affected by swollen veins, but not excessively pale.
Is there any discharge from the eyes or nose, and is the nose free from encrusted material?
Is the mouth a healthy pink colour and do the teeth look normal and white, without any marked discoloration? Look into the dog's opened mouth. Pieces of wood or bone can be wedged between the upper teeth for months without being recognized.
Are the ears clean, free from waxy deposits, or do they smell? Healthy ears have a clean, pink look. There should not be matted hair in the ears, often a problem with poodles, as this can lead to more serious ear infection. The head, limbs and trunk of a healthy dog's body will have no unusual swellings and the skin no wounds, other than perhaps minor scratches, and no sign of hair loss or sore inflamed patches. Standing or moving, the dog should appear comfortable; a 'haunched' stance or lameness always indicates that something is wrong.
Location of a lameness may be extremely difficult (or blindingly obvious) but remember the old dodge of imagining a stone in your own shoe, it will remind you how a lameness affects movement. The dog's head or rump drops when the sound limb has weight on it, and lifts by comparison when the lame leg is on the ground. After that it becomes a matter of gentle, but firm pressure with the hand to find where the pain is, but once again this is often easier when the dog is relaxed at home, instead of tense in the surgery.

The skin should be elastic, and spring back into place rapidly after it is lifted away from the animal's body. This varies from breed to breed. A Labrador puppy's skin, for example, always seems several sizes too large, but it still feels elastic and somehow 'healthy'.

The most popular guide in determining health is the dog's temperature, which is normally between 38° and 39° Celsius. In good health it is unlikely to fall much below 38° except just before whelping, when it is usual to record rectal temperatures as low as 37°. Excited or nervous healthy dogs may go as high as 39·5° for short periods.

There is no reason why a careful dog-owner should not take a dog's temperature. Use a snub-nosed clinical thermometer and grease the end. Make certain it is shaken down to well below the 38° mark. Insert *and hold it* into the dog's rectum for approximately half the thermometer's length, applying slight sideways pressure to hold the bulb against the wall of the rectum. Nearly all thermometers are '30 second' tested, but it is usual to keep it in place for a full minute to make sure. Wipe it before reading and wash it afterwards in cold water with disinfectant.

Pulse and respiration rate are probably not worth recording in most circumstances, but difficult or heavy breathing and unusual sounds should be noted.

Vomiting and diarrhoea, alterations in the pattern or type of urination and vaginal discharges should never be

Below: Detecting illness can be a simple matter of being able to tell from general appearance when a dog is 'off colour'. The Setters are clearly in the best of health.

Above: A dog injured in a road accident can be quickly treated if moved gently in a blanket to the veterinarian's surgery. Left: A dog's temperature is taken in the rectum.

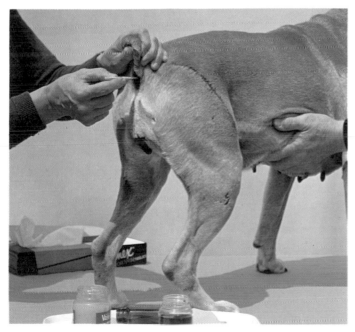

ignored by the conscientious animal-owner.

People rarely have difficulty in deciding that a particular problem in their dog is urgent. Most are inclined to over-emphasize the urgency of need for attention, and it is understandable that they do so. It is more difficult to decide what first aid measures to take. The question to ask yourself is: should you do anything? Most people have the feeling that they should do something, but, although they rarely do harm with first aid, they often do little good at some hazard to themselves. A dog having a fit is a case in point. Forget about it swallowing its tongue and choking – it won't. But if you try to put a gag in its mouth in the traditional way you will probably get your fingers bitten, so just leave it alone, and move all the breakable objects out of its way.

Similarly with a dog in collapse, forget the heart massage and just get it to the vet.

On the other hand, animals which are bleeding badly do need rapid first aid, preferably not by tourniquet but with a pressure bandage applied tightly to the wound. A dog's life can even be saved by a sensible owner using a school scarf in this way. Open wounds which are not bleeding badly, but which look large enough to need stitching, should simply be kept clean, and old cotton sheets are probably ideal for the purpose. But do not cover such wounds in antiseptic ointment or wound dressing powder – it only means a longer cleaning job for the nurse before the veterinary surgeon can see what he is meant to be sewing up.

Leg injuries and possibly broken bones should be disturbed as little as possible, conducive with reasonably rapid transportation to a veterinary surgeon. Nevertheless, it is certainly better to take the slight risk of further injury by movement rather than leave the animal in an exposed place. All dogs involved in a road accident, however trivial, should be checked by a veterinary surgeon because of the risk of shock or internal injury.

Most veterinary surgeons prefer to treat dogs at their surgery, some even refuse to make house calls under any but the most exceptional circumstances, and the reasons are primarily medical. Proper examination demands suitable facilities and these are rarely to be found in domestic surroundings. When a receptionist tries to persuade a client to bring the patient in to the surgery, she is not doing so merely because the veterinarian 'cannot be bothered' to call, but because experience has taught that in nine cases out of ten attention at the surgery is likely to be more satisfactory.

It is important that pet-owners know the consulting hours of the veterinary surgeon, whether such times are given over normally to consultations by appointment or are run as 'open' surgeries on a first come first dealt with basis, and whether the surgery's telephone number is the same as the out of hours emergency number. Anyone with a pet who does not already have this information should obtain it without delay as a precaution against future need. Even though it may not be necessary for your dog to be seen by the veterinarian at the moment it could be a sensible precaution just to call in on the receptionist and register your intention to use the practice should the need arise.

If the practice holds open surgeries only, prior arrange-

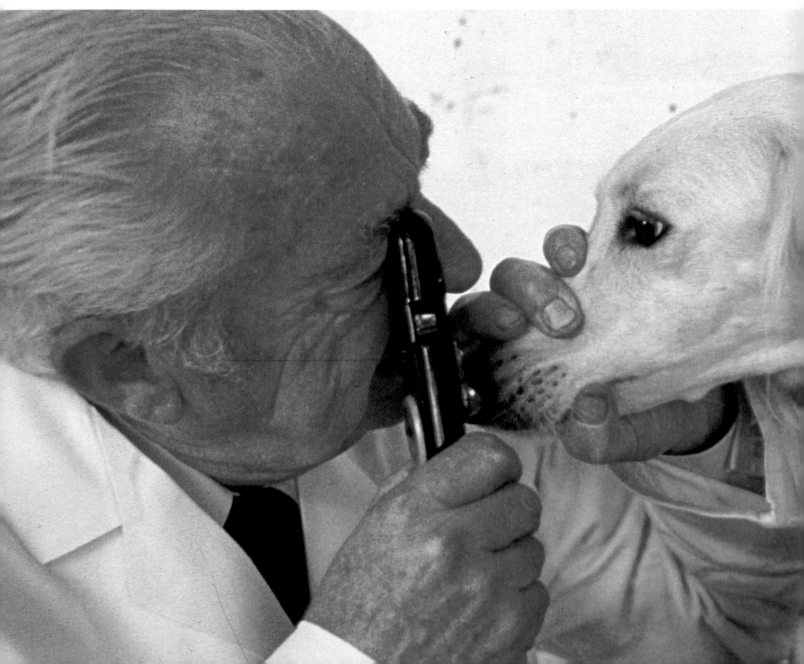

ments for attendance are not necessary and most people for most purposes will simply go along and form the queue. But a telephone call beforehand is appreciated if you intend to present anything out of the ordinary, such as a case which may take longer than normal to deal with, or a dog that may be suspected of suffering from an infectious disease which could affect other pets.

Practices which run an appointment system require you to telephone beforehand. The receptionist answering the phone will routinely ask about the problem in order to make the most suitable placement on the list. She will not need the case history, just your name and address, the dog's name and briefly the reason for the desired visit.

All services that have to deal with emergencies recognize that a routine procedure is the quickest way to handle problems and that short cuts rarely work. If veterinary staff do not *seem* to respond adequately to your demand for emergency attention it is because they are viewing the situation dispassionately but efficiently. If an accident occurs either at home or in the road, and an emergency arises, telephone first. Few veterinary practices can

guarantee to have professional staff on the premises at all times, although all will have a veterinary surgeon available for recall at short notice. An advance telephone call will often be the quickest way to obtain attention..

In an emergency most veterinary practices will advise you to bring the dog into the surgery as quickly as possible (although practices with an equipped ambulance may prefer to send it out). If the instruction is to bring the dog in do not be put off by the first-aid manual's advice about not moving the patient. Moving a dog as carefully as possible is far less likely to harm the animal than leaving it where it is, to suffer from shock or haemorrhage for a possibly prolonged period. Common sense in careful handling is a safe guide in almost all circumstances. If a leg is hanging uselessly, support it. If the dog is unable to move, carry it, if necessary in a blanket. And remember, if you cannot get close enough to it to restrain it, neither can the veterinary surgeon. Dogs which are not able to run away because of injury, but are nevertheless defending themselves by biting at all comers, can usually be restrained by throwing a blanket over them; they won't suffocate. Injured animals are often very frightened and need calm and quiet handling, but it is sometimes necessary to be firm yet careful in order to restrain them without getting perhaps severely bitten.

Left: Most veterinarians' surgeries have a reception and a waiting system. **Below:** A calm and helpful owner can be of great assistance when a dog is injured and in pain and needs reassurance during examination and treatment.

Most people are probably more familiar with their medical GP's office than with veterinary surgeries. There are obvious similarities, but many essential differences, and the first may arise as you go through the door. It is a basic difference: all floors in veterinary surgeries have to be impervious to liquids and easily cleaned. Occasional accidents occur in doctors' waiting rooms but they are everyday occurrences in veterinary reception rooms.

Reception and waiting rooms may be separate or combined, it is a matter of choice. On the one hand there may be the consideration that a client wants to discuss something confidentially with the receptionist, an arrangement about an account perhaps; on the other hand the veterinary surgeon may feel that a receptionist working in the waiting room is more welcoming, and can help to put clients, and perhaps patients, at ease.

Most veterinary surgeries will have one or more examination rooms, the equivalent of the doctor's consulting room, which will probably have only minimal equipment for clinical examination of the patient. The two essential items are good lighting and a firm examination table. Once again the system may vary. Immediate treatment following diagnosis may be carried out in the examination room, an injection perhaps or irrigation of an ear, or this may be passed on to a side-room where a nurse may do the same thing on the veterinary surgeon's instructions. A particular difference in British medical and veterinary practice is that a prescription for treatment of an animal will almost certainly be dealt with on the premises, usually immediately by a nurse or assistant, whereas the majority of doctors write a prescription to be filled by the local pharmacist.

Another matter for some measure of choice is whether the owner or a nurse holds the dog for examination. The writer believes that many dogs are less disturbed if their owner holds them during the course of simple examination, and this method is preferred if it is apparent that no harm is likely to occur to anyone. If the owner cannot safely restrain the dog the veterinary assistant takes over. Quite often a calmer firmness is all that is needed,

although every owner must understand that considerably firmer handling, including a nose bandage to muzzle the dog, may be required occasionally. As a matter of policy the writer insists that nose bandages are not kept in the examination room, to make plain to staff that they are to be considered only after less severe techniques are exhausted. For prolonged examination or treatment, sedation is probably more widely used in veterinary than in human medicine.

There are a very few practising veterinaries who will not carry out surgical techniques more complicated than

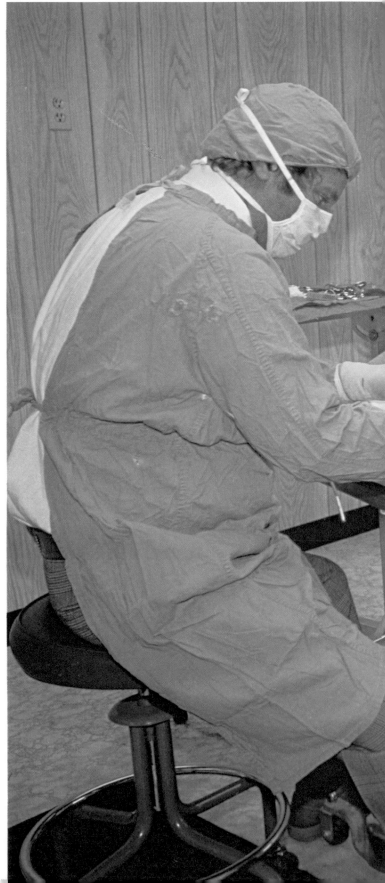

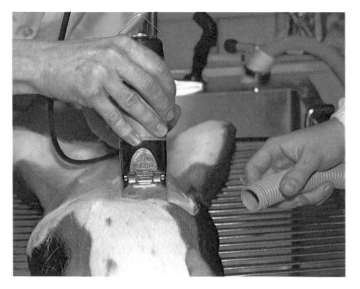

Above: Under anaesthesia a dog is prepared for an abdominal operation. Right: A veterinarian operates on a dog under much the same conditions that humans have created for themselves. The equipment and skill required are the same.

injections or lancing an abcess (although these are close to the limits of the modern-day medical GP). Much of the interest in practice to many veterinary surgeons is in the development of their surgical skills. The tradition of general veterinary medical and surgical treatment by the same person has led to a low degree of specialization in veterinary surgery, and one man's morning might well consist of seeing a series of patients with the usual, or perhaps some unusual diseases, followed by a hysterectomy and a spell of orthopaedics. Both types of operations will have been done as competently as you could have expected in a human operating theatre, but the chance of a heart transplant being done next by the same surgeon is remote. Regrettably, considering the cost and benefit, the demand for heart transplants in dogs is also uncommon.

Most veterinary surgeons are equipped to exercise their surgical skill to reasonable limits, which will vary from person to person. Most know their limits. If a particular operation seems desirable but is beyond a veterinarian's technique, the owner will be referred to a colleague who is better qualified and equipped to perform the task.

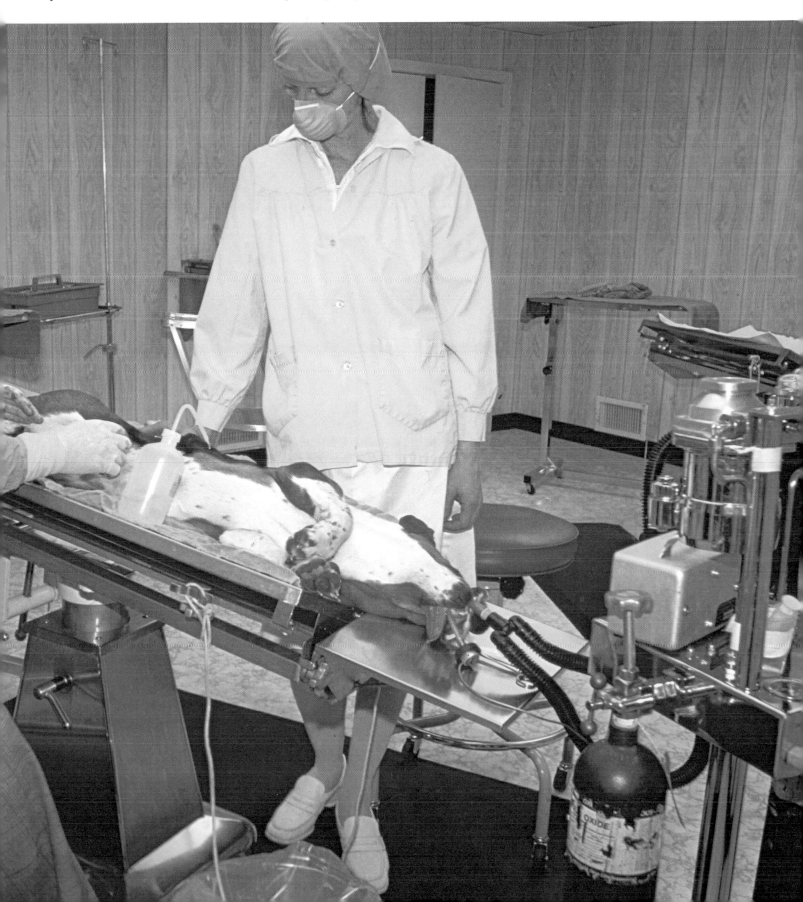

One of the interesting contrasts between human and veterinary medicine is in the use of hospitals. In Britain the extensive state hospital service is among the largest employers in the country. Hospitals have become frequently massive and impersonal centres for the administration and treatment of ill-health rather than their traditional role of the provision of nursing care.

The lack of tax-payers' money has forced the British veterinary profession to move slowly into hospitalization of its patients, and given its members the opportunity to evaluate the use of a hospital system of treatment in terms of their patients, and their clients, rather than 'efficiency'. It has become noticeable that in both the United States and Europe, the growth of veterinary hospitals has slowed considerably, being displaced by smaller units offering necessary hospitalization facilities but with treatment based on out-patient attendance.

The decision to hospitalize a dog for treatment is primarily one for the veterinary surgeon, but it will be influenced strongly by the owner's attitude and circumstance. After much routine surgery and in the management of many diseases, the main ingredient is still 'tender loving care' and in most cases this is best given by the owner. The point at which care becomes special nursing is

not easily defined. There may be, rarely, reasons why a dog which has not fully recovered from an anaesthetic may be allowed home into the care of an owner who is experienced, competent and in whom the veterinary surgeon has considerable trust. For many owners, however, a dog which is only slightly depressed after an anaesthetic for minor surgery still poses problems outside their experience or ability to cope, and anaesthetic recovery cases probably occupy more hospital space in the average veterinary clinic than all others combined.

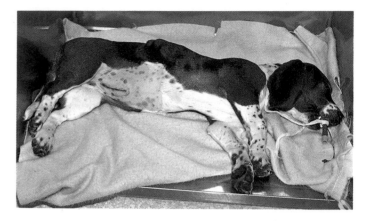

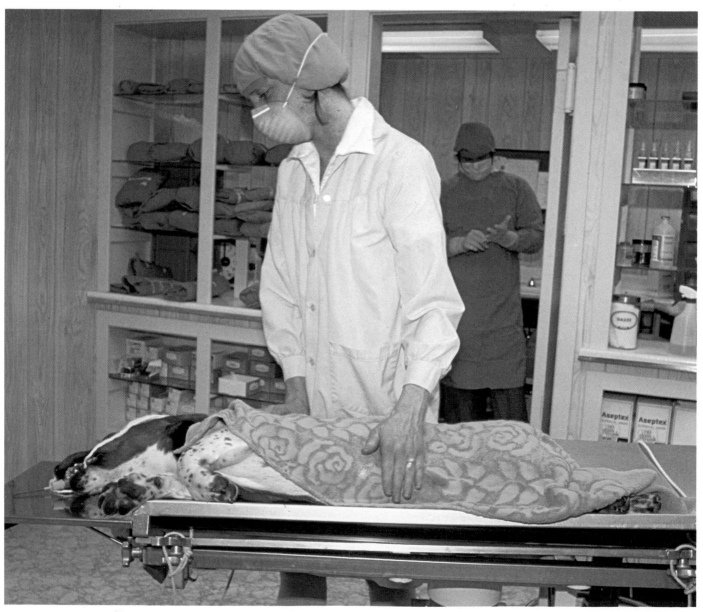

Apart from this routine use of hospitalization, in-patient care is mostly concerned with special attention which cannot be given by the owner. This is usually determined by the nature of the treatment and use of particular equipment, or by the need for frequent observation and assessment. The use of an intravenous drip is a good example. The equipment has to be set up by trained hands and then continuously monitored and adjusted. Most critically, however, it requires efficient restraint of the patient. Most drips are given when the dog is in no condition to move about, but every veterinary nurse has had to cope with dogs that suddenly decide they feel much better and try to get up.

Some hospital care facilities must be available for dogs with 'owner problems', and it is important that owners discuss the question of care with the veterinarian. If an owner is out at work all day, for example, difficulties in home care could arise that may well delay the dog's recovery. Take, for instance, the routine operation of spaying a bitch. Most such cases are sent home the same day or the day after on the assumption that the owner will keep an eye on them. Most bitches will lick the operation wound, but only very rarely will one attempt to bite the stitches out. But if this happens, and the chances are

multiplied if the bitch is on her own at home and is bored, veterinary attention is needed urgently.

In this situation no nursing ability is required on the part of the owner, but observation can be critically important. If the owner is forced to be away from home it is worthwhile considering hospitalization for two or three days.

Hospitalization should also be considered where, for emotional or other reasons, home treatment is not acceptable to the owner. Perhaps an owner cannot bear the sight of an unpleasant sore on a dog's body, or is unable to administer the prescribed tablets (and it can be extremely difficult). But if for any reason care or treatment of a sick dog cannot be carried out at home, alternative arrangements must be made by talking matters over with the veterinary surgeon.

Below left: After an operation is complete the nursing staff take over the post-operative recovery and care of the dog. Left: The dog has been gently removed from the operating table and laid down in a recovery stall with all the medical aid that it needs. Below: Nursing staff keep a careful eye on the gradual process of return to full health. If the owner is unable to take on the full-time nursing of a sick pet, hospitalization is recommended where possible. This can speed recovery and an early and happy return home.

3 | Management and Training

To get the most from a new family pet it is necessary to know how to train it and give it proper care so that it will become a social asset and a pleasure to its owners.

Below: Choosing a pet is a decision to be enjoyed by the whole family.

The decision to have a dog should be a family decision. It is not one that can be made lightly and without a great deal of thought. The dog, when you get it, will soon become an integral part of your family and is likely to remain so for many years. It is important therefore, that every member of the immediate family should want a dog and be prepared to accept the duties that responsible ownership entails.

If you decide to have a puppy you should not buy one less than eight weeks old. It should be fully weaned and wormed. Having a puppy in the house is similar to looking after a new baby as it requires regular feeding, play, sleep and training. Anyone who tells you that a puppy is no trouble has never looked after one properly, but the pleasure of the task brings its own reward. If you choose an adult dog it will take a little longer than a puppy to adapt to your way of life.

The most important considerations in purchasing a purebred puppy are predictability and pride of ownership. Each breed follows a pattern and breeders will be able to tell you how the adult dog will look and what personality and temperament to expect from their stock. Pride of ownership can be increased by having a special sort of dog that you are proud of and with whom you are proud to be seen.

If you acquire a mongrel or 'cross breed', as they are sometimes called, you can have no real idea how big the puppy will grow or how it will look when mature.

Once you have decided to buy a purebred dog you will be able to choose from more than 120 breeds. Avoid the temptation of being swayed by the appearance of dogs seen on TV commercials or in glossy magazines.

It is no use thinking about a Great Dane, Afghan Hound, Old English Sheepdog or German Shepherd if you live in a flat or very small town house. These dogs need plenty of room. By the same token if you live in the country and are looking for a companion for long walks a Pekingese is not for you. If you are looking for a playmate for your children and they are at the 'toddler' stage, most of the breeds classified as 'toys' would not be suitable as they are too much of a temptation for a small child to pick up. A puppy can be easily dropped – and does not like the experience. Children have to be taught how to treat a dog properly. They must not, for example, squeeze a puppy as if it was a teddy bear. A larger, tougher breed would be more suitable for young children.

Christmas is never a good time to introduce a puppy into a family, especially when children are around. There are too many other things demanding the owner's attention which make it difficult for a puppy to settle and be properly cared for and appreciated at this time of year. Late spring and early summer have the advantage of fine weather and make house training easier. But it is grossly unfair and unsettling to introduce a dog into the household and then, two or three weeks later, to put it into kennels while the family goes on holiday.

There are advantages in buying from a breeder rather than from a large department store, a pet shop or an advertised dog hypermarket, or a puppy farm that stocks many breeds and sells them on hire purchase terms. No reputable breeder, who has the welfare of his dogs at heart, sells to any of these establishments. He likes to know that the puppies he has carefully raised are going to the right homes. A breeder has a reputation to uphold. A puppy bought from him will be a planned puppy. The stud dog will have been carefully chosen and the dam will have

Left: Small children are occasionally afraid of big dogs, but mature dogs rarely lack patience with children. A calm introduction, however, can be the beginning of a lasting friendship. Above: The company that a dog can offer old people can be invaluable, but again the right breed needs to be carefully chosen.

had the best possible care and the puppy itself reared to the highest possible standard.

The breeder will make sure you know exactly how to look after and feed your puppy. If your puppy has not been vaccinated against distemper, hepatitis and leptospiroses the breeder will tell you when to take it to your veterinary surgeon to have this done and what precautions to take in the meantime. If you buy a puppy which has had vaccinations, demand to see proof.

If you buy from a pet shop or puppy farm the puppy will have been bought by these dealers as cheaply as possible for resale. Or it may come from a bitch they own and which is bred every time it comes in season. Such puppies do not receive the devoted attention to rearing given to those bred by reputable breeders. You may save a little on the purchase price but it may involve costly visits to the veterinary surgeon to restore the pup to good health.

The best method of finding a breeder in your area is to contact the Kennel Club. Breeders sometimes have older dogs they are willing to sell for a very reasonable sum to a good home. Nearly always these dogs will give many happy years of companionship and love. They are ideal for people who feel a puppy may be too exuberant.

Write or telephone the breeder, do not visit him casually as he is a busy person. Make an appointment to see the puppies and when you go take only immediate members of your family with you as too many people can confuse the issue. Good breeders will be able to help you make the right choice of breed for your particular circumstances.

The aim of every serious breeder of pedigree dogs is to breed something as close as possible to the standard of the breed approved by the Kennel Club, to improve the stock and to produce a champion. Some puppies, very attractive but not quite up to show standard, will make wonderful pets. Sometimes a breeder will offer you 'pick of the litter,' but most of them breed for show and will want to keep the dogs with the best show prospects.

When making your final choice of a puppy there are several additional factors to bear in mind. Look for a confident, enquiring puppy, a lively youngster with bright, sparkling eyes, and a shining coat and a moist nose free from mucous. It should be a 'firm' puppy, not one whose ribs stick out or with a tummy that is disproportionately large. Discard a sluggish-looking puppy and choose an extrovert instead. A puppy should be a mixture of appeal, mischief, curiosity, sensitivity, playfulness and, when asleep, serenity.

If you want a show-type puppy, say so, although it will be more expensive than the obvious pet puppy. The 'pick of the litter' does not always live up to its early promise. If you really want a show dog it is better to buy something between five and eight months old.

The best time to collect your puppy is in the morning, which gives it time to settle in its new surroundings before the loneliness of the night. If you are going by car remember that this will be the puppy's first outing and the first time away from the litter. Take some old towels, newspaper and paper towels in case it is car sick. Any animal when moved from one environment to another experiences stress, and dogs are no exception.

When you get home take the puppy into the kitchen. First associations are important and the kitchen, usually warm and with a lingering smell of food, makes a happy introduction to new surroundings. A house pet will always live in the house but it is a good idea to keep any puppy indoors until it has received its initial training and is mature.

The puppy should have its own sleeping quarters. A bed in a draft-free area in the kitchen or utility room is necessary. Initially when you bring a puppy home a cardboard carton, with a piece cut out of the front to allow easy access, or a crate lined with newspaper and a piece of old blanket is ideal. Gradually, as the dog grows older this can be replaced with a bed. There are a variety of dog beds on the market and it is a matter of personal preference which one you finally select.

The old wicker-basket type is hard to keep clean and tends to harbour dust and dirt. New plastic beds in bright colours can be lined with a choice of the special washable pile polyester fur fabrics which are veterinary-approved. All dogs love this type of bedding. These beds are inexpensive and easy to keep clean as they can be wiped over inside and out daily with a wet cloth and disinfectant. They come in a variety of sizes.

A canvas base camp-type bed strung between metal supports with its own attractive washable cover will blend with any decor. These are available from small to Great Dane size. Some of the small smooth-coated dogs appreciate the hooded, padded material beds into which they can snuggle and hide. These beds are machine washable. Still another hygienic type of bed, in every size, is the one filled with polystyrene beads which take on the shape of the dog. Whichever type you use, clean it out daily and make sure it is in a warm, draught-free area of the house.

For dogs that are kept outside, a good weatherproof outbuilding with a comfortable bed is ideal. Make sure the building has a window that gives light and ventilation during the warm weather. If the floor is concrete the bed should be raised from the floor. A large wooden box especially designed as a dog bed with wooden blocks attached to the bottom and filled with shredded paper is very acceptable. Purpose-built kennels are available on the market with enclosed runs attached. Most of these are constructed of wood and are therefore easy to scrub and keep clean.

Sleep and periods of rest from the excitement of human companionship during the day are of the greatest importance to a growing dog, so put the puppy firmly in his box for a rest after each meal.

The best plan at night is to play with the new puppy until it is sleepy then take it outside for a final elimination. Put it in the bed (which you have surrounded with clean newspaper), place a loud ticking alarm clock nearby, turn out the light and leave your pet to sleep. It may give a few whimpers at first but will soon nod off.

House training is achieved by patience and persistence. Dogs should be trained where to defecate. Never slap a puppy for being dirty. As far as daytime habits are concerned house-training can usually be achieved within one week.

The puppy should be taken to the same spot in the

Below left: Whatever you offer your dog as a bed should be free from draughts and must be easily cleaned. The Spaniels are making good use of a child's cot which is raised from the ground and has a washable blanket for warmth and comfort. Below: A final elimination before turning in for the night is a must in a good training regime. Bottom: Giving a puppy a shoe or slipper to play with is inviting it to play with all shoes and slippers. It needs its own toys which cannot be confused with its owner's precious belongings.

garden first thing in the morning, preferably immediately it awakens, again after each feed, drink and nap, and last thing at night. When the puppy is taken to the selected spot the command 'Be quick!' should be repeated several times whilst it sniffs around. Once it has obliged, spoken praise such as 'Good boy' or 'Good girl' will soon start to register in the puppy's mind. It is important to remember that this comes under the heading of schooling. It is a serious matter and under no circumstances should you indulge in playing with the puppy on these occasions until after the object of the exercise has been achieved.

People in flats or people who have toy breeds such as Chihuahuas may prefer to 'paper train' their dogs. This involves placing several sheets of newspaper in a convenient position. When you wish the puppy to relieve itself just adopt the procedure outlined above. A word of warning, however. Many a 'paper trained' pup takes a greater than usual interest in any piece of newspaper after this training. If a newspaper has been left lying open on the floor, a table or chair it is inviting use.

Most breeders will give a diet and instruction sheet when you buy a puppy and this diet should be followed as closely as possible (see Chapter 2). The general rule is to feed little and often and as the dog grows older decrease the number of meals but increase the amount until at six months of age the animal is on two meals a day.

Whilst the dog must be allowed to enjoy his own home he will appreciate it all the more if he knows what is his to use. This theory applies to toys, too. If you give a puppy a slipper to play with how can you expect him to understand that he can't pick up any shoes and slippers left lying about? One of the most satisfying toys for small puppies is a man's old sock knotted into a 'dolly' which the puppy can easily carry around in its mouth and shake. It will provide him with endless enjoyment.

Most communities have obedience training or ringcraft classes that will help you help your dog to act in a responsible way in society. Neverthless, there are some elementary points that need to be kept in mind.

Unnecessary barking is a nuisance both to the owner of a dog and to others. While you should praise the dog for warning you of the approach of strangers to your house, you should not tolerate barking just for the sake of it.

A fully and properly trained guard dog must be able to 'switch off' when it is not on duty. Owners of dogs used for guarding must see that they are kept under proper control. If they are used to patrol specific areas and left loose at night, the area must be fully and securely fenced so that there can be no likelihood of children wandering into the area and being attacked. Guard dogs should be treated with respect for their training at all times.

Do not let your dog foul the pavement when it is out for a walk. If it starts to defecate, put it into the gutter immediately. Disposable plastic scoop bags are available which fit easily into the pocket and can be disposed of in a suitable place after use. Increasingly, people are setting aside a part of their garden for their dog to use to relieve itself without damage to lawns.

Parks and beaches have long been favourite exercising and playing areas for dogs, but a little thought needs to be given to the people using these areas. Dogs should not be permitted to use children's play areas as toilets, and there are few things more annoying to sun bathers than the dog that races out of the sea and shakes itself all over them, or pelts them with sand because it has decided to have a dig.

Do not take your dog for a walk without a lead. It should be allowed to run loose only in an area completely cut off from traffic. It is all too easy for a dog to spot another dog or a cat across a busy street. If the owner is momentarily distracted the dog can dart off and tragedy can quickly result.

Teach your dog to respect other animals. Most dogs will chase livestock unless they are taught not to do so. Farmers in Britain are within their rights to shoot a dog found worrying sheep. If the dog is not shot the owner can be liable for heavy penalties if his dog is found committing this offence.

Most dogs enjoy car rides but it is not advisable to feed a dog just before a journey. And do not allow it to put its head out of a window of a moving car. This can irritate and

Top and above: Specially provided places for dogs to get a drink or to use as toilets make life pleasanter for them as well as their owners and the general public. Left: Classes in ringcraft and in general obedience training for the dogs with their owners are run in many places and advantage should be taken of their existence.

damage the eyes, and in some circumstances can be a hazard to other drivers.

If you have to leave a dog alone in a car make sure it has plenty of ventilation. Do not leave a lead on it and the window open, for the dog could jump out and strangle itself if the lead catches on the door handle or window winder. If the weather is warm take a flask of cold water and a bowl so that the dog may have a drink. In hot weather leave the dog at home. Never keep a dog in the car with the windows closed, no matter what the weather.

The amount of exercise required each day depends on the breed and the living circumstances. If you have a large fenced-in garden or paddock and your dog is allowed to run freely several times a day, further exercise is unnecessary. Toy breeds that have a garden in which to run require very little else. If you have no garden you must exercise your dog. The ideal solution is to take the dog for a good brisk walk first thing in the morning, another short walk in mid-morning or lunchtime, again late in the afternoon and in the evening.

Every dog owner should acquaint himself with the laws relating to dogs and see that these are kept. British owners have to licence annually every dog over six months old. Some countries require proof each year of rabies vaccination before a licence is issued. The owner of a dog that causes an accident or serious damage is liable under the law; this can be covered by insurance for a nominal cost.

A well-behaved dog, like a well-behaved child, is a source of enormous pleasure once it has been taught to live as part of a family group. Initially all training should be done by one member of the family. It is not necessary to spank or punish a dog when it disobeys – the tone of the human voice is sufficient to make it feel ashamed – but it is essential to give lavish praise when you are pleased with your pet. The learning process should be enjoyable for the dog and for its owner.

Training a dog requires patience and self-control. Commands should be short. The words 'No,' 'Sit,' 'Stay' and 'Come' must be understood before your dog can claim to be a welcome guest.

Let your puppy master one thing at a time and do not make the mistake of trying to teach it too much at once. Make sure the dog fully understands each stage of a new exercise before proceeding further. Keep training sessions to 10 minutes at most, but start with periods of two or three minutes and increase the time gradually. Always end a lesson by giving an order that the dog understands, so that it earns praise and the lesson ends on a happy note. Repetition and praise feature strongly in any training programme.

The first thing your dog will learn is its name. It is important that you talk to your dog when it is with you. The next command is 'No!' This means 'Stop it now!' If the puppy is chewing something or doing something that you want to stop, say 'No!' and repeat the instruction followed by its name. This should all be done in a commanding tone of voice. If it does not desist, repeat the command and use the index finger to show what you want the dog to stop doing. When it stops, praise it and try to distract the puppy by encouraging it to otherwise occupy itself.

Many puppies indulge in 'catch me if you can' games when called. This can be overcome by attaching a length of thin cord to the dog's collar and leaving it to trail when the animal is off the lead. If the dog tantalises you just out of reach the game can be soon stopped by putting a foot on the trailing cord followed by a sharp tug and the command 'Heel!' As usual, praise the dog when it obeys.

To teach a small dog to sit it is usually sufficient to say 'Sit!' while putting your hand over the rump of the dog, very gently pushing it down. With a larger dog it is sometimes necessary to put one hand on the hind quarters and the other on the chest so that you are gently encouraging the dog to assume the sitting position. When this has been mastered the follow-on command is 'Stay!' with 'No!' then 'Stay!' being used when the dog starts to rise from the sitting position.

Start your training at home. When the dog has mastered the art of coming, sitting and staying on command next try issuing these commands without warning when it is running loose in the garden. When the dog can be sufficiently relied on to obey, try them when you are out for a walk.

Do not let your dog jump up on people, either at home or outside. Teach it to welcome you with its four feet on the ground. To discourage a large dog from jumping up, repeat the word 'Down!'. If it persists raise your knee so that you catch the dog on the chest or brisket as it jumps, at the same time saying 'Down!' It is slightly more difficult with a small dog. In this case you must use your hand to push the dog, firmly but gently, down saying 'Down!' as you do so.

Training your dog can be a most rewarding experience and well worth the patience and effort you put into it. Below left and below: Train your dog to walk obediently to heel so that in any situation, town or country, you have control over it. Always congratulate and reward such obedience. Right: Until you are absolutely sure of your dog responding to your command, training should be undertaken while the dog is on a lead and can be controlled by it if necessary.

Dogs should never be let out on the street on their own, or left to roam without supervision. The ideal dog is one which follows on the lead when in a built-up area and enjoys his freedom, but is ready to return to heel at once, when in the open country. Certainly it is essential that the dog is taught that there are times when its freedom has to be restricted. It is a most important part of the entire training programme.

It is important for every dog to walk properly on a lead. Some puppies take immediately to a collar and lead but others need more patience and encouragement. When you put a collar on the puppy, it is preferable to use a light one rather than a heavy one. It should be fastened securely yet be loose enough for you to insert two fingers between the neck of the dog and the inside of the collar.

At first the dog may be irritated by the collar and scratch and try to remove it. If you put the collar on just before feeding or play time it will soon be distracted and forget the irritation.

Once the puppy has become accustomed to the collar go into the garden and attach a light lead. Keep the lead very slack and start walking, simultaneously calling the puppy by name. If it starts to move in another direction, keep the lead slack and go with the dog, but continue talking to it. This is to get it used to the feel of a lead attached to the collar and someone controlling the other end of the lead.

The puppy may sit down and decide it does not like this 'game.' Such a response, or lack of response, should be met with encouragement and the offer of a tidbit as a

reward when the puppy eventually moves.

The puppy should start its lead training at an early age. As soon as the prescribed time after the final vaccination has elapsed it can be taken out for walks. First lessons can take place in the garden and gradually be increased. After five or six lessons and a lot of praise it should be happy to go on the lead.

You may find, especially with the larger breeds, that they are so confident they start to pull. This must be checked immediately and in such cases it is advisable to teach the dog to 'heel.' For a dog to walk at heel it must walk on your left side with its head close to your leg. The dog must walk at your pace. If it pulls give the lead a sharp jerk telling the dog to 'heel.' When it is again in the desired position walking in pace with you, slacken the lead. It will soon learn that if it leaves that position by going too fast or too slow it will receive a jerk to bring it into position.

With some dogs it will be necessary to replace the ordinary collar with a 'choke' collar. This is a special piece of chain which fits loosely round the neck but is extremely firm when jerked. It is not advisable, however, to leave a choke collar on a dog when running free.

Left: Dog owners often need help to train their pets. Schools exist for the training of both. After initial indoor instruction, owners and their puppies or mature dogs go out into the street where mutual understanding is of great importance and obedience is essential. Below: Choke chains provide a useful adjunct to a voiced command. Pressure with the hand on the lead and chain reminds the dog to obey. Bottom: A dog walker in the United States with her hands full.

All dogs need grooming, some more so than others; it depends on their coat. A Shih Tzu, Afghan or Old English Sheepdog will take a lot of time to keep attractive, but Dobermanns, Boxers and other smooth-coated breeds require a minimum of grooming. Terriers and Poodles need regular professional attention if they are to look their best. The glamour of a long coat without hours of tedious grooming is combined in such breeds as the Japanese Chin, Saluki or Cavalier King Charles Spaniel.

The ability to keep still while being groomed is a lesson the dog must learn. It should be stood on a sturdy table; if it ever has to go to the veterinary surgeon for treatment it will then know how to behave on a table and have no fears.

For smooth-coated dogs, have two pieces of cotton wool, one dampened with warm water and one dry. You will also need a hound glove, an old towel and a dry, soft chamois leather or piece of velvet. First wipe over the eyes with the moist cotton wool and then the dry. Lift up the flaps of the ears to see that the ear is not red, inflamed or dirty inside. If it is and you see the dog scratching, take it to a veterinary surgeon.

Brush the dog well with the hound glove. This removes any loose or dead hairs. About 100 strokes from nose to tail (not forgetting chest and sides) is a good rule. Repeat with the towel and chamois or velvet.

Terrier breeds will have to be stripped professionally or clipped twice a year, but should be groomed daily with a brush and wire glove in a similar manner to the smooth-coated dog. Their legs and whiskers should be combed daily with a steel comb.

Below: The Poodle having its beard trimmed stands calmly while the task is carried out. Bottom: Long-haired dogs need frequent grooming. The Collie is being held quietly while its coat is stripped. Right: The rough-haired Lakeland Terrier is being smartened up by careful brushing and trimming. Below right: The coat of the Italian Greyhound, as with other smooth-haired dogs, responds well to grooming with a hound glove. The glove gives the coat a healthy sheen.

Long-coated breeds do not need brushing down to the skin every day. Once or twice a week will be sufficient and it is best to use a pure bristle brush for this. If you do find any 'knots,' which tend to form behind the ears, under the front legs and in the 'armpits,' sprinkle them liberally with talcum powder and ease them out with your fingers, finishing off with the brush. If you have a long-coated dog you should especially examine the hind end to see that there is no excreta sticking to the hair.

A 'slicker' is the best type of brush to use for thick, harsh-coated dogs. It is an oblong wire pin brush on a handle and effectively removes the dead hair.

Always dry your dog thoroughly if it gets wet in rain or snow. For smooth-coated breeds a chamois and a towel are ideal. Use a towel with a squeezing motion rather than rubbing long-coated breeds, as rubbing tends to matt the coats. Terriers enjoy a good rub with a rough towel.

Most dogs do not often require a bath, but when you do bath your dog use a reputable medicated shampoo. A baby shampoo can be used for small long-coated dogs and in this case finish off with a cream rinse. Dry the dog well. Many dogs soon get used to a blow-drier.

At certain times of the year, mainly in the summer, your dog can pick up a flea or tick from grass (see Part 2, Common Ailments). Look out for these when grooming. Your veterinary surgeon will be able to advise you of a good spray, powder or special shampoo to use depending upon the severity of the problem. If your dog does pick up any parasites it is equally important to treat the bedding as well as the dog.

Below: Long-haired, rough-haired and smooth-coated dogs all need bathing occasionally. Stand the dog in the bath, use a gentle soap, not a detergent, and use a shower or cups of water to rinse the coat thoroughly. Top right and far right: A hot air blower can be used to dry the coat quickly. Below right: Claw clipping should only be undertaken by a veterinarian or other trained person.

Suitable arrangements must be made for the care of your dog at holiday time. If you are camping or caravanning it will not be too difficult to take the dog with you, although you may find that it is at times inconvenient. Some camping areas do not permit dogs, so be sure to check before you depart.

When you book your holiday make sure that you also book your pet into a reputable boarding kennel. It is important to know that your dog is being well looked after while you are away. It is fair neither to your pet nor neighbours to leave it in their care. Ask the breeder or your veterinary surgeon to recommend a good kennel. Word of mouth is the best recommendation.

Make your reservation at the kennels in plenty of time. Let them know the day and time you will bring your dog in and the day and time you will collect it. Most kennels will ask for a deposit to confirm the booking. They will also insist on seeing a current vaccination certificate. Usually they will ask you what you have been feeding the dog because they will want to follow the same diet to avoid any upsets that may be caused by changing the food.

They may ask you to bring the dog's bed or blanket. This is so that the dog will feel familiar and settle more quickly in strange surroundings. Do not take your dog's feeding dishes unless you are asked to do so. Many kennels charge a small weekly fee for insurance in case of the need for veterinary attention.

When you are considering holiday accommodation for your dog it is quite in order for you to telephone the kennels and ask about the facilities they offer and if the dogs are housed singly in sleeping compartments with adjacent runs. Ask if you can make an appointment to view the kennels before making a booking. When you go to see them ask if you can take the dog to meet the staff, but do not expect to be allowed to take it down to inspect the kennels. It is better to leave children at home when you go on this exploratory visit.

When you actually take your dog to the kennels you will usually leave it at the reception area and collect it from the same place. This is because other dogs already in the kennels would be disturbed and excited by a stream of strangers and it is the kennel owner's responsibility to keep the dogs as quiet and content as possible during the duration of their stay.

Responsible boarding kennel owners love animals and know how to care for them, but do not expect them to be pleased if you telephone or arrive out of hours. A great deal of work goes on behind the scenes, and boarding reception and kennel office hours are arranged so that kennel work is disturbed as little as possible. In many countries boarding kennels have to be licensed and inspected by local government authorities at regular intervals.

If your dog has recently received any veterinary treatment or is in season let the receptionist know. And it is always advisable, before you leave your dog, to give the name, address and telephone number of a friend or relative who can be contacted in case of an emergency.

Choose your pet's holiday home as carefully as you would choose your own, and make certain to book up well in advance of your departure date. Left: Kennel hands do their job for many reasons, but you can be sure that, in a reputable establishment, they like the animals they care for. Above: It may be possible for you to have your dog collected and given five-star treatment. Right: The receptionist will be able to tell you what the kennel offers its temporary guests by way of training or extra comforts.

Transporting dogs abroad is a specialized business. For anyone moving overseas it is necessary to contact one of the kennels or agencies that specialize in shipping. Countries have different requirements and a dog may need to have vaccinations and blood tests as much as 28 days before departure. Documentation also varies from country to country. It is important that this is carried out correctly otherwise the dog may be refused admission upon arrival at its destination.

It is preferable to let the experts in this field carry out the actual shipping of the dog. They can provide a travelling crate of the correct size for the comfort of the dog and one that will be in accordance with the relevant regulations. Documentation can take several weeks, especially where import permits are needed from the country to which the dog is being consigned. It is thus necessary to start making arrangements for your dog well in advance of the date of departure in order to be sure that everything is completed in good time.

Most dogs adapt well to air travel and arrive in excellent condition. It is wise to get the dog accustomed to its travelling crate for a week or so before the journey. This can be done by locking it in the container for short periods, initially for feeding, and gradually increasing the length of time until it willingly stays there all night. If this is done the dog will not find its confinement strange, or be frightened, when the time for the journey finally comes.

Dogs are carried on passenger ships and kennels are usually provided, often staffed by kennel-maids on long voyages on some vessels owned by the large shipping lines. Container ships plying between Britain and Australia also carry dogs and an attendant is employed to look after them. He is not necessarily a trained person but rather someone who is working his passage. A sea journey is often too long for a dog, and temperature changes and a lack of proper exercise and care can mean that the animal may arrive in poor condition.

Several countries apart from Britain have quarantine regulations. The reason for this is simple. Any warm-blooded animal can contract rabies and this disease, nearly always fatal, can be transmitted to humans. Rabies is transmitted by an infected animal through a bite, lick or scratch, or from saliva. Vaccination of animals against rabies is still not 100 per cent effective so the laws of some countries require animals to undergo a period of quarantine on entry.

Quarantine is a very serious business and must be left to government approved bodies. Left: Kennel hands move a dog in its specially designed quarantine box to its stall in the kennels shown in the large picture below. The external appearance is forbidding, but with kindness from kennel staff and plenty of room to run, dogs quickly become accustomed to their new homes and settle down well. Below: throughout air or sea travel, animals' welfare is attended with great care. A short air journey is obviously preferable to a long sea journey. On board ship kennels are often provided.

Every dog brought into Britain from abroad, even from a rabies-free country, has to spend six months in a government-approved quarantine kennel. If during quarantine the dog does not develop the symptoms of rabies it is released to its owners. During this period it does not come into contact with any other animal. Smuggling an animal into countries that have quarantine regulations quite properly carries severe penalties. These range from very large fines to a period of imprisonment. In addition the animal may be destroyed.

Many people wonder what the effects of quarantine will be on their dog and how it will settle down after spending a long time away from home and loved ones. There is no cause for worry. Dogs soon become established in the quarantine quarters and its routine. They receive plenty of care and never seem to forget their families and friends, no matter how long the parting. Dogs do not seem to have a sense of the passage of time.

4 | The Breeds

The following section is derived from official standards of the Kennel Club (KC) in Great Britain, the American Kennel Club (AKC), the *Fédération Cynologique Internationale* (FCI) in Europe, and the Royal Agricultural Society for Kennel Control (RASKC) in Australia.

Top left: Samoyed;
far left: Curly-coated Retriever;
above left: Chihuahua;
left: Tervuerens;
above: Kuvasz.

A

Affenpinscher

Origins

Dogs which look very like the modern breed are to be seen in many paintings dating from the 14th century, but it was not until the turn of the century that the breed attracted enough attention in Germany, its country of origin, to be scheduled at shows. The dog is closely related to the Smooth Miniature Pinscher, but differs from it in temperament, in the shape of the head and in coat. It has also enjoyed a lower level of popularity, having been introduced recently.

Characteristics

Facially the Affenpinscher has a strong resemblance to a monkey and also has some of that animal's mischievousness and humour. The face is flat with round forward-looking dark eyes. The teeth fit closely together and many dogs are slightly undershot. The ears are small and pointed, in America they may be

Afghan Hound

Affenpinscher

Alaskan Malamute

Anatolian Karabash Dog

cropped. The body is short, compact and square with a docked tail, and it is set, fore and rear, on straight legs.

Group
Toy. Pet Dogs (FCI).

Size
Height: In KC, 24 – 28cm (9½ – 11in). Not exceeding 26cm (10¼in) at the shoulder in AKC. In FCI and RASKC 25 – 28cm (10 – 11in).
Weight: In KC, 3 – 4kg (6½ – 9lb).

Coat
Colour: Usually black but black and tan, red, grey and other mixtures are permitted in North America. Light colours and white are not allowed.
Texture: Short and dense, hard and wiry.

The head should carry a good crop of whiskers.

Afghan Hound

Origins
This is a coursing hound from two distinct types which are now almost entirely intermingled from the mountains and plains of Afghanistan, its country of origin. There is some evidence that Afghans moved eastwards along the trade routes and originated in the hounds of the eastern Mediterranean. They were first imported into Britain in 1894, but failed to make much of an impression until, in 1907, Zondin appeared at shows and attracted Royal attention. They were imported into North America in 1926.

Characteristics
A dignified hound, but capable of playing the wilful fool. It needs a lot of excercise and its profuse coat needs frequent grooming. Given proper care it is one of the most striking of breeds and for this reason enjoys the mixed blessing of great popularity. The movement of the Afghan should be smooth and springy with considerable style. The dog gives the impression of strength and dignity combined with speed and power. The head is long and lean, the body strong and deep, with very muscled forequarters and powerful hind-quarters.

Group
Hound. Greyhounds (FCI).

Size
Height: Dogs 68·5 – 73·6cm (27 – 29in), bitches 5 cm (2 – 3in) smaller. In AKC, dogs 68·5cm (27in), bitches 63·5cm (25in), both plus or minus 2·5cm (1in).
Weight: In AKC, dogs about 27·2kg (60lb), bitches 22·6kg (50lb).

Coat
Colour: All colours acceptable.
Texture: Long and fine and allowed to develop naturally.

Alaskan Malamute

Origins
First used as a sledge dog by the Mahlemut people in Alaska, its country of origin, the Malamute is one of the northern Spitz breeds and the largest of sledge dogs. Fable claims that the breed was subject to frequent crosses with wolves; this is disputed by some authors, but authenticated by such authorities on wolves as Canadian biologist, Farley Mowat. These dogs are very tough, capable of great feats of endurance and will survive in conditions to which other dogs would quickly succumb.

Characteristics
A powerful and substantially built dog with deep chest and strong, compact body. The head is strong and like a wolf's with a distinctive white cap or mask. The ears are pricked, the eyes alert and wolf-like. The tail, as in all Spitz breeds, is carried over the back and is thickly plumed. The dog is affectionate, friendly, loyal, an excellent guard and formidable fighter when roused.

Group
Working.

Size
Height: Dogs 63·5cm (25in) at the shoulder, bitches 58·4cm (23in).
Weight: Dogs 38·5kg (85lb), bitches 34kg (75lb).

Coat
Colour: From light grey through intermediate shadings to black, always with white underbodies, legs, feet and part of the face. Only white allowed as a solid colour.
Texture: Thick, dense guard coat, not long nor soft, with a dense undercoat which is deep, oily and woolly. Coat is shorter when the winter coat is shed.

Anatolian Karabash Dog

Origins
The Karabash is a herding and guard dog much valued by Anatolian shepherds who developed the breed over very many centuries from the mastiff dogs which existed in the Babylonian Empire over 3000 years ago. The breed retains a considerable likeness to these ancient mastiffs. Only recently recognized as a show dog, the breed is now finding a degree of popularity well beyond its country of origin.

Characteristics
The head is large and broad, the ears V-shaped and pendant. The back is long, and the powerful loins slightly arched. The tail is long and carried low.

Group
Working.

Size
Height: 66 – 76cm (26 – 30in).
Weight: 40·8 – 67·9kg (90 – 150lb).

Coat
Colour: Cream, fawn or brindle with black points.
Texture: Short and dense.

Australian Cattle Dog

Origins
From imported stock Australia has produced two distinctive and impressive working breeds, the Kelpie and the Cattle Dog. The Cattle Dog has been

known as the Australian, Blue or Queensland Heeler, Heeler being an old British word applied to cattle dogs. In its veins runs the blood of several working breeds which have combined to produce this superlative cattle dog. Black Bobtailed sheepdogs, the Smithfield Drover, two breeds now extinct, as well as Dingos, Kelpies, Smooth Collies and Dalmatians have all contributed to the breed.

Characteristics
The head is broad and wedge-shaped, the ears pricked, and the eyes dark. The chest is broad and the ribs well sprung, the loin is powerful. Hindquarters are well angulated and powerful. The tail is long, carried and furnished like a fox's.

Group
Working.

Size
Height: Dogs 45·7 – 50·8cm (18 – 20in), bitches 43 – 48·2cm (17 – 19in).

Coat
Colour: Blue, blue mottled with or without black markings, some tan is allowed on legs and feet.
Texture: Short.

Australian Cattle Dog

B

Basenji

Origins
This breed originated in Zaire. It is unique as a dog which doesn't bark though it is an accomplished yodeller, and as a Spitz breed from Africa, still very close to its wild ancestors. Known as a guard, hunter and companion in Western Africa for centuries, it was not known in the Western world until two were brought to Britain in 1895; unfortunately both died shortly afterwards. It was not until 1937 in Britain and 1941 in America that imports became more successful and breeding stock became established.

Characteristics
The breed is remarkable for its great cleanliness, produced not only by its short coat but by its personal habits. Basenjis are lightly built, finely boned aristocratic animals, tall, poised, alert and intelligent. The wrinkled head, with pricked ears, is carried proudly on a well-arched neck.

Group
Hound. Terriers (FCI).

Basenji

Size

Height: Dogs 43cm (17in) at the shoulder, bitches 40·6cm (16in).
Weight: Dogs 10·9kg (24lb), bitches 9·5kg (21lb). In FCI, dogs 10·6kg (23½lb), bitches 9kg (20lb).

Coat

Colour: Pure bright red, or pure black, black and tan, all with white feet, chest and tail tip. White legs and white blaze and collar optional.
Texture: Short, sleek and close, very fine.

Basset Griffon Vendéen

Origins

A descendant of the white variety of the

Basset Griffon Vendéen

ancient St Hubert hound. As a hunting hound the breed is said to lack stamina.

Characteristics

The Basset Griffon Vendéen is an intelligent dog, sure of itself, distinguished in physique and gait. The head is well rounded, not too broad, with the stop accentuated by bushy eyebrows. The eyes are large, dark and vivacious and the pendulous ears, soft, narrow, fine and covered with long hair. The overall build is that of a Basset; other varieties, including the Briquet, follow the conformation of the Foxhound.

Group

Hound. Hounds for smaller game (FCI).

Size

Height: Two varieties exist: 38 – 41·8cm (15 – 16½in) and 34·2 – 38cm (13½ – 15in).

Coat

Colour: Fawn, white and orange, white and grey, tricolour.
Texture: Long, bushy, heavy and hard. The skin should not be too fine.

Basset Hound

Origins

This breed originated with the old French hounds, which were crossed with Bloodhounds to produce the dog which Shakespeare compared with Thessalian bulls. The breed was developed in Britain from a litter imported in 1872 from Comte de Tournour by Lord

Onslow. Bassets are a slow-moving, ponderous, deep-voiced pack hound used for hunting the hare. Hounds bred for work and those bred for the show ring may nowadays be very different animals.

Characteristics

A short-legged hound of considerable substance, capable of moving smoothly. The head is big, domed and heavy, owing a lot in appearance to the Bloodhound; the ears are long and pendulous. The body from prominent breastbone to the long, strong stern is of considerable length with well-sprung ribs, a broad level back and arched loins.

Group

Hound. Hounds for smaller game (FCI).

Size

Height: 33 – 38cm (13 – 15in) more than 38cm (15in) is regarded as a disqualifying fault in AKC and FCI.

Coat

Colour: Generally black and white and tan or lemon and white but any recognized hound colour is acceptable. The American standard says that the distribution of colour and markings is of no importance.
Texture: Smooth, short and close without being too fine. The American standard requires a hard coat and loose skin.

Beagle

Origins

This English breed is the smallest of the pack hounds and is used for hunting the hare with followers on foot. By the time Thomas Bewick was writing his *History of Quadrupeds* in 1790, he was able to speak of these small hounds which had already been known for over 300 years. In those days there were two sizes of Beagle, with the name 'vaches' being reserved for the larger variety. Eventually the smaller sort ceased to be used, but attempts have been made in America to recreate the pocket Beagle.

Characteristics

Certainly one of the most popular hounds and one which makes a cheerful companion. The Beagle is compactly built and should convey the impression of great stamina and activity. The standard asks for a short body, fairly well-sprung ribs, powerful loins, clean shoulders and very muscular hind-quarters. The tail, or stern, is of moderate length, carried proudly, but not over the back.

Group

Hound. Hounds for smaller game (FCI).

Size

Height: Not greater than 40·6cm (16in) or less than 33cm (13in). In AKC, there

Basset Hound

Beagle

are two varieties: not exceeding 33cm (13in), and 33 – 38cm (13 – 15in), with hounds over 38cm (15in) being disqualified.

Coat

Colour: Any recognized hound colours.
Texture: Close, hard and of medium length. In Britain the standard differentiates between smooth with a very dense coat, not too fine or soft, and a rough variety with a very dense and wiry coat.

Belgian Shepherd Dog (Groenendael)

Origins

The herding dogs of mainland Europe are all closely related and share several strong family characteristics. However it was not until Professor Reul at the end of the 19th century embarked on a study of these dogs, then generally simply referred to as Chien de Berger, that the various local breeds were accorded separate recognition. Among the three basic types recognized by Professor Reul was one with rather long black hair. The principal breeder of this type was Monsieur Rose of Groenendael whose stock was all descended from a single black pair, Petite and Picard D'Uccle, black being a colour not traditionally favoured by the Belgian shepherds. From this pair developed the Groenendael.

Characteristics

The breed should be intelligent, courageous, alert and faithful, protective of the person and property of its owners, but it should show no viciousness by unwarranted attack. The Belgian Shepherd Dog is a well balanced, square dog, elegant in appearance with a pronounced proud carriage of the head and neck. The head is strong, the ears stiffly erect, the topline slopes from withers to croup, the chest deep but not broad. Forelegs are straight and strong, set into long and

oblique shoulders, hindquarters are broad and heavily muscled. The tail is long and undocked.

Group

Working. Shepherd Dogs (FCI).

Size

Height: Dogs 61 – 66cm (24 – 26in), bitches 56 – 61cm (22 – 24in) at the withers. In KC and FCI, the ideal height for a dog is 62cm (24½in), a bitch is 58·4cm (23in).

Coat

Colour: Black.
Texture: Long, well-fitting, straight and abundant, of medium harshness. The undercoat should be extremely dense, depending on climatic conditions.

Belgian Shepherd Dog (Malinois)

Origins

One of the three breeds of Belgian herding dogs now growing in popularity throughout the world. The three breeds, the Groenendael, Tervueren and the Malinois, share a common heritage and very similar conformation and characteristics, the principal difference between them being coat colour and texture.

Characteristics

As for the Belgian Shepherd Dog (Groenendael).

Group

Working. Shepherd Dogs (FCI).

Size

As for the Belgian Shepherd Dog (Groenendael).

Coat

Colour: Rich fawn to mahogany with black overlay, black mask and ears.
Texture: Comparatively short, straight with dense undercoat.

Belgian Shepherd Dogs: right
Groenendael, top right
Malinois, far right Tervueren.

Belgian Shepherd Dog (Tervueren)

Origins

One of the Belgian sheepdog breeds.

Characteristics

This breed differs from the Groenendael in little other than colour.

Group

Working. Shepherd Dogs (FCI).

Size

Height: Dogs 62cm (24½in), bitches 58·4cm (23in).

Coat

Colour: Fawn with black points.
Texture: Long-haired.

Bernese Mountain Dog

Origins

This is another of the European herding dogs which have been developed from herding dogs left behind by Roman legions. Switzerland is home to four varieties of mountain dogs but it is the breed developed in the canton of Berne which, because of its rich black and tan silky coat, is the most distinctive. By the late 18th century the breed had degenerated, but was rescued by Franz Schertenlieb and Professor Albert Heim so that by the beginning of the 20th century a breed club was founded.

Characteristics

The Bernese Mountain Dog is well balanced, active and alert, combining sagacity, fidelity and utility. The skull is flat with a well-defined stop, eyes are dark, hazel-brown and full of fire, and the ears are V-shaped, set on high and in repose hang close to the head. The body is rather short, compact and well ribbed-up, the chest broad and with a good

depth of brisket. Loins are strong and muscular, and the forelegs are straight and muscular. The hindquarters have well-developed thighs and well-bent stifles. The tail is carried low.

Group
Working. Guard Dogs (FCI).

Size
Height: Dogs 58·4 – 70cm (23 – 27½in); bitches 53·3 – 66cm (21 – 26in).
In FCI, dogs 64 – 70cm (25 – 27½ in), bitches 58 – 66cm (23 – 26in).

Coat
Colour: Jet black with russet-brown or deep tan markings in the traditional black and tan pattern.
Texture: Soft and silky with bright, natural sheen, long and wavy not curly.

Bichon Frise

Origins
Italian traders returning from the Canary Islands in the 14th century brought with them some of the small and very attractive little dogs which they had found in the islands. The dogs probably were descended from the Old Barbet or Water Spaniels from which the original name of Barbichon was derived. Later the name was contracted to 'Bichon' or changed to 'Teneriffe' and the breed began to gain favour in the Royal Courts of Europe. After the French Revolution, the breed became popular as a circus dog but by the 19th century much of its popularity had been lost. After the First World War its potential was again recognized and, in 1933, the present name was adopted, since which time the breed has regained much of its former popularity.

Characteristics
The breed is sturdy and lively with a stable temper, has a stylish gait and an air of dignity and intelligence. The skull is broad and somewhat round with a dense topknot. The ears are dropped and covered with long flowing hair; the large, round eyes are dark and expressive. The neck is rather long and proudly carried behind the erect head. The shoulders are well laid back into a body slightly longer than it is tall, the ribs well sprung, the loin arched and muscular, the brisket well let down. The tail is covered with long flowing hair, carried gaily and curved to lie on the back. The legs are straight and strong boned.

Group
Toy. Non-sporting (AKC). Pet Dogs (FCI).

Size
Height: Not to exceed 30cm (12in) or less than 20cm (8in).

Bernese Mountain Dog

Bichon Frise

Coat
Colour: Solid white, or white with cream, apricot or grey on the ears and on body.
Texture: Profuse, silky and loosely curled. There is an undercoat.

Black and Tan Coonhound

Origins
This is the only recognized breed of half a dozen Coonhounds which include the very impressive Redbone Coonhound, the surprisingly named English Coonhound, and the more American-flavoured Bluetick, Treeing Walker and Plott. These hounds hunt by night as the raccoon is a nocturnal animal. The Black and Tan Coonhound is only recognized in America and was admitted to registry by the AKC in 1945.

Characteristics
Slightly resembles a lightly built Bloodhound, essentially a working dog, capable of withstanding the rigours of winter and the heat of summer. The general impression should be one of power, agility and alertness. His expression should be alert, friendly, eager and aggressive. He should impress with his easy, powerful rhythmic movement.

Group
Hound (AKC). Hounds for smaller game (FCI).

Size
Height: Dogs 63·5 – 68·5cm (25 – 27in), bitches 58·4 – 63·5cm (23 – 25in).
Weight: In AKC dogs 29·5 – 36kg (65 – 80lb), bitches 22·5 – 29·5kg (50 – 65lb).

Coat
Colour: Coal black, rich tan markings.
Texture: Short and dense.

Bloodhound

Origins
In 1553, Dr Caius was able to describe the Bloodhound very much in terms which are applicable today and was perhaps one of the first to mistakenly attribute the source of the breed's name

Black and Tan Coonhound

to their ability to follow a blood trail. In fact the word is used in the same sense as in 'blood stock' as a reference to aristocratic breeding. Even so the breed's reputation as a formidable tracking dog had obviously already been established and has survived up to the present day. The breed is yet another of the English hound breeds originally derived from French stock.

Characteristics

The Bloodhound is a powerful animal, larger than most hound breeds. He is characterized by a thin loose skin which hangs in deep folds, especially about the head, and imparts that lugubrious expression for which he is so often caricatured. In temperament the Bloodhound should not be quarrelsome with other dogs, as his nature tends to be reserved.

Group

Hound. Hounds for larger game (FCI).

Size

Height: On average 63·5cm (25in) for dogs, 61cm (24in) for bitches; in FCI and RASKC 66cm (26in) for dogs.
Weight: Dogs average 40·8kg (90lb), bitches 36.2kg (80lb).

Bloodhound

Greater heights and weights preferred, provided character and quality are maintained.

Coat

Colour: Black and tan, red and tan, red, called fawny in America. White is permissible only on chest, feet, tip of stern. *Texture:* Smooth, short and glossy.

Borzoi

Origins

Until comparatively recently, when the Borzoi's name was changed from Russian Wolfhound, its origins could be easily and correctly assumed. Before the Revolution every Russian nobleman maintained a pack of these hounds which were used in pairs for coursing wolves. It is amusing to note that early dog writers complained that the breed had become so effete that it was no longer able to pull down a wolf without assistance.

Characteristics

A very graceful, aristocratic and elegant dog possessing courage, muscular power and great speed. The head is long and lean, the neck is slightly arched and powerful, the back comparatively short, rising in a graceful curve at the loins, more marked in dogs than bitches. The legs are long, the feet hare-like with well-arched knuckles.

Group

Hound. Greyhounds (FCI).

Size

Height: Dogs from 73cm (29in) upwards, bitches from 68·5cm (27in) upwards. In AKC, dogs 71cm (28in) minimum at withers; bitches 66cm (26in) minimum. In FCI, dogs 75cm (29¾in), bitches 71cm (28in).

Weight: In AKC, dogs 34 – 47·6kg (75 – 105lb), bitches 27·2 – 40·8kg (60 – 90lb).

Coat

Colour: Any, white predominating. Lemon tan, brindle, grey, black. *Texture:* Long and silky, flat, wavy or rather curly, never woolly.

Bouvier des Flandres

Origins

This dog is one of a small group of Flemish drovers' dogs used partly for herding cattle and partly as guards. After the First World War in which they had acted as ambulance and messenger dogs, very few animals survived, but an army vet had saved one dog, Nic, who was to become virtually the father of the entire breed. Bouviers are now used as police and army dogs.

Borzoi

Characteristics

A compactly bodied, powerfully built dog of upstanding carriage and alert, intelligent expression.

Group

Working. Shepherd Dogs (FCI).

Size

Height: In AKC, dogs 59·7 – 69·8cm (23½ – 27½in), bitches a minimum of 57cm (22¾in). In FCI and RASKC, dogs 65cm (25½in), bitches 62cm (24½in).

Weight: 35 – 40kg (77 – 88lb) for dogs, 27·2 – 35kg (60 – 77lb) for bitches.

Coat

Colour: Fawn to black. Pepper and salt, grey and brindle. A white spot on the chest is allowed.

Texture: Rough, tousled and unkempt in appearance, the coat is capable of withstanding the hardest work in the most inclement weather. Topcoat harsh, rough and wiry, undercoat fine and soft.

Boxer

Origins

A German breed, this is one of several European breeds which have their origins in the mastiffs of Southern Europe, and which in the Middle Ages were developed as hunting dogs. Nowadays Boxers are mainly used as police dogs and guard dogs. During the First World War this breed, in common with others of Germanic origin, went through a period of unpopularity, but the Boxer's virtues as a companion and guard dog soon restored it to favour.

Characteristics

A medium-sized sturdy dog of square build with a short back, strong limbs and short, tight-fitting coat. He is clean and hard in appearance and has a firm, springy stride. The head is square and short, a distinctive feature of the breed, with skin forming deep wrinkles. In America the ears may be cropped, but in Britain, where cropping has long been illegal, the ears lie flat and close to the cheeks. The mouth is normally undershot, though the teeth of the underjaw should not be seen when the mouth is closed.

Group

Working.

Size

Height: Dogs 55·8 – 61cm (22 – 24in), bitches 53·3 – 58·4cm (21 – 23in) at the withers. In AKC, dogs 57 – 63·5cm (22½ – 25in), bitches 53·3 – 60cm (21 – 23½in). In FCI, dogs 61cm (24in), bitches 58·4cm (23in).

Weight: About 30kg (66lb) for dogs, about 28kg (62lb) for bitches; in FCI 24·9kg (55lb) for bitches.

Coat

Colour: Fawn, brindle and fawn in various shades from light yellow to dark deer red.

Texture: Short, shiny, lying smooth and tight to the body.

Briard

Origins

The Briard comes from one of several ancient sheepdog breeds which probably came to Europe with the Mongol invaders and which developed into different and localized breeds. This one is from France. By 1809, Abbé Rozier was able to differentiate between the Berger

Boxer

Bouvier des Flandres

Briard

de la Brie (Briand) and the de la Beauce, the difference being in coat length. A club was formed in France in 1900 to protect the breed and by 1930 an agreed standard had finally been adopted. The breed came to Britain after the First World War and to America in 1922.

Characteristics
A strong and substantially built dog, fitted for field work, lithe, muscular, well proportioned, alert and active. Like a number of other European herding dogs, the hind legs each carry two dewclaws.

Group
Working. Shepherd Dogs (FCI).

Size
Height: Dogs 58·4 – 68·5cm (23 – 27in) at the shoulders, bitches 55·8 – 64·7cm (22 – 25½in). In FCI, dogs 61·5 – 68cm (24¼ – 26¾in), bitches 55·8 – 63·5cm (22 – 25in).

Coat
Colour: Dark colours are preferred, but all solid colours except white are acceptable.
Texture: Long, slightly wavy, stiff and strong.

Bulldog

Origins
An excellent choice of breed to represent Britain in that, in spite of numerous hereditary abnormalities, the breed is thriving. The Bulldog was originally used for bull-baiting, a sport which began in the early 13th century and continued until it was made illegal in 1835. The Bulldog as a distinct breed had evolved by the mid-17th century from crosses between mastiffs and more active terriers, and was then more like a Boxer or an old-type Staffordshire Bull Terrier. After bull-baiting became illegal the breed evolved to its present exaggerated form.

Characteristics
The general appearance is of a thickset dog, rather low in stature but broad, powerful and compact. The head is strikingly massive and large in proportion to the dog's size. The face is extremely short, the muzzle very broad, blunt and inclined upwards. The tail is short and screwed, the forelegs are bowed.

Group
Non-sporting. Utility (KC). Working (FCI).

Size
Weight: In KC, 25kg (55lb) for a dog, 22·6kg (50lb) for a bitch. In AKC, 22.6kg (50lb) for dogs, 18kg (40lb) for bitches.

Coat
Colour: Whole or smut, brindles, reds with their varieties, fawns, fallows, white and also pied.
Texture: Fine in texture, short, close and smooth, (hard only from shortness and closeness, not wiry).

Bulldog, French

Origins
This breed has descended from Bulldogs introduced from Britain into France, probably at the end of the 19th century. However there are 17th-century paintings which show dogs very like the present-day Frenchie, which does not necessarily mean that they are any relation of the breed. Whatever its origins, there can be no doubt about the speed at which this stylish miniature Bulldog swept to popularity among the fashion-conscious French.

Characteristics
A French Bulldog should be sound, active and intelligent, of compact build, medium or small-sized, with good bone. The head is massive, square and broad, with a domed forehead and loose skin forming symmetrical wrinkles. The bat ears are distinctively different from the ears of other Bulldog breeds.

Group
Utility. Non-sporting (AKC). Pet Dogs (FCI).

Size
Weight: 12·7kg (28lb) for dogs and 10·8kg (24lb) for bitches. In AKC, there is a lightweight class for dogs under 10kg (22lb) and a heavyweight class for dogs 10 – 12·7kg (22 – 28lb). In FCI, 7·9 – 14kg (17½ – 31lb).

Coat
Colour: Brindle, pied and fawn.
Texture: Fine, smooth, lustrous, short and close.

Bullmastiff

Origins
Shakespeare commended the British mastiffs as being very valiant creatures of unmatchable courage. The Bullmastiff is a nineteenth-century development of these ancient mastiff breeds, the product of a cross with terriers to produce a smaller, more active dog. He was used as and often referred to as the Gamekeepers' Dog and because he often worked at night was sometimes called the Night Dog. A sagacious guard and one feared by even the boldest poacher, quick enough to catch the fastest runner and capable of throwing down and holding the strongest of intruders. First

Bullmastiff

Bulldog

officially recognized as a breed in 1924.

Characteristics

His temperament combines high spirits, reliability, activity, endurance and alertness. He is a powerfully built dog, showing great strength but not cumbersome. The head is large and square, and the skin wrinkles when the dog becomes interested in something. The neck is well arched and very muscular, the chest broad and deep, the back short and straight. Hindquarters are wide and muscular.

Group

Working. Non-sporting (RASKC).

Size

Height: Dogs 63·5 – 68·5cm (25 – 27in) at the shoulder, bitches 61 – 66cm (24 – 26in).

Weight: Dogs 49·8 – 59kg (110 – 130lb), bitches 40·8 – 49·8kg (90 –110lb). In AKC, bitches 45·3 – 54·3kg (100 – 120lb).

Coat

Colour: Any shade of brindle, fawn or red. A dark muzzle is essential.

Texture: Short and hard, lying flat to the body.

C

Chien Français

Origins

The French hound derives from the Billy and the Poitevin and in 1957 was divided into three varieties, by size and colour. The Blanc et Noir is the largest of the three and, apart from having a more domed skull, longer and narrower head, and thinner stern, is similar in appear-

French Bulldog

Chien Français

Chihuahua, Long Coat

Chihuahua, Smooth Coat

Chinese Crested Dog

ance to the Foxhound. The Blanc et Orange and the Tricolore are similar in appearance, smaller than the Blanc et Noir; the Tricolore may have light coloured eyes.

Group
Hounds for larger game.
Size
Height: Dogs 65 – 71cm (25½ – 28in), bitches 62 – 68·5cm (24½ – 27in).
Coat
Colour: White and black, tricolour or white and orange depending on the variety.
Texture: Short, dense and rugged.

Chihuahua, Long Coat

Origins
Popularly and correctly accepted as the world's smallest breed of dog with the smallest specimens weighing little more than ·45kg (1lb). The breed's origins are shrouded in myth and mystery. Certainly its immediate origin was the Mexican state after which the breed is now named, but whether it arrived there via trade routes with China and Japan or whether the breed was developed by the native Aztecs or Toltecs it is not possible to say. The first Chihuahua to be registered by the AKC was Midget registered in 1904, though there had been reliable references to Mexico's little dogs for the previous 25 years, before which there existed neither archeological remains nor reliable references which would prove satisfactorily the existence of the breed.
Characteristics
The most obvious characteristic is its extremely small size. The head too is very distinctive, being round with an 'apple dome' skull, with or without molero, a characteristic also sometimes found in

toy Japanese breeds. The eyes are full and round, though not protruding, and the ears large, set at an angle of about 45°. The dog is alert and swift with a saucy expression, it is small with a dainty compact appearance which is coupled with a brisk and forceful personality.
Group
Toy. Pet Dogs (FCI).
Size
Weight: Up to 2·7kg (6lb) with 0·9 – 1·8kg (2 – 4lb) preferred.
Coat
Colour: Any colour or mixture of colours.
Texture: Long, soft, and either flat or slightly waved. Feathering on feet, legs, pants and ruff. The tail should be long and full as a plume.

Chihuahua, Smooth Coat

Origins
Originally much more popular than the Long Coat, but now the two are very much on a par. Interbreeding between

the two varieties is permitted though each has separate classification.
Characteristics
The standard for the Smooth Chihuahua is as for the Long Coat except:
Group
Toy.
Coat
Texture: Smooth, soft, close and glossy.

Chinese Crested Dog

Origins
This is a breed from China. Hairless dogs exist in many parts of the world, such as Africa, Turkey, China and Mexico. Whether each shares a common origin or whether each is a mutant produced from a local breed it is not possible to say. Even in Mexico the Mexican Hairless Dog has been called the Chinese Hairless, because it possibly originated in China.
Characteristics
A small, active and graceful dog, medium

hills, with only local recognition. In 1860, however, Queen Victoria visited Balmoral for the first time, saw the breed, fell in love with it and so assured its future popularity. Popularity understandably changed the breed, bringing with it a greater emphasis on elegance and beauty and less on working ability.

Characteristics

The standard seeks to protect the breed's working ability by asking for a strong and active dog, free from cloddiness and without coarseness. It places great emphasis on expression, a product of the shape of the head, size and shape of eyes and position and carriage of ears.

Group

Working. Shepherd Dogs (FCI).

Size

Height: Dogs 55·8 – 61cm (22 – 24in) at the shoulder, bitches 50·8 – 55·8cm (20 – 22in). In AKC, 5cm (2in) higher.

Weight: Dogs 20·4 – 29·5kg (45 – 65lb), bitches 18 – 25kg (40 – 55lb). In AKC, dogs 27·2 – 34kg (60 – 75lb), bitches 22·6 – 29·4kg (50 – 65lb).

Coat

Colour: Three recognized colours, sable and white, tricolour, and blue merle, each with white markings.

Texture: Very dense, the outer coat straight and harsh, the undercoat soft, furry and very close. Mane and frill very abundant, mask smooth, legs well feathered, and the hair on the tail profuse.

Collie, Smooth

The standard is as the Rough except:

Coat

Texture: Hard, dense and smooth.

Left Smooth Collie, *below* Rough Collie

Long-haired Dachshund

Smooth-haired Dachshund

Wire-haired Dachshund

Dachshund, Long-haired.

Origins
As for the Smooth-haired Dachshund.

Characteristics
As for the Smooth-haired Dachshund.

Group
Hound.

Size
Weight: In KC, middle weight up to and heavy weight over 8kg (18lb) for dogs and 7·7kg (17lb) for bitches.

Coat
Colour: Black and tan, dark brown with lighter shadings, dark red, light red, dappled, tiger marked or brindle.
Texture: Soft and straight or slightly waved, of shining colour.

Dachshund, Smooth-haired

Origins
Dachshunds represent a small and distinctive subgroup within the hound group, differentiated from other hounds by their small size, the work for which they were intended and to some extent by the quarry they used to hunt. 'Dachshund' simply means 'badger dog', but must not be taken to mean that these diminutive hounds, whose history dates back to the 15th century, were used exclusively for that quarry. Larger hounds, weighing 13·6kg (30lb) or 15·8kg (35lb) were used for badger, while smaller ones were kept for stoat and weasel. Not only did size vary, so did coat, as it still does with many hounds and terriers bred exclusively for work. It was not until 1915 that the Dachshund was differentiated by its different coats. The breed has achieved considerable popularity as a pet and show dog and so, inevitably perhaps, outside Europe it has become a very different animal from the one so carefully bred in Germany as a working hound.

Characteristics
First and foremost a sporting dog, but is equally adaptable as a house pet. The general appearance is long and low, but with a compact and well-muscled body, not crippled, cloddy or clumsy, with a bold defiant head carriage. The head is long, the stop not pronounced. The eyes are of medium size, oval and set obliquely, dark in colour, though choco-

lates may have lighter eyes and wall eyes are permitted in dapples. The neck is long, muscular and clean, with no dewlap. The forelegs are very short, the lower arms slightly crooked. The body is long and muscular, the chest very oval and the breastbone very prominent. The hindquarters are full and broad, the hocks hard and plastic. The tail is high set, strong and tapering.

Group

Hound. Dachshunds (FCI).

Size

Weight: Dogs not to exceed 11·3kg (25lb), bitches not to exceed 10·4kg (23lb).

Coat

Colour: Any colour, other than white.

Texture: Short, dense and smooth, but strong.

Dachshund, Wire-haired

Origins

As for the Smooth-haired Dachshund.

Characteristics

As for the Smooth-haired Dachshund.

Group

Hound.

Size

Weight: Dogs 9 – 10kg (20 – 22lb), bitches 8 – 9kg (18 – 20lb).

Coat

Colour: All colours are allowed.

Texture: Short, thick, hard and rough; any sort of soft hair is faulty as is long, curly or wavy hair.

Dachshund, Miniature

The standards for the miniature versions are as other Dachshunds, except:

Size

Weight: Must not exceed 4·9kg (11lb) in KC and RASKC.

Dalmatian

Origins

Said to have originated in Dalmatia on the Adriatic coast, though spotted dogs are found in many parts of the world. However, the breed has been established for so long in Britain, where it was used as a carriage guard, that it can perhaps be recognized as a British breed. In America its affinity with horses and carriages earned it a place with the horsedrawn fire engines and it became the Firehouse Dog. Unfortunately its image, fostered by films, novels and adverts, in part contradicts the fact that the Dalmatian is a big strong dog.

Characteristics

Dalmatians should be strong, muscular and active, and of good demeanour. They are graceful in outline, elegant and capable of great endurance. The most obvious characteristic is the spotted coat. Dalmatians have great freedom of movement, a smooth powerful rhythmic action with a long stride which enables them to cover considerable distances.

Group

Non-sporting (AKC). Utility (KC). Pet Dogs (FCI).

Size

Weight: In FCI, dogs 24·9kg (55lb), bitches 22·4kg (49½lb).

Height: In KC, dogs 58·4 – 61cm (23 – 24in), bitches 55·8 – 58·4cm (22 – 23in). In AKC, any dog or bitch over 61cm (24in) at withers is disqualified. In FCI, dogs 55 – 61cm (21½ – 24in), bitches 50 – 58cm (19½ – 23in).

Coat

Colour: The ground colour is pure white, evenly covered with black or liver spots each separate and ideally about the size of a 10 pence piece.

Texture: The coat should be short, hard and dense, sleek and glossy in appearance.

Dalmatian

Deerhound, Scottish

Origins

A breed which demonstrates in the most eloquent manner possible that some breeds have no need of improvement or to be altered in order to follow the latest fashion. The Deerhound of today is just as it has always been when, having been produced out of the hounds used by Pictish hunters, the breed was used to bring deer to bay and were the prized possessions and constant companions of their masters. A good brace of Deerhounds was almost above price, credited with sufficient value to purchase the reprieve of an Earl condemned to death. When the Battle of Culloden (1746) put a virtual end to the clan system, the Highland Chieftains assumed exclusive ownership so that the breed declined. It was only rescued from ignominy by Lord Colonsay around 1825, and nowadays the breed is in every way comparable with the hounds which graced Scotland in earlier days, and which were so remarkable for their courage in the field and their courteous dignity in the home.

Characteristics

The general conformation is similar to

Deerhound

Doberman(n) Pinscher

Dogue de Bordeaux

that of a Greyhound, but of larger size and bone. The head is long without stop and is flat in skull. The eyes are dark and moderately full, the ears set on high and folded back. The neck is long, though not overlong, and strong. The shoulders are well sloped and the forelegs are straight. The chest is deep rather than broad, powerful and drooping, with well-bent stifles. The tail is long, thick at the root and reaches almost to the ground. A curl or ring tail is very undesirable.

Group
Hound. Greyhounds (FCI).

Size
Height: Dogs not less than 76cm (30in), but 76 – 81cm (30 – 32in) or even more in AKC, bitches not less than 71cm (28in).
Weight: Dogs 38·5 – 47·6kg (85 – 105lb), bitches 29·4 – 36·2kg (65 – 80lb). In AKC, dogs 38·5 – 50kg (85 – 110lb), bitches 34 – 43kg (75 – 95lb).

Coat
Colour: Dark blue-grey is preferred, but darker or lighter greys or brindles, yellow and sandy-red or red-fawn are also accepted, the last three perhaps being the oldest colours.
Texture: Harsh and wiry on body, neck and shoulders and about 7·6 – 10cm (3 – 4in) long. A woolly coat is bad; the correct coat is thick, close-lying, ragged and harsh or crisp to the touch.

Doberman(n) Pinscher

Origins
This breed is the second most popular breed in the USA. It is of such recent origin that it can be traced to the person who first produced it, Louis Dobermann, a German tax collector. Between 1865-70 he set about producing a first class guard dog based on the concept of a giant terrier, combining agility with strength, speed and great intelligence. So well did he succeed that the Dobermann Pinscher is now sometimes too quick, too intelligent for those who seek to control it. Such a dog demands the highest standards of its handlers.

Characteristics
A medium-sized dog with a well-set body, muscular and elegant, proud carriage and bold alert temperament. The breed is compact and tough with light, elastic movement. Neither shyness nor viciousness are characteristic of the breed. The head is long and clean, the eyes deep and almond-shaped. Ears may be erect or dropped, cropped in countries where the operation is permitted. The body is square, the back short and firm.

Group
Working. Non-sporting (RASKC).

Size
Height: Dogs 70cm (27½in), in KC and RASKC 68·5cm (27in); bitches 65cm (25½in).

Coat
Colour: Black, red, brown or blue with rust-red markings which must be sharply defined. Markings of any kind are undesirable.
Texture: Smooth-haired, short, hard, thick and close lying. The British standard says 'invisible grey undercoat on neck is permissible.'

Dogue de Bordeaux

Origins
The Dogue de Bordeaux may lay claim to being the national dog of France.

Characteristics
In appearance the breed is very similar to the English Mastiff and is descended from the same stock as other European mastiff breeds, that is from the Roman mastiffs originally imported from the East. In France, the breed was developed as a fighting dog and was used as such until the beginning of the 20th century. Nowadays, the breed makes an excellent watchdog as it is vigilant, faithful and has great strength.

Group
Working (FCI).

Size
Height: 70 – 76cm (27½ – 30in).
Weight: 54·3 – 65·7kg (120 – 145lb).

Coat
Colour: Apricot, silver, fawn or dark fawn-brindle with black points.
Texture: Smooth and short.

Elkhound

Origins
The Elkhound is another of the Scandinavian Spitz breeds. It has arrived at its present distinctive appearance as a result of selection based on its ability to hunt the elk, bringing the animal to bay while summoning the hunters with its shrill barking. Careful selection for very many years has made the Elkhound a very versatile hunting dog for a variety of quarry and it has not in any way changed as a result of its popularity as a show dog and companion.

Characteristics
The Elkhound is a hardy sporting dog of Nordic type with a bold and virile nature. Its disposition should be friendly and intelligent, with great energy and independence of character and without any sign of undue nervousness. In general appearance it is compactly built with a short body, thick, abundant coat, pricked ears and a tail curled tightly over the back. The head is broad in the skull, the eyes as dark as possible with a fearless and friendly expression. The forelegs are straight and firm with good bone and the hindquarters straight at the hock, without dewclaws. The feet are compact, oval in shape.

Group
Hound. Hounds for larger game (FCI).

Elkhound

Size

Height: Dogs 52cm (20½in), bitches 47cm (18½in) and 49·5cm (19½in) in AKC and RASKC.
Weight: Approximately 22·6kg (50lb) for dogs; 19·5kg (43lb) bitches. AKC, dogs 24·9kg (55lb), bitches 21·7kg (48lb).

Coat

Colour: Grey of various shades with black tips on the long outer coat, and lighter on the chest, stomach, legs and the underside of the tail.
Texture: Thick and abundant, coarse and weather resistant with a longish, coarse top coat and a light coloured, soft woolly undercoat.

Estrela Mountain Dog

Origins

The Estrela Mountain Dog from Portugal, like so many of the European dual-purpose herding and guard breeds, is a large and very powerful dog with great courage and stamina. It is independent by nature and needs careful training.

Characteristics

The head is massive, broad and moderately long. The skull is slightly domed with a well-defined stop and strong muzzle. The eyes are almond-shaped, dark and wide-set. The ears are small and carried folded back. The body is rectangular in outline, rather longer than it is tall with a broad, muscular back, deep chest and slightly arched loin. The tail is

Estrela Mountain Dog

long and carried low.

Group

Working.

Size

Height: 58·4 – 68·5cm (23 – 27in).
Weight: 40·8 – 49·8kg (90 – 110lb).

Coat

Colour: Grey, tawny and red, red or light tan.
Texture: Short, thick and rather coarse, smooth and very slightly wavy.

Finnish Spitz

F

Finnish Spitz

Origins

Internationally this is one of the least numerous of the Spitz breeds, but deserving of a greater popularity. In its own country it is very popular indeed and still does the job for which it was bred as well as acting as a companion. Originally the breed was used to track down and mark with their piercing bark the position of a variety of game in the Finnish woodland; now they are principally regarded as bird dogs. During the 19th century the breed's purity was restored after a number of dogs which had not been crossed with other breeds had been found in Lapland. In 1927, the breed was introduced into Britain where it is admired by a few enthusiasts.

Characteristics

The general outline is square, the head with its keen eyes, erect pointed ears and pointed muzzle is distinctly fox-like. The back is short and straight, the chest deep. Forelegs are straight, hindquarters strong, but without a great bend of stifle. The bushy tail, in the typical Spitz manner, is carried over the back.

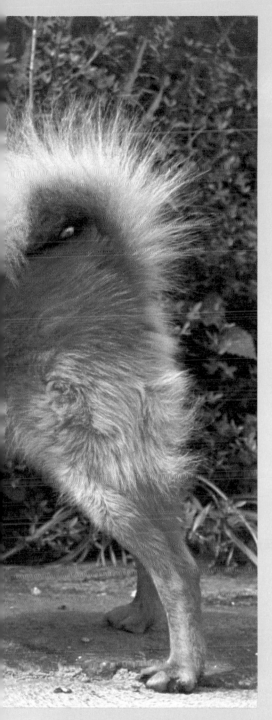

Group
Hound. Hounds for smaller game (FCI).
Size
Height: Dogs 43 – 50·8cm (17 – 20in),
bitches 39·2 – 45·7cm (15 – 18in).
Weight: Dogs 14 – 16·3kg (31 – 36lb),
bitches 10·4 – 13kg (23 – 29lb).
Coat
Colour: Reddish brown or yellowish red.
Texture: Short and close on the head
and legs, longer on the body, with a
mane of coarser hair.

Foxhound

Origins
A breed which has been developed
exclusively for a single purpose and
which in Britain has not been diverted
from its original purpose by popularity
either as a pet or as a show dog, for in
neither role has it achieved a place.
Intense selection over many years, a
careful breeding programme and a freedom from the major influences of
fashion have brought the Foxhound to a
peak of perfection.

Characteristics
The British standard is the shortest for
any standard and concentrates on purely
physical attributes. The skull is broad, the
neck long and not thick, the shoulders
free from lumber and the legs well
boned. The body has plenty of heart
room and the chest is well ribbed. The
coupling should not be short. The hind
quarters are full and muscular, the hocks
well let-down. The feet are not open.

Group
Hound. Hounds for larger game (FCI).

Coat
Colour: A good 'hound colour' – black,
tan, white in any combination.
Texture: Weather-resistant, short, dense,
hard and glossy.

Foxhound, American

Origins
Foxhunting in America is very different
from fox hunting in Britain and it follows
that the hounds used will also be very
different. The American breed, however,
is to a large extent the product of a pack
of hounds imported into the country in
1650 by Robert Brooke and of later
imports, such as those in 1742 made by
Thomas Walker and by the Gloucester
Foxhunting Club in 1808. Hounds from
other countries too were imported –
George Washington, for instance, recorded his interest in hounds from
France – and over the years a very
distinctive breed has been formed. In
America, Foxhounds are run in field
trials, used for hunting a fox with a gun or
raced along a predetermined trail.

Characteristics
The skull is fairly long and domed, the
ears set moderately low, fine in texture,
broad, long and pendulous. The eyes are
large with a soft expression, the muzzle is
fairly long with a well-defined stop. The
neck is of medium length, strong and
clean, set into sloping shoulders. The
chest is deep and narrower than in the
English hound, the ribs are well sprung.
The forelegs are straight and well boned,
the hindquarters strong and well muscled. The stern is set moderately high
and carried gaily with a slight brush.

Group
Hound (AKC). Hounds for larger game
(FCI).

Size
Height: Dogs 56 – 63·5cm (22 – 25in),
bitches 53·3 – 61cm (21 – 24in).

Coat
Colour: Any colour.
Texture: Close, hard, medium length.

Foxhound

American Foxhound

German Shepherd Dog (Alsatian)

Origins

A breed with origins and uses as indicated by its name. The first breed club, the Verein für Deutsche Schäferhund, was formed in 1899. By 1926 it was the most popular dog in Britain, where it was called the Alsatian Wolf Dog. Thoughtless breeding and ignorant handling contrived to give the breed a dubious reputation which only the worst deserve. Of the best it is difficult to praise too highly their intelligence and sagacity, resourcefulness and desire to please, but all these virtues must be in the hands of an owner able to develop them.

Characteristics

The characteristic expression of the German Shepherd Dog gives the impression of perpetual vigilance, fidelity, liveliness and watchfulness, alert to every sight and sound; fearless, but with a decided suspiciousness of strangers. This dog possesses highly developed senses. It is a well-proportioned dog, showing great suppleness of limb, with a long strongly boned body with plenty of muscle. Obviously capable of endurance and speed and of quick, sudden movement. The gait is supple, smooth and long-reaching.

Group

Working. Shepherd Dogs (FCI).

Size

Height: 55·8 – 61cm (22 – 24in) for bitches, 61 – 66cm (24 – 26in) for dogs to shoulders.
Weight: 27·2 – 31·7kg (60 – 70lb), bitches, 34 – 38·5kg (75 – 85lb) dogs.

Coat

Colour: Not important, though all white or near white unless possessing black points are undesirable.
Texture: Smooth and double texture with a thick, close, woolly undercoat and a close, hard, straight, weather-resistant outercoat.

Great Dane

Origins

In spite of its name the breed has no close association with Denmark. Indeed because drawings of very similar dogs were found on Fourth Dynasty tomb walls, some people might put its origins in Egypt, but it was in Germany that the breed was developed and achieved popularity. The breed was the one favoured by Bismarck and used to hunt wild boar. In spite of its present group classification the Great Dane's original work was that of a hound.

Characteristics

Great Danes should be very large, very muscular, strongly though elegantly built. Their heads are carried high and the whole outline should be elegant. Size however is of paramount importance for the breed.

Group

Working. Non-sporting (RASKC).

Size

Height: Minimum for an adult dog 76·2cm (30in) in FCI 79·5cm (31½in), and for a bitch 71cm (28in).
Weight: Minimum for an adult dog 54·3kg (120lb) and for a bitch 45·3kg (100lb).

Coat

Colour: Brindle, fawn, steel blue, black or Harlequin.
Texture: Very short and thick, smooth and glossy.

Greyhound

Origins

There can be no doubt that Greyhounds are of very ancient origin. As early as 1016 Canute's law forbade 'mean persons' from keeping Greyhounds and, in 1408, Dame Juliana Berners used an older description of the breed in her Book of St Albans.

'The Condyscyons of A grehound and of his propyrteys.
  Thy grehounds most be
    heddyd lyke a snake
    y neckyd lyke a drake.
    foted lyke a Kat.
    Syded lyke a Bream.
    Chyned lyke a Beam.
Then ys grehounde well y schapte.'

Various attempts have been made to explain one origin of the name which refers not to colour, but is possibly derived from the Latin 'gradus' meaning 'rank'. Others look to the old British word 'grach' meaning 'dog', or even 'Grais' meaning 'Grecian'.

Characteristics

The Greyhound possesses remarkable stamina and its long-reaching movement enables it to move at great speed; indeed the Greyhound over a measured sprint is probably the fastest of all dogs. The head is long and elegant, the eyes bright and intelligent, the neck long and muscular, set into well-laid shoulders. The chest is deep and capacious with flanks well cut-up, the legs are strong, well boned and powerfully muscled.

Group

Hound. Greyhounds (FCI).

Size

Height: Dogs 71 – 76cm (28 – 30in), bitches 68·5 – 71cm (27 – 28in).
Weight: Dogs 29·4 – 31·7kg (65 – 70lb), bitches 27·2 – 29·4kg (60 – 65lb).

Coat

Colour: Black, white, red, blue, fawn,

German Shepherd Dog (Alsatian)

Great Dane

Greyhound

fallow, brindle or any of the colours broken with white.

Texture: Fine and close.

Greyhound, Italian

Origins

A breed of ancient origin which was certainly widely known and admired among the civilizations around the Mediterranean 2000 years ago, but which probably achieved its peak of popularity in 16th-century Italy and in the courts of James I, Frederick the Great and Catherine the Great. It is the smallest of the sight hounds, though its fragile proportions preclude any active participation in the chase. The Italian Greyhound is prized today as it always has been for its elegance, its sweet nature, its great beauty, its small size and the ease with which it is kept.

Characteristics

A miniature Greyhound, very slenderly made and of great elegance, with a high-

Italian Greyhound

stepping and free action. The skull is long, flat and narrow, the muzzle very fine, the eyes rather large, bright and full of expression and the ears are rose-shaped, soft and delicate. The neck is long, gracefully arched and set into long, sloping shoulders. Forelegs are straight with small delicate bones, hindquarters carry muscular thighs. The chest is deep and narrow, the back curved and drooping to the hindquarters. The tail is rather long and fine with low carriage.

Group
Toy. Greyhounds (FCI).
Size
Height: In AKC, 33 – 38cm (13 – 15in). In FCI, 31·5 – 38cm (12½ – 15in).
Weight: In KC, 2·7 – 3·6kg (6 – 8lb), but not exceeding 4·5kg (10lb). In FCI, maximum weight 4·9kg (11lb).
Coat
Colour: All shades of fawn, white, cream, blue; black and fawn, and white pied are acceptable. Black or blue with tan markings and brindle are regarded as faults.
Texture: Thin and glossy, like satin.

Griffon Vendéen, Grand

Origins
This dog is a descendant of the white variety of the ancient St Hubert hound of France.
Characteristics
The Griffon Vendéen is an intelligent dog, sure of itself and distinguished in physique and gait. The head is well rounded, not too broad, with the stop accentuated by bushy eyebrows. The eyes are large, dark and vivacious, and the pendulous ears are soft, fine, narrow and covered with long hair.
Group
Hounds for larger game (FCI).
Size
Height: 60 – 65cm (23½ – 25½in).
Coat
Colour: Fawn, white and orange; white

Griffon Vendéen Grand

and grey; tricolour.
Texture: Long, bushy, heavy and hard. The skin should not be too fine.

Griffon, Bruxellois

Origins
Originally the Griffon was a humble adjunct of stables, used to keep down vermin and as an effective early warning system of unauthorized intrusion. Probably the breed has origins in the more ancient Affenpinscher, but certainly owes a debt to a number of other breeds, including Black and Tan Terriers, Pugs and Yorkshire Terriers. Although small and toy-like, the breed retains many of its terrier characteristics.

Characteristics
The Griffon is a smart little dog with a pert monkey-like expression. It is well balanced, square in outline, lively and alert. The head is large and rounded, the eyes also large and round. Ears are semi-erect and high set, the smaller the better. The chest is wide and deep, the back short, level from withers to tail root. Hind-quarters are well muscled, with short hocks, carried well bent. The tail is short, docked and carried high.

Group
Toy. Pet Dogs (FCI).
Size
Weight: 2·3 – 5kg (5 – 11lb), most desirable 2·7 – 4·5kg (6 – 10lb). In AKC, 3·6 – 4·5kg (8 – 10lb), not to exceed 5·4kg (12lb). In FCI, small Griffons not over 2·9kg (6½lb); large, over 2·9kg (6½lb) to 4·5kg (10lb) for bitches and 4·9kg (11lb) for dogs.
Coat
Colour: Red, black or black and rich tan.
Texture: Short and tight.

Griffon, Rough

Origins
This Griffon has basically the same origins as the smooth variety but possibly owes its harsh red coat to the judicious introduction to the stock of Irish Terrier blood.
The Standard is the same as the Smooth Griffon except:
Coat
Texture: Harsh, wiry and free from curl, preferably with an undercoat.

Top Griffon Bruxellois, *bottom* Rough Griffon

Hamiltonstövare

Origins
The Hamiltonstövare is a breed produced by crosses between the Holstein, Hanover and Kurland Beagles and the Foxhound made by Adolf Patrick Hamilton, hence the breed's name..

Characteristics
The appearance is very much that of a small and lightly built Foxhound.

Group
Hounds for smaller game (FCI).

Size
Height: On average, dogs 57cm (22½in); bitches 53·3cm (21in).

Coat
Colour: The back black, shading to brown on the head and legs, with white on the muzzle, chest and legs.
Texture: Short and dense.

Harrier

Origins
No matter what opinion John Jorrocks held about hunting the hare, the quarry was already highly prized in 400BC when Xenophon was able to describe two types of hounds, the Castorean and the fox-breed said to be the product of a fox-dog cross. Xenophon listed the qualities necessary in hare hounds, qualities which were still relevant when Sir Elias de Midhope of Penistone gathered the first pack of Harriers together in 1260.

Characteristics
In every respect a small Foxhound.

Group
Hound. Hounds for smaller game (FCI).

Size
Height: 48·2 – 53·3cm (19 – 21in). The FCI adds 2·5cm (1in) on upper limit.

Coat
Colour: Any hound colour.
Texture: Short, smooth and dense.

Ibizan Hound

Origins
One of the ancient sight hound breeds with origins in the lands around the Mediterranean and with a history which reaches back into ancient Egypt and the courts of the Pharaohs. In the tomb of Hemako was found a carved dish which carries the image of an Ibizan Hound; this dish was made during the 1st Dynasty between 3100 and 2700BC. Other tombs of Tutankhamen and Ptolemy also provide evidence of the breed's ancient origin. The hounds probably were first taken to Ibiza by Phoenician traders, where selection based on survival of the fittest produced a breed capable of hunting with skill, endurance and tenacity.

Characteristics
The head is long and narrow, the eyes oblique, small and ranging in colour from amber to caramel. The neck is long, slender, slightly arched and strongly muscled, set in sloping shoulders. The chest is deep and long with flat ribs, the underbelly well tucked-up. Forequarters are straight and fine boned, with long forearms, and hindquarters are strong with hocks close to the ground. The hare feet have long, close, strong toes.

Group
Hound. Setters (FCI).

Size
Height: In KC, 56 – 73·6cm (22 – 29in). In FCI, dogs 60 – 66cm (23½ – 26in), bitches 57 – 63·5cm (22½ – 25in).
Weight: Average weight for dogs 22kg (49lb); bitches 19kg (42lb).

Hamiltonstövare

Harrier

Coat

Colour: Red and white, red with white, or solid red only.

Texture: Short-coated hounds have a short hard coat; wire-haired hounds have a hard coat from 2·5 – 7·6cm (1 – 3in) in length.

Irish Wolfhound

Origins

In AD 391. Consul Quintus Aurelius recorded that a gift of seven wolfhounds had filled 'all Rome with wonder'. The breed was obviously already well established, but the extinction of the wolf led to the breed's decline, so that by the mid-19th century, Stonehenge, a usually reliable authority, was able to record that the breed was extinct. However, in the 1860s, Captain George Graham, a Scot living in Dursley in Gloucestershire, set himself the task of recreating those massive hounds from the few remaining specimens he was able to gather together. So well did he succeed that the breed now exists in healthy numbers.

Characteristics

The breed's most obvious characteristics are its great size, its commanding appearance and the impression of considerable strength it conveys. The head is long, the skull not too broad, the ears small and Greyhound-like in carriage. The neck is rather long, and very strong and muscular. The chest is very deep, the back rather long with arched loins and the belly well drawn-up. The forequarters are muscular, the hindquarters long and strong as in the Greyhound, with large, round feet.

Group

Hound. Greyhounds (FCI).

Size

Height: 78·7cm (31in) for dogs, 71cm (28in) for bitches. In AKC, minimum 81cm (32in) for dogs, 76cm (30in) for bitches. Great size is to be aimed at.

Weight: 54·5kg (120lb) as a minimum for dogs, 40·9kg (90lb) for bitches, in AKC 47·6kg (105lb).

Coat

Colour: Grey, brindle, red, black, white or fawn.

Texture: Rough and hard on the body, wiry and long over eyes and underjaw.

Ibizan Hounds

Irish Wolfhound

Japanese Chin

Origins
Like so many of the toy breeds which originated in the Orient, the Japanese Chin, sometimes called the Japanese Spaniel, has long been associated with the Royal courts. The breed's ancestors probably arrived in Japan as gifts from the Chinese Emperor to his Japanese counterpart. It is interesting to note that they were introduced into Britain in just the same way, as a gift to Queen Victoria. The breed makes an excellent and attractive companion, but one with a mind of its own.

Characteristics
The Japanese Chin is a lively little dog of dainty appearance, smart compact carriage and with a profuse coat. It is stylish in movement, lifting the feet high, and carries its plumed tail over the back. The head is large in proportion to the size of the dog, with a broad and rounded skull, and the muzzle very short. The dark eyes are large and set wide apart, the ears small, V-shaped and carried slightly forward. The neck is of moderate length and held proudly. The body is squarely and compactly built, wide in the chest and cobby in shape. Forelegs are straight and finely boned, giving them a slender appearance; hindquarters have a good turn of stifle and like the forelegs are profusely feathered. Feet are slender, hare-shaped and feathered at the tips. The tail is set high and profusely feathered, closely arched or plumed over the back.

Group
Toy. Pet Dogs (FCI).

Size
Height: In FCI, dogs average 30·4cm (12in).
Weight: Classes may be divided between dogs under and over 3kg (7lb). In KC and RASKC, 1·8 – 3kg (4 – 7lb), the daintier the better.

Coat
Colour: Black and white or red and white.
Texture: Profuse, long, soft and straight, of silky texture, free from curl or wave.

Japanese Spitz

Origins
This dog was bred from Spitz breeds taken to Japan which were used to form a breed with similarities to the Pomeranian.

Characteristics
The muzzle is pointed, the ears are erect and pointed. The tail, richly fringed, falls on the back. The forequarters and hindquarters are well proportioned. The body is compact and the general appearance handsome. The Japanese Spitz is characterized by great courage and its intelligent and cheerful disposition.

Group
Pet dogs (FCI).

Size
Height: Dogs 30·4 – 40·6cm (12 – 16in), bitches 25·4 – 35·5cm (10 – 14in).

Coat
Colour: Pure white.
Texture: Straight and standing away from the body. The undercoat is short, soft and abundant.

Keeshond

Japanese Chin

Japanese Spitz

K

Keeshond

Origins

The breed shares origins with its close neighbour, the Pomeranian, and is named after a Dutch Patriot Kees de Gyselaer of Dordrecht. It was adopted as a mascot of the Patriotten during the revolutionary times before the French Revolution. The breed had long existed as a watchdog used on the barges of Holland, but has its origins among other more northerly Spitz breeds, the Samoyed, the Norwegian Elkhound and the Finnish Spitz, among others. Since its rise to popular recognition some two centuries ago, the breed has changed little and is still easily identified in the paintings and drawings of the period. However political changes as well as changes in the design of barges reduced the breed's popularity. In 1920 the Baroness van Hardenbroek began to breed Keeshonds and was responsible for making the breed well known and admired.

Characteristics

Keeshonds have short, compact bodies, alert carriage and fox-like heads. They carry their well feathered tail curled over their back in the typical Spitz manner.

Movement should be clean and brisk. Temperament should be bold.

Group

Non-sporting. Utility (KC).

Size

Height: Dogs 45·7cm (18in), bitches 43cm (17in). Type is of more importance than size.

Coat

Colour: Wolf, ash grey, never either all black or all white; the undercoat should be light coloured.

Texture: Dense and harsh, standing away from the body with a thick soft undercoat, never silky or wavy.

Kelpie

Origins

The Kelpie appears to have emerged, from crosses between imported herding dogs, as a distinct breed in the 1870s and itself produced the smaller and more aggressive Australian Cattle Dog. Nowadays the Kelpie works side by side with

Kelpie

the ubiquitous Border Collie on the huge sheep farms of Australia where its keen sight, scenting powers and hearing make it highly valued.

Characteristics

The Kelpie is a tough and muscular dog, rather fox-like in appearance with a strong, arched neck, moderately long back, and bushy tail carried low.

Group

Working.

Size

Height: Dogs 45·7 – 50·8cm (18 – 20in), bitches 43 – 48·2cm (17 – 19in).

Coat

Colour: Black, black and tan, red, red and tan, fawn, chocolate or smoke-blue.

Texture: Short, straight, thick and harsh to the touch.

Komondor

Komondor

Origins
The herding breeds of Hungary and Russia form a loose family group with several family likenesses; many are probably descended from the Aftschowka, an ancient breed from Eastern Europe. The Komondor probably has retained the closest resemblance to this ancient breed which the Magyars have bred for more than a thousand years as guards to the flocks of sheep which graze the Puszta. The modern breed is now in the capable hands of the Hungarian Komondor Club whose standard for the breed has been translated for use in North America.

Characteristics
The Komondor is characterized by imposing strength, courageous demeanour and pleasing conformation. In general it is a big muscular dog with plenty of bone and substance covered with an unusual heavy white coat. The breed make excellent guards, being wary of strangers, earnest, courageous and loyal. The head is short and wide with a powerful muzzle, ears are pendulous, the neck of moderate length and arched. The body is characterized by the powerful deep chest which is wide and muscular. Forelegs are straight, well-boned and muscular set into moderately sloping shoulders, hindquarters have well-bent stifles and highly developed muscles. Feet are strong and rather large with close arched toes. Movement is light, leisurely and balanced with a long straight stride.

Group
Working (AKC). Shepherd Dogs (FCI).
Size
Height: Dogs 65cm (25½in) and upwards at withers, bitches 60cm (23½in). Type should not be sacrificed for size.
Weight: In FCI, dogs 50 – 60kg (110 – 132lb), bitches 39·9 – 50kg (88 – 110lb).
Coat
Colour: White; any other colour is a disqualification.
Texture: Dense, weather-resisting and very soft in the puppy, but growing into heavy tassel-like cords in the mature dog; these cords form naturally.

Kuvasz

Origins
The breed is said to have been introduced into Hungary in the 12th century by the Kurds, its name being a corruption of the Turkish 'Kawasz', meaning 'the protector'. Originally it was used to protect farm stock from marauding wolves and bears, but was also used, though purely as a side line, as a hunting dog. The similarity between the Kuvasz, the Maremma and the Pyrenean Mountain Dog point to a common origin.

Characteristics
A strongly boned dog, big and powerfully built, the head is noble with an intelligent expression, the chest deep and powerful. Forelegs are straight and well boned, hind-quarters powerful. The tail is undocked and reaches below the level of the hock.

Group
Working (AKC). Shepherd Dogs (FCI).
Size
Height: In AKC, dogs 71 – 76cm (28 – 30in), bitches 66 – 71cm (26 – 28in). In FCI, dogs 71 – 74·8cm (28 – 29½in), bitches 66 – 70cm (26 – 27½in).
Weight: In AKC, dogs 45·3 – 52kg (100 – 115lb), bitches 31·7 – 40·8kg (70 – 90lb). In FCI, dogs 39·9 – 52kg (88 – 115lb), bitches 29·9 – 42kg (66 – 93lb).
Coat
Colour: Pure white.
Texture: Long, straight or slightly wavy.

Kuvasz

Lhasa Apso

Origins
In Tibet, the Lhaso Apso's homeland, the breed is known as Abso Seng Kye, the Bark Lion Sentinel Dog, a name which sums up its function. The Apso is one of four breeds now justly popular in the West which for very many years acted as guards within the precincts of the lamaseries in and around the sacred city of Lhasa. This task is one for which the Apso's intelligence, alertness, acute hearing and distrust of strangers aptly fits it.

Characteristics
The Apso should give the appearance of a solid dog with a gay and assertive character, yet chary of strangers. The head is narrow, but with hair completely covering its face. The ears are pendant and heavily feathered. The body is longer than the height to the withers, the topline level, the forelegs straight and the hindquarters well developed with good muscle. The tail is high-set and carried over the back. The Apso carries a considerable abundance of coat.

Group
Utility (KC). Non-sporting (AKC and RASKC). Pet Dogs (FCI).

Size
Height: Dogs 25·4cm (10in) to the shoulder, slightly smaller for bitches.

Coat
Colour: Golden, sandy, honey, dark grizzle, slate, smoke, parti-colour, black, white or brown.
Texture: Straight and hard, not woolly or silky, long and with dense undercoat.

Lhasa Apso

Löwchen

Maltese

Löwchen

Origins
From the Middle Ages, dogs very like the modern breed of Löwchen appeared in paintings and Lion Dogs are described by Bewick. Whether the modern Löwchen is the same as these dogs is a matter for conjecture, since it seems unlikely that these dogs had to be clipped in order to produce their lion-like appearance.

Characteristics
A small intelligent dog with an affectionate and lively disposition combining all the good qualities of a companion dog. The body is clipped in the traditional lion clip.

Group
Toy. Pet Dogs (FCI).

Size
Height: 20·3 – 35·5cm (8 – 14in) at the withers.
Weight: 1·8 – 4kg (4 – 9lb).

Coat
Colour: Any colour permissible; the most sought after colours are white, black and lemon.
Texture: Fairly long and wavy, but not curly.

M

Maltese

Origins
This breed has been known in the Mediterranean islands probably since the time of the Phoenicians. Certainly the breed existed very much in its present form since, at the time of the Apostle

Maremma

Paul, Publius, the Roman Governor of Malta, owned a Maltese which was described by the poet Martial as being 'more frolicsome than Catulla's sparrow . . . purer than a dove's kiss . . . gentler than a maiden . . . more precious than Indian gems.' Throughout the intervening years, the breed has attracted the admiration of successive writers and their extraordinary grace and beauty have found them a place in the courts of Ancient Greece, Egypt and of Queen Elizabeth I.

Characteristics
The breed should be sweet tempered and very intelligent, smart, lively and alert. The profuse white coat covers a well-made little dog with dark brown eyes, long pendant ears, a level or scissors bite, and a neck of medium length set into well-sloped shoulders. The forelegs are short and straight and the hindquarters nicely angulated. The body is short and cobby with good spring of rib and a level topline. The tail is well arched over the back and feathered. The

standard lists bad mouths, gay tails, curly or woolly coats, brown noses, pink eye rims and any unsoundness as points to be avoided.

Group
Toy. Pet Dogs (FCI).

Size
Height: Not over 25·4cm (10in). In FCI, dogs 20 – 25·4cm (8¼ – 10in), bitches 18·9 – 22·8cm (7¾ – 9in).
Weight: In AKC, under 3kg (7lb), 1·8 – 2·7kg (4 – 6lb) preferred. In FCI, 2·9 – 4kg (6½ – 9lb).

Coat
Colour: Pure white, but slight lemon markings are acceptable.

Texture: The coat should be of good length, but not so long as to impede movement, of silky texture and straight. It should not be woolly or crimped. There should be no woolly undercoat.

Maremma

Origins
The Maremma is a large, heavy-coated herding dog from Italy, very much in the pattern of other European herding breeds to which it is undoubtedly closely related. It is now beginning to be more

Mastiff

widely appreciated as a show dog and companion, though it was first imported and recognized in England in 1935.

Characteristics
The breed is large and strongly built, majestic in appearance, distinguished, robust and courageous. In general appearance the breed much resembles the Pyrenean Mountain Dog.

Group
Working.

Size
Height: Dogs 65 – 73·6cm (25½ – 29in), bitches 60 – 70cm (23½ – 27in).
Weight: Dogs 34·9 – 44·9kg (77 – 99lb), bitches 29·9 – 39·9kg (66 – 88lb).

Coat
Colour: Solid white, ivory, pale orange, or lemon.
Texture: Very abundant, long and rather harsh with a soft undercoat.

Mastiff

Origins
One of the ancient mastiff breeds of Europe with origins in the war dogs of Europe, which fought alongside their masters to repel the invasion of the Roman legions of Britain in 55BC. The

Romans recognized their great courage and imported them to Rome to take part in gladiatorial contests against bulls, bears, lions and tigers. The breed was so greatly admired that mastiff like dogs, generally called 'dogues', eventually were to give their particular name to all domestic dogs. The present-day English Mastiff is largely based on the strain which, since 1415, had been bred at Lyme Hall, near Stockport in Cheshire, and the Duke of Devonshire's strain kept at Chatsworth.

Characteristics
A large, massive and powerful dog with a symmetrical and well-knit frame, combining grandeur with good nature and courage with docility. The head is square in appearance, the muzzle short and broad. The stop between the eyes is well defined. The eyes are small, dark, and set wide apart. The ears are small and thin, lying flat and close to the cheek. The neck is very muscular, moderately long and slightly arched, set into heavy, muscular and slightly sloping shoulders. The forelegs are heavily boned, straight and strong, the hindquarters broad, wide and muscular. The chest is wide and

deep, ribs well arched and carried well back, the back and loins are wide and muscular. The tail is wide at the root, then tapering.

Group
Working. Non-sporting (RASKC).
Size
Height: In AKC, minimum height for dogs is 76cm (30in) and 70cm (27½in) for bitches.
Coat
Colour: Apricot or silver, fawn or dark fawn, brindle. The muzzle, ears and nose should be black with black also round and between the eyes.
Texture: Short and close-lying, but not too fine over shoulders, neck and back.

Mastiff, Neapolitan

Origins
Many of the European Mastiff breeds are of ancient origin and the Neapolitan Mastiff is no exception for, although it made its appearance in the show ring only after World War II, it is descended from the Roman fighting dogs.
Characteristics
Columella described the breed and said it should be black 'so that during the day a prowler can see him and be frightened by his appearance. When night falls the dog, lost in the shadows, can attack without being seen. The head is so massive that it seems to be the most important part of the body. The ears fall towards the front, the brilliant and penetrating eyes are black or grey, the chest is deep and hairy, the hind-legs powerful.'
Group
Working.
Size
Height: Dogs 65 – 72cm (25½ – 28½in), bitches 60 – 68·5cm (23½ – 27in).
Weight: 50 – 68kg (110 – 150lb).
Coat
Colour: Black, or lead or mouse grey.
Texture: Dense and smooth.

Munsterlander, Large

The standard is as the Small Munsterlander, except:
Size
Height: 58·4 – 62cm (23 – 24½in).

Munsterlander, Small

Origins
The breed is the product of crosses made at the turn of the century between the then numerically small Brittany Spaniels and the Deutsch Langhaar.
Characteristics
The small Munsterlander is a working gundog with sharp intelligence, vigour

Neapolitan Mastiff

Munsterlander

and fidelity, able to adapt quickly to any type of terrain or quarry. At home it is an excellent guard and a good-natured companion. The head is lean and distinguished, the nose brown, the muzzle is long and not too heavy. The eyes are dark, the ears light and pointed with good feathering. The neck is slightly arched and very muscular, the chest deep and broad with well-sprung ribs. The croup is well developed and the loins well filled-out. The tail is carried straight out. The angulation of fore-quarters and hindquarters must be such as to enable the dog to work in rough country and move freely.
Group
Gundog (KC). Setters (FCI).

Size
Height: Dogs 48·2 – 56cm (19 – 22in),
bitches 44 – 52cm (17½ – 20½in).
Coat
Colour: White with black spots or white
with spots and speckling or black and
white roan.
Texture: Smooth and slightly wavy.

Newfoundland

Origins
The Newfoundland breed was primarily
developed not, as is often suggested, as a
canine lifeguard, but as a draught dog,
big and strong enough to pull carts or
carry heavy loads. However, its affinity
with the fishermen of Newfoundland
made it a superb water dog and its loyalty
and great intelligence certainly have enabled it to save the lives of many people
in danger of drowning. Early prints suggest that the breed has its origins among
the Huskies of Northern Canada, other
writers have argued that its blood carries
that of Pyreneans or French Boar-
hounds. Whatever its origins there can
be no dispute that the breed is today a
magnificent and aristocratic animal.

Characteristics
The breed should have an exceptionally
gentle and docile nature and should be
strong and active. Movement should be
free, with a slight rolling movement not
being objectionable. The head is broad
and massive, the eyes small and dark, the
ears small, set well back and falling close
to the head, and the mouth should be
soft and the lips well covered, the bite
level or scissors. The chest should be
deep and fairly broad, the loins strong
and muscular. The forelegs are straight
and well feathered, the hindquarters very
strong and without dewclaws. Feet
should be large and well shaped. The tail
should be of a fair thickness and well
covered with hair.

Group
Working. Non-sporting (RASKC).

Size
Height: Dogs 71cm (28in), bitches 66cm
(26in).
Weight: Dogs 63·5 – 68kg (140 – 150lb),
bitches 50 – 54·5kg (110 – 120lb). In
AKC, 68kg (150lb) and 54·5kg (120lb)
are regarded as average weights.
Coat
Colour: Dull jet black, a slight tinge of
bronze or white on the chest and toes is
not objectionable. Other than black, colours most to be encouraged are white
and black or bronze.
Texture: Flat and dense, of a coarsish
texture and oily nature, and water-
resistant.

Norwegian Buhund

Origins
A typical Spitz breed, used as a general
farm dog and guard, which inexplicably
has not achieved the same degree of
popularity which some other less attractive Spitz breeds enjoy. The breed formed
the basis for the Icelandic Dog which was
bred from stock taken to Iceland in
AD 874. The ancient origin of the breed is
thus established.

Newfoundland

Characteristics
The breed is fearless, brave and energetic, typically Spitz in appearance, of medium size, lightly built with a short compact body.

Group
Working. Shepherd Dogs (FCI).

Size
Height: Dogs 45cm (17¾in), bitches smaller.

Coat
Colour: Biscuit, ripe wheat, light red, sable, black. The lighter colours are preferred.
Texture: Close and harsh with soft undercoat.

Norwegian Buhund

O

Old English Sheepdog

Origins
The breed was probably developed, if it did not originate, in the West of England, either by using indigenous herding breeds, such as the Bearded Collie or, less likely, imported stock like the Russian Owtchow. The Old English Sheepdog was not used so much as a herding dog but as a drover's dog for driving sheep and cattle to market. Drover's dogs were exempt from taxes if they were docked, hence the tailless outline of the Old English Sheepdog; hence also its popular nickname of 'Bobtail'.

Characteristics
A strong compact-looking dog, profusely coated all over, very elastic in a gallop, but when walking or trotting has a characteristic ambling or pacing movement. The bark should be loud with a

Old English Sheepdog

peculiar 'bell-like' ring to it. The head is large and rather squarely formed, the jaw fairly long and strong; dark or wan eyes are preferred and the ears are small and carried close to the head. The body is short and very compact, with well-sprung ribs and deep brisket. The loin is gently arched, forelegs are straight and well boned, hindquarters round and muscular with hocks well let-down. Feet are small, round and the toes well arched with thick pads. The tail in puppies born with tails is docked short.

Group

Working. Shepherd Dogs (FCI).

Size

Height: Dogs 56cm (22in) and upwards, slightly less for bitches.

Weight: Type, symmetry and character are of greatest importance and must not be sacrificed for size.

Coat

Colour: Any shade of grey, grizzle, blue or blue merle, with or without white markings. Any shade of brown or sable is objectionable.

Texture: Profuse and of good hard texture, not straight but shaggy and free from curl. The undercoat should be a waterproof pile.

Otter Hound

Origins

Although otter hunting in England dates back to the early 12th century, it was not until the reign of Edward II (1307-27) that a description of hounds which fits the modern breed was set down. For over 800 years otter hunting provided sport for the few packs which existed in Britain, by no means all of which were composed of pure-bred Otter Hounds, but it was only recently that they were declared responsible for the otter's sudden decline. When, in 1977, otter hunting became illegal in England and Wales, there was a danger that the comparatively few remaining pure-bred Otter Hounds might be lost, but, after a campaign conducted in the pages of *Our Dogs*, the Kennel Club moved quickly to accept registrations so that hounds could be shown as they had been in the USA since 1907.

Characteristics

The Otter Hound is a large, rough-coated, squarely built hound, with an exceptionally good nose and deep musical voice. The head is large and narrow, the chest deep, with ribs carried well back, the topline is level and the stern long and sickle-shaped. The legs are heavy boned, forelegs straight, hindlegs moderately angulated and well muscled. The feet are large, broad, compact and webbed, dewclaws are removed. Movement is smooth and effortless, with the feet only just coming off the ground, and the dog's strength and stamina have proved capable of carrying the hound for many miles.

Group

Hound (AKC). Hounds for smaller game (FCI).

Size

Height: In AKC, dogs 61 – 68·5cm (24 – 27in) at the withers, bitches 56 – 66cm (22 – 26in). In FCI, dogs 60 – 65cm (23½ – 25½in), bitches proportionately smaller.

Weight: In AKC, dogs 34 – 52kg (75 – 115lb), bitches 29·4 – 45·3kg (65 – 100lb). In FCI, 29·9 – 34·9kg (66 – 77lb).

Coat

Colour: Any colour or combination of colours.

Texture: The rough outer coat is hard and 7·6 – 15cm (3 – 6in) long; the weather-resistant inner coat is short and woolly.

Otterhound

Papillon

Pekingese

P

Papillon

Origins

Arguably Papillons or their Miniature Spaniel progenitors appear in more paintings by artists, such as Rubens, Watteau, Boucher and Fragonard, than any other breed of dog. As companions to the ladies of the courts of Europe, these elegant little creatures led a noble existence. Today they have lost none of their elegance or their great charm and vivacity. They have also to a large degree retained much of the toughness inherited from gundog ancestors.

Characteristics

A dainty, balanced little toy dog which should have an attractive, slightly rounded head with finely pointed muzzle and round, dark eyes showing an alert, lively expression. The bearing should be alert, movement sound, light and free. The ears should be large, rounded at the tips, heavily fringed and carried obliquely like the spread wings of a butterfly, hence the name Papillon. The body should have plenty of length and be well formed with well-sprung ribs, a strong loin of good length and slightly arched belly. Forelegs are straight, slender and fine-boned, set into well-developed, sloping shoulders. Hindquarters have well-bent stifles and are without dewclaws.

Group

Toy. Pet Dogs (FCI).

Size

Height: 20·3 – 27·9cm (8 – 11in) at the withers. In AKC, 30·4cm (12in) disqualifies.

Weight: In FCI, there are two classes, below 2·4kg (5½lb) and over 2·4kg (5½lb) to 4·5kg (10lb) for dogs and 4·9kg (11lb) for bitches.

Coat

Colour: White with patches which may be any colour except liver. A tricolour must be black and white with tan spots over the eyes, tan inside ears and under root of tail and on cheeks. Head markings should be symmetrical about a white, narrow, clearly defined blaze.

Texture: Abundant and flowing, but without undercoat, long, fine and silky, with a profuse frill on the chest. Short and close on skull, muzzle and front part of the legs. A harsh, curly or stand-off coat is a fault.

Pekingese

Origins

In ancient times the Pekingese was the sacred dog of China, its presence and appearance recorded in intricately carved statues of ivory, jewel-studded wood or cast in bronze or precious metals. Certainly during the Tang Dynasty in the 8th century these Foo Dogs were already highly prized, carefully bred and jealously guarded. The Foo Dogs were of three types: the strongly built Lion Dogs, the golden Sun Dogs and the tiny Sleeve Dogs. Their introduction into the West came after the Imperial Palace in Peking had been looted, part of this loot was a fawn and white Pekingese which passed into the hands of Queen Victoria. Lord Hay and the Duke of Richmond had other Chinese Pekingese.

Characteristics

Should be a small, well-balanced, thick-set dog with great dignity, a fearless carriage and an alert, intelligent expression. The head is massive, the skull broad, wide and flat between the ears and eyes. The nose is very short and

Miniature Pinscher

broad, well wrinkled with a firm under-jaw, giving a flat profile. The eyes are large, clear, dark and lustrous, the ears heart-shaped and carried close to the head, with long profuse feathering. The body is short with a broad chest, falling away behind, lion-like with a distinct waist. The forelegs are short, thick and heavily boned, bowed but firm at the shoulder. Hindquarters are light but firm and well shaped, absolutely sound, giving a slow, dignified rolling gait in front, with a close gait behind.

Group

Toy. Pet Dogs (FCI).

Size

Weight: Dogs 4·9kg (11lb), bitches 5·4kg (12lb). The dog should be surprisingly heavy when picked up. In AKC, extreme limit is 6·3kg (14lb).

Coat

Colour: All colours and markings are

permissible and equally good, except albino and liver. Parti-colours should be evenly broken.

Texture: Long and straight with a profuse mane forming a frill round the neck, and profuse feathering on ears, legs, thighs, toes and tail, which is carried over the back. The top coat should be rather coarse with a thick undercoat.

Pharaoh Hound

Origins

This dog originated in Egypt and North Africa. The only significant differences between the various breeds of Greyhound rest in the coat and in the size, the one dependent on the climatic conditions in which they are expected to work, the other on the quarry they are intended to hunt. It follows, therefore, that the breeds change very little over long periods of time, while in their own countries doing the job for which they were bred. The Pharaoh Hound or Balearic Greyhound is just such a breed. It was much admired by Phoenician traders who introduced the breed throughout the Mediterranean countries where it has formed the foundation stock for other breeds.

Characteristics

Much the same in type as the Greyhound, but distinguished from it by its triangular head and large erect ears, unique among gaze hounds. The eyes are quite small and deep set, amber or light brown, the neck slender and rather long set into long lean fore-quarters. The back is straight with a long curve of loin running into a slightly falling croup.

Group

Hound. Greyhound (FCI).

Size

Height: Dogs 56 – 63·5cm (22 – 25in), bitches 53·3 – 61cm (21 – 24in). In FCI, dogs 63·5 – 70cm (25 – 27$\frac{1}{2}$in), bitches, smaller than dogs but not less than 57 – 66cm (22$\frac{1}{2}$ – 26in).

Coat

Colour: White with chestnut or rich tan or yellow tan markings.

Texture: Short, fine and glossy, with a soft skin.

Pinscher, Miniature

Origins

Contrary to popular misconception the Miniature Pinscher is not a small Dobermann; its original name 'Reh Pinscher' referred to the breed's resemblance to small forest deer. It has existed for several centuries in Germany and Scandinavia, where it was valued as a very alert watchdog. It was however only during the early years of this century that it began to find international favour.

Characteristics

The Miniature Pinscher is structurally a well-balanced, sturdy, compact, elegant, short-coupled, smooth-coated toy dog, naturally well groomed, proud, vigorous and alert. Its natural high-stepping gait, its fearless animation, complete self-possession and its spirited presence differentiate the breed from other toy dogs. The head is narrow, without coarseness, the ears upstanding, cropped in countries where the operation is still allowed.

Pharaoh Hound

The body is compact, muscular with well-sprung ribs, the tail set high and docked short. Legs are well boned with clean joints, feet cat-like.

Group
Toy. Pet Dogs (FCI).

Size
Height: 25·4 – 30·4cm (10 – 12in). In AKC, 27·9cm (11in) to 29cm (11½in) is the ideal. Dogs of either sex which are less than 25·4cm (10in) or over 31·5cm (12½in) are disqualified.

Coat
Colour: Red or black with tan markings, solid brown or chocolate.
Texture: Smooth, hard and short, straight and lustrous, closely adhering to and uniformly covering the body.

Pointer

Origins
Pointers have been used in Britain since the mid-17th century to indicate by pointing just where game was hidden, to locate, for instance, the forms of hares for coursing. Early in the 18th century, when guns came into use, the Pointer began to function as a gundog. The breed's distinctive appearance owes something to the Foxhound, its elegance to the Greyhound and its attitude to game-birds may be derived from the same stock from which Spaniels are descended. This perhaps accounts for the insistence by some authorities that the breed originated in Spain.

Characteristics
The Pointer is bred for work in the field and should look and act the part, giving an impression of compact power and agile grace allied to intelligence and alertness. The head is aristocratic with an unusual dish-shaped muzzle, the ears pendulous, the eyes rounded and dark. The neck is long, clean, muscular, and slightly arched, the shoulders long and sloping. The body is of moderate length, falling slightly to the croup, the chest is deep and the tuck-up pronounced. Fore-legs are straight, hindquarters muscular and powerful with great propelling leverage, with long thighs and well-bent stifles. Feet are oval, compact, well padded and deep. The tail is not docked. The gait is smooth and powerful with the head carried high.

Group
Gundog. Sporting (AKC). English Hunting Dogs (FCI).

Size
Height: Dogs 63·5 – 68·5cm (25 – 27in), bitches 61 – 66cm (24 – 26in). In AKC, dogs 63·5 – 71cm (25 – 28in), bitches 58·4 – 66cm (23 – 26in).
Weight: In AKC, dogs 24·9 – 34kg (55 – 75lb), bitches 20·4 – 29·4kg (45 – 65lb). In FCI, 19·9 – 20·8kg (44 – 46lb).

Coat
Colour: Liver, lemon, black, orange solid or combined with white. A good Pointer cannot be a bad colour.
Texture: Short, dense, smooth with a sheen.

Pointer, German Short-haired (Kurzhaar)

Origins
There are few records of the breed before the Klub Kurzhaar stud book was started in the 1870s, but as with so many working breeds it had long been established among those who appreciated its working qualities. The breed probably has its origins in the dogs introduced by homecoming crusaders intermingled with indigenous bird dogs and the Spanish Pointer, with style and elegance being largely dependant on the blood of the English Pointer. Nowadays the breed has a deservedly high reputation as a general purpose gundog.

Characteristics
An aristocratic, well-balanced, symmetrical animal displaying power, endurance and agility. Its expression should show enthusiasm for work without any sign of a nervous or flighty disposition. The head is clean cut, the shoulders sloping, the chest deep and the back short and powerful. Strong quarters provide propulsion for well-co-ordinated economical movement.

Group
Gundog. Sporting (AKC). Setters (FCI).

Size
Height: Dogs 58·4 – 63·5cm (23 – 25in), bitches 53·3 – 58·4cm (21 – 23in) at the withers. In FCI, dogs 62 – 65cm (24½ – 25½in), bitches not less than 58·4cm (23in).
Weight: Dogs 25 – 31·8kg (55 – 70lb), bitches 20·4 – 27·2kg (45 – 60lb).

Coat
Colour: Solid liver or any combination of liver and white.
Texture: The skin is close and tight, the hair short and thick.

Pointer, German Wire-haired

Origins
This dog was developed by selectively crossing several indigenous gundog breeds – the wirehaired Pointing Griffon, the Stichelhaar, the Puderpointer and the German Shorthair which, apart from in coat, it very closely resembles. The breed has been slow to gain recognition outside Germany, but now has a growing band of enthusiastic followers who appreciate the breed's outstanding abilities as an all-purpose gundog, able to point and to retrieve either on land or in water, and brave and hardy.

Characteristics
Essentially a dog of the Pointer type, of sturdy build, lively manner and with an intelligent, determined expression. In disposition the breed has been described as energetic, rather aloof, but not un-

friendly. The head is moderately long with a broad skull, the ears are rounded but not too broad and hang close to the sides of the head. The body is a little longer than it is high, the back short, straight and strong, the back line perceptibly sloping from withers to croup. The chest is deep and capacious with well-sprung ribs. The forelegs are straight, the hindlegs strong and muscular, moderately angulated. The feet are round in outline, webbed and high-arched.

Group
Gundogs. Sporting (AKC). Setters (FCI).

Size
Height: Dogs 60 – 65cm (23½ – 25in), bitches smaller, but not under 56cm (22in).
Weight: Dogs 25 – 32kg (55 – 70½lb), bitches 20·5 – 27kg (45 – 59½lb).

Coat
Colour: Liver and white, liver roan. Any black on the coat is very objectionable.
Texture: Weather-resistant and to some extent water-repellant. Outer coat straight, harsh, wiry, lying flat, 2·5 – 5cm (1 – 2in) in length; the undercoat is dense in winter, thinner in summer.

Pomeranian

Origins
Possibly the smallest of the Spitz breeds, but one which retains all the courage and character of its larger cousins. During the last century the Pomeranian has been reduced in size, but seems to have avoided many of the problems often associated with miniaturization. Now it is

Pointer *Top left* German Short-haired Pointer and *Top right* German Wire-haired Pointer

Pomeranian

Pug

no longer used to herd sheep, but it remains an alert housedog, capable of giving warning of intruders with a surprisingly deep bark, giving the impression that a larger animal is on duty.

Characteristics
The Pomeranian is a short-coupled, compact dog, alert in character and deportment. His head is fox-like in shape and expression, the eyes bright and dark in colour, the ears small and erect. The neck is rather short, a shortness which is accentuated by the characteristic Spitz ruff. The shortness of the cobby body too is accentuated by the curled Spitz tail. Movement is smooth and free.

Group
Toy. Pet Dog (FCI).

Size
Height: In FCI, 27·9cm (11in) maximum.
Weight: Dogs 1·8 – 2kg (4 – 4½lb), bitches 2 – 2·5kg (4½ – 5½lb). In AKC, 1·3 – 3kg (3 – 7lb), ideally from 1·8 – 2·2kg (4 – 5lb). In FCI, not more than 3·3kg (7½lb).

Coat
Colour: Any solid colour with or without lighter or darker shadings of the same colour.
Texture: Double-coated: a short, soft thick undercoat with a longer, coarse, harsh-textured outer coat.

Poodle, Miniature

Origins
Of later origin than the Standard Poodles and used exclusively as a companion. The standard is the same as the Standard Poodle except:

Size
Height: Under 38cm (15in) but not less than 27·9cm (11in). In AKC, 38cm (15in) maximum with disqualification at aheight of 25·4cm (10in) or less. In FCI, 34·8 – 45cm (13¾ – 17¾in).

Poodle, Standard

Origins
Originating in France, the poodle was used as a gundog over a wide area, including France, Germany and Russia. Their adaptability, intelligence and unusual appearance soon led them to be used for a wide variety of purposes, as well as in the production of other gundog breeds.

Characteristics
A very active, intelligent and elegant dog with a good temperament, carrying itself proudly. The head is long and fine with almond-shaped eyes, the chest deep and moderately wide with well-sprung ribs. The back is short and strong. The tail is docked.

Group
Non-sporting. Utility (KC). Pet Dogs (FCI).

Size
Height: 38cm (15in) and over. In AKC, over 38cm (15in). In FCI, 45 – 54·5cm (17¾ – 21½in).

Coat
Colour: All solid colours, clear colours preferred.
Texture: Very profuse and dense and of harsh texture. The coat has the advantage that it does not shed like most other breeds and lacks the distinctive and sometimes objectionable doggy smell. The distinctive appearance is achieved by careful and laborious clipping and grooming. The lion clip in one or other of its variations is customary for adult show dogs and is claimed to have a functional basis with long hair being left where the dog requires protection either from cold, wet or undergrowth. The Dutch clip is usually favoured by pet owners since it needs less dedicated grooming and is within the capabilities of

the average poodle parlour.

Poodle, Toy

The standard is the same as the Standard Poodle except:

Group
Toy (AKC).

Size
Height: Below 27·9 (11in). In AKC, not more than 25·4cm (10in). In FCI, less than 34·8cm (13¾in).

Pug

Origins
The Pug is another of the toy breeds with roots in ancient China, where it has flourished for the past 2000 years. Many carvings were made of Pugs in Netsuke, which show how little the breed's appearance has changed. Although very much a toy dog, the Pug has all the characteristics of some of the Eastern mastiff breeds which it so closely resembles. In Europe, its fortunes were based on it being taken up, rather like the Keeshond, as a political mascot. It was the breed associated with the Dutch House of Orange after it had saved the life of William, Prince of Orange, by warning of Spanish intruders. Josephine, Napoleon's wife, was so captivated by the breed that she was able to ignore its history of royal patronage and chose Pugs as her companions during her husband's imprisonment. She even contrived to get her pet to carry messages to Napoleon.

Characteristics
The Pug is a square and cobby little dog, giving an impression of considerable substance packed into small size. The head is round, massive, and deeply wrinkled. The muzzle short and blunt, the eyes very large, bold and dark. The body is short, wide in the chest and well

ribbed-up. The forelegs are strong and straight, the hindquarters muscular. The tail is curled tightly.

Group

Toy. Pet Dogs (FCI).

Size

Weight: 6·3 – 8kg (14 – 18lb).

Coat

Colour: Silver or apricot fawn with black trace and mask, black.

Texture: Fine, smooth, soft, short and glossy, neither hard nor woolly.

Standard Poodle: *right* unclipped, *below* with lion clip.

Puli

Origins

This breed is a working partner of the Komondor and the Kuvasz and shares the same origins among the herding dogs which invading Magyars brought into Hungary. The Puli was used to herd and drive sheep while the larger Komondors played their parts as guards.

Characteristics

A medium-size breed, vigorous, alert and extremely active, even to the point of being distinctly bouncy. By nature Pulis are affectionate and loyal, but being excellent guards are suspicious of strangers. The construction of the Puli is not exaggerated in any way, the head is of medium size, the neck strong and muscular and of medium length. The chest is deep and fairly broad and the body of medium length, straight and level. Forelegs are straight and well boned, hindquarters well developed with well-bent muscular stifles. The tail is never docked and is carried over the back.

Group

Working (AKC). Shepherd Dogs (FCI).

Size

Height: Dogs 40 – 44cm ($15\frac{3}{4}$ – $17\frac{1}{2}$in), bitches 36·7 – 40·6cm ($14\frac{1}{2}$ – 16in). In AKC, dogs about 43cm (17in) and not to exceed 48·2cm (19in), bitches 40·6cm (16in), not to exceed 45·7cm (18in).
Weight: Dogs 12·9 – 14.9kg ($28\frac{1}{2}$ – 33lb), bitches 9·9 – 12·9kg (22 – $28\frac{1}{2}$lb).

Coat

Colour: Solid colours, principally a distinctive rusty black, various shades of grey and white.
Texture: The coat is characteristic of this and related breeds and hangs in tight, even cords.

Puli

Pyrenean Mountain Dog

Origins

This dog is a descendant of the South European herding and guard breeds, originating in the mountains on the borders of France and Spain. It was the guard dog of the region, protecting the flocks against wolves, bears and thieves. The Chien de Berger des Pyrénées, a smaller version, is used as the herding dog. The Mountain Dog is an impressive animal, and captured the interest of the Dauphin who, in 1675, brought some of the breed to the Court in Paris.

Characteristics

The dog is serious in play and at work. He should exemplify gentleness and docility even to the point of self-sacrifice. A dog of immense size, great majesty,

Pyrenean Mountain Dog

keen intelligence and kindly expression. Soundness is of the greatest importance in the breed. The head is large.

Group

Working. Guard Dogs (FCI). Non-sporting (RASKC).

Size

Height: In KC and RASKC, minimum height for dogs 71cm (28in), bitches 66cm (26in). In AKC, dogs 68·5 – 81cm (27 – 32in), bitches 63·5 – 73·6cm (25 – 29in).

Weight: Dogs 50kg (110lb), bitches 40kg (90lb). In AKC, dogs 45·3 – 56·7kg (100 – 125lb), bitches 40·8 – 52kg (90 – 115lb). In FCI, 45·3 – 54·5kg (100 – 120lb).

Coat

Colour: All white or principally white, with markings of badger, grey or shades of tan.
Texture: Created to withstand severe weather, with a fine undercoat and thick overcoat of coarser hair.

R

Retriever, Chesapeake Bay

Origins
In the early part of the 19th century the nondescript indigenous Retrievers used in Maryland, USA, received an unexpected influx of new blood as a result of two dogs having been rescued from a wrecked English brig. The new blood so improved the native stock that other crosses were used and by the end of the century a distinct breed of Retriever had emerged. This dog was expected to work in the icy waters of Chesapeake Bay retrieving fallen duck. It has thus achieved a great reputation as a retriever of water fowl, though this reputation has not led to great popularity.

Characteristics
The head and body, to some degree, resemble the Labrador Retriever. The skull is broad and round, the muzzle short, the ears small and pendulous and the eyes fairly large, clear and yellow or amber in colour. The neck is of medium length, set into sloping shoulders. The chest is barrel round and deep, the body of medium length with flanks well tucked-up. Hindquarters are especially powerful to supply driving power for swimming, and the stifles are well angulated. The forelegs are straight, well boned and muscled with well-webbed harefeet of good size. The tail is long, straight or slightly curved and medium heavy at the base.

Group
Sporting (AKC). English Hunting Dogs (FCI).

Size
Height: Dogs 58·4 – 66cm (23 – 26in), bitches 53·3 – 61cm (21 – 24in). Oversized or undersized specimens are severely penalized.
Weight: Dogs 29·4 – 36·2kg (65 – 80lb), bitches 24·9 – 31·7kg (55 – 70lb). In FCI, the standard is 2·2kg (5lb) less for both maximum weights.

Coat
Colour: Any colour varying from dark brown to a faded tan or deadgrass, which varies from a tan to a dull straw colour.
Texture: The coat is thick and short with a dense fine woolly undercoat. The outer coat is harsh and oily and should resist water as does a duck's feathers.

Retriever, Curly-coated

Origins
The Curly-coated Retriever had been established as a distinct breed by 1860 when it was first exhibited at Birmingham City Show. The breed had been produced as a gundog superbly adapted to working in water, on a basis of the Old English Water Spaniel, with the judicious introduction of Irish and English Water Spaniels, St John's Newfoundland and Poodle.

Characteristics
A smart upstanding dog which shows activity, endurance and intelligence. The head is long and well proportioned, with black or brown eyes, and rather small, low-set ears lying close to the head. The

Chesapeake Bay Retriever

Bottom Curly-coated Retriever,
below Golden Retriever, *right* Labrador
Retriever, *below right* Flat-coated Retriever.

neck is moderately long, the shoulders very deep, muscular and well laid-back. The body has well-sprung ribs, deep brisket and little tuck-up. The hindquarters are strong and muscular with hock low to the ground. The tail is moderately short, carried straight and covered with curls.

Group
Gundog. Sporting (AKC). English Hunting Dogs (FCI).

Size
Height: 63·5 – 68·5cm (25 – 27in). In FCI, approximately 66cm (26in).
Weight: 31·7 – 36·2cm (70 – 80lb).

Coat
Colour: Black or liver.
Texture: It should be one mass of crisp small curls all over. This is the main characteristic of the breed.

Retriever, Flat-coated

Origins
The breed is a subtle mixture of the St John's Newfoundland, a smaller version of the Newfoundland, with setters, sheepdogs and spaniels, and is a first class retriever of water fowl. The breed was first shown in Britain in 1859 under a classification which included curly coats, wavy or smooth-coated Retrievers, but had to wait until 1873 when Mr E. Shirley, founder of the Kennel Club, took an interest in it and stabilized type. The breed then was overtaken in popularity by other gundog breeds, but in recent years has justly found itself coming back into popularity and now appears in the ring in healthy numbers and is re-establishing its reputation in the field.

Characteristics
A bright, active dog of medium size with an intelligent expression, showing power and raciness. The head is long and nicely moulded, the skull flat and moderately broad, the jaw long and strong. The eyes are dark brown or hazel of medium size and the ears small and fitting close to the side of the head. The neck is long, the chest deep and fairly broad, the forelegs straight and well feathered, the back short. Hindquarters are muscular, the stifle neither too straight nor too bent. The tail is short, straight and well set on, carried gaily, but never above the level of the back.

Group
Gundog. Sporting (AKC). English Hunting Dogs (FCI).

Size
Weight: Should be 27·2 – 31·7kg (60 – 70lb).

Coat
Colour: Black or liver.
Texture: Dense, of fine quality and texture, and as flat as possible.

Retriever, Golden

Origins
It has been suggested that the breed has its origins in a troupe of Russian circus dogs which Lord Tweedsmuir saw and bought in Britain. It is perhaps a pity that there is no factual evidence to support such a story. What really happened was that in 1865 he bought, from a cobbler in Brighton, a yellow wavy-coated Retriever bred by Lord Chichester. This he mated to a Tweedwater Spaniel, a breed local to his home county, and then bred on to further crosses with Tweedwater Spaniels, black Retrievers, an Irish Setter and a Bloodhound, so that by 1913 the Kennel Club was able to recognize the result as a separate breed. They were first known as Retrievers (Golden or Yellow) but, in 1920, the name was changed to Retrievers (Golden). From inception to recognition as a breed had taken a mere 45 years, simply because breeders were selecting stock against their name as gundogs. The breed does good service as a guide dog for the blind.

Characteristics
The Golden Retriever is symmetrical, active and powerful, a good level mover, sound and well put together. The head is broad, the expression kindly, the eyes dark. The neck is clean and muscular, set into long-bladed, well laid back shoulders. Forelegs are straight with good bone, the body well balanced, short coupled and deep, the ribs well sprung. Hindquarters are strong and muscular with well-bent stifles. Feet are round and cat-like. The tail should not be carried too gaily or curled at the tip.

Group
Gundog. Sporting (AKC). English Hunting Dogs (FCI).

Size
Height: Dogs 56 – 61cm (22 – 24in), bitches 50·8 – 56cm (20 – 22in). In AKC, dogs 58·4 – 61cm (23 – 24in), bitches 54·5 – 57cm (21½ – 22½in).
Weight: Dogs 32 – 37kg (70 – 80lb), bitches 27 – 32kg (60 – 70lb). In AKC, dogs 29·4 – 34kg (65 – 75lb). In FCI, dogs 29·4 – 31·7kg (65 – 70lb).

Coat
Colour: Any shade of gold or cream, but neither red nor mahogany.
Texture: Flat or wavy with good feathering and dense, with a water-resistant undercoat.

Retriever, Labrador

Origins
In 1822 reports of 'small water dogs . . . admirably trained as retrievers in fowling and are otherwise useful' indicated that there existed in Newfoundland a breed of gundog which British sportsmen were quick to recognize as being first class. Colonel Hawker, a noted sportsman described them as 'by far the best for any kind of shooting' while the Earl of Malmesbury described the breed as having 'close coat which turns the water off like oil and (have) a tail like an otter'. The Earl's knowledge of gundogs far surpassed his knowledge of geography, for he referred to the dogs which came from Newfoundland as Labradors. When new stock from Newfoundland became hard to get attempts were made to introduce the blood of other gundogs, but the strong characteristics of the original breed proved to be dominant and survived. Labradors have frequently won the Kennel Club Best in Show cup at Crufts. To qualify as a champion in England a Labrador needs a working certificate.

Characteristics
The general appearance is that of a strongly built, short-coupled, very active dog, with a broad skull, broad and deep through the chest and ribs, and broad and strong over the loins and hindquarters. The dog must move neither too wide nor too close in front or behind, but must stand and move true all round on legs and feet. The tail is a distinctive feature of the breed and should be very thick at the base gradually tapering towards the tip and giving that peculiar rounded appearance which has been described as the 'otter' tail.

Group
Gundog. Sporting (AKC). English Hunting Dogs (FCI).

Size
Height: Dogs 50·8 – 57cm (20 – 22½in), in RASKC 55·8 – 57cm (22 – 22½in), bitches 54·5 – 56cm (21½ – 22in). In AKC, dogs 57 – 62cm (22½ – 24½in), bitches 54·5 – 60cm (21½ – 23½in).
Weight: In AKC, dogs 27·2 – 34kg (60 – 75lb), bitches 24·9 – 31·7kg (55 – 70lb).

Coat
Colour: Colour is generally black or yellow but other whole colours are permitted. The AKC expressly mentions chocolate.
Texture: The coat is short and dense and without wave, with a weather-resistant undercoat, and should be fairly hard.

Rhodesian Ridgeback

Rottweiler

Rhodesian Ridgeback

Origins

The European farmers, who in the 16th and 17th centuries settled in South Africa, brought with them a collection of dogs from which they developed a hound suitable for the conditions and game encountered in South Africa, and which was also willing to act as a guard. They did this by crossing their dogs with a native hunting dog which had a ridge on its back. The dog had to be tough to withstand hard work in extremes of temperature, sufficiently versatile to either retrieve a partridge or put down a wounded buck, had to be easily kept and fit well into the family. The breed, which was developed by the Boer farmers, was introduced into Rhodesia in 1877 by the Reverend Helm who used it for hunting lions, from which activity it got the name of African Lion Hound.

Characteristics

The peculiarity of the breed is the ridge on the back formed by hair growing against the nap of the rest of the coat; this ridge is regarded as the escutcheon of the breed. The Ridgeback is a strong, muscular and active dog, symmetrical in outline and capable of great endurance with a fair amount of speed; its movement is similar to that of a Foxhound. The head is of fair length, flat and broad between the ears, which are set high and carried close to the head. The eyes are bright and coloured to harmonize with the colour of the dog. Forelegs are straight and heavily boned, shoulders sloping, clean and muscular. The chest is deep and capacious, the back powerful with strong, muscular and slightly arched loins. The tail is carried with a slight upward curve, but never curled.

Group

Hound. Hounds for smaller game (FCI).

Size

Height: Dogs 63·5 – 68·5cm (25 – 27in), bitches 61 – 66cm (24 – 26in).
Weight: Dogs 36·3kg (80lb) and bitches 31·7kg (70lb) with a variation of 2·2kg (5lb) either way. In AKC and FCI, dogs 34kg (75lb) and bitches 29·4kg (65lb).

Coat

Colour: Light wheaten to red wheaten, with only a little white on the chest and toes.
Texture: Short and dense with a sleek, glossy appearance.

Rottweiler

Origins

Yet another of the European mastiff breeds which probably have their origins among the dogs which guarded and helped drive the herds of cattle which accompanied the Roman armies. Rottweil itself was founded by the Romans and was an important cattle trading centre in the 12th century. In such circumstances it is not surprising that a distinctive breed of working dog developed. The Rottweiler Metzerhund was an integral part of the region's prosperity until its use declined with the coming of the railways and mass transport of cattle. At the beginning of this century a club was formed to protect the Rottweiler and, soon after, its qualities earned it a place in police work. The breed's ability as a guard dog is still recognized, its courage, strength and forbidding aspect make it a marvellous guard for those able to control it.

Characteristics

The Rottweiler is a compact dog, well proportioned and powerfully built to permit great strength, manoeuverability and endurance. His bearing displays boldness and courage, while his tranquil gaze manifests a good nature and devotion. The head is distinctive, broad, of medium length, with well-muscled cheeks and moderately wrinkled. The neck is of fair length, strong, round and very muscular, set into long and sloping shoulders. Forelegs are muscular, with plenty of bone and substance, the body is broad and deep, the back straight, strong and not too long. Hindquarters are broad and strongly muscled with well-angulated hocks. Movement should be supple giving an impression of strength, endurance and purpose.

Group

Working. Non-sporting (RASKC).

Size

Height: Dogs 63·5 – 68·5cm (25 – 27in), bitches 58·4 – 63·5cm (23 – 25in). In AKC, dogs 60 – 68·5cm (23¾ – 27in), bitches 54·5 – 65cm (21¾ – 25¾in). In FCI, dogs 60 – 68cm (23½ – 27in), bitches 55 – 63cm (21½ – 25in).

Coat

Colour: Black with clearly defined tan markings on cheeks, muzzle, chest and legs, as well as over the eyes and under the tail.
Texture: Coarse and flat, with a medium-length topcoat.

S

St Bernard

Origins
The St Bernard's ancestors were probably brought to Switzerland by invading Roman armies. These dogs were crossed with native dogs to produce the Talhund and Bauernhund which, by the 11th century, were in common use on Swiss farms. At the beginning of the 18th century, a passing reference to the work of rescue dogs, working from the Hospice founded by Archdeacon Bernard de Menthon, implies that rescue work was a well established part of the dog's uses, although 100 years earlier the Hospice appears to have been without dogs.

St Bernard

Characteristics
The head of the St Bernard is massive and round with an expression of benevolence, dignity and intelligence. The neck is long, thick and muscular, and slightly arched. The muzzle has a well-developed dewlap. Forelegs are perfectly straight, and strong in bone, shoulders are broad and sloping. The back is broad and straight, the chest wide and deep. Hindquarters should be heavy in bone with well-bent hocks. The standard draws attention to the need for sound movement and regrets that the breed has often failed in this direction, hind legs being especially faulty. The feet are large and compact; the tail set on rather high.

Group
Working. Non-sporting (RASKC).

Size
Height: Dogs 69·7cm (27½in) minimum, bitches 65cm (25½in) minimum.

Coat
Colour: Orange, mahogany-brindle, red-brindle, white with patches on body of these colours.
Texture: Rough specimens have a dense, flat coat; smooths have a close, hound-like coat.

Saluki

Origins
Northern Africa has produced some of the best of the sight hound breeds and it is possible that all owe something to what might be the oldest of these breeds, the Saluki. The breed certainly existed when Alexander invaded India, four centuries before the birth of Christ, while carvings on Sumerian and Egyptian tombs dating from 7000 BC are recognizable as Salukis. Throughout a long history, the breed has been recognized as an aristocrat, for instance the Moslems, who regard dogs as unclean animals, make an exception of 'the noble one', the dog given to them by Allah. The high esteem in which the breed was held resulted in them being given extraordinary privileges, which they nowadays find less readily available in a 20th-century home. The breed was first brought to Britain in 1840.

Characteristics
The appearance of the breed is one of grace and symmetry, suggesting great speed and endurance coupled with the strength and activity to enable it to catch and kill a gazelle over deep sand or rocky mountains. The head is long and narrow, the eyes dark to hazel and bright. The ears are long and mobile and covered with long silky hair. The neck too is long,

Saluki

supple and well muscled, set into sloping shoulders set well back. The chest is deep and moderately narrow, the forelegs straight and long in postern. The back is muscular and slightly arched. Hindquarters are strong with stifle close to the ground. The tail is long, low set and carried in a graceful curve, well feathered with long silky hair.

Group
Hound. Greyhounds (FCI).

Size
Height: Dogs 58·4 – 71cm (23 – 28in), bitches proportionately less. In AKC, dogs 70cm (27½in) minimum, bitches 65cm (25½in).
Weight: In FCI, 22·6 – 29·9kg (50 – 66lb).

Coat
Colour: White, cream, fawn, golden, red, grizzle and·tan, tricolour and black and tan or variations of these colours.
Texture: Smooth and silky, with elegant silky feathering on ears, legs and tail, except in the smooth variety.

Samoyed

Origins
Just as the Saluki may lay claim to being the oldest of the Mediterranean sight hounds, so the Samoyed may claim to be the oldest of the Northern Spitz breeds. It shared the hard life of the Sayantsi in ancient times and more recently accompanied Nansen, Shackleton, Scott and Amundsen on their expeditions. Originally bred as a guard for herds of reindeer, the breed also acted as companion, guard and sledge dog in which capacity it accompanied Polar expeditions. The breed's strength, stamina and hardiness are belied by its child-like good nature and fairy-tale and soft appearance.

Characteristics
The Samoyed is intelligent, alert, full of action, but above all displays affection towards all mankind. The breed should be strong, active and graceful, with a muscular back of medium length allowing liberty of movement. The chest is deep and well sprung, the neck proudly arched, the front straight and the loins exceptionally strong, giving an impression of great endurance. A short-legged dog is to be deprecated. The head is powerful and wedge-shaped, the eyes almond-shaped with an intelligent expression. The ears are erect and thick, covered inside with hair. The tail is long and profusely coated, carried over the back when alert, but sometimes dropped when at rest.

Group
Working. Non-sporting (RASKC).

Size
Height: Dogs 50·8 – 56cm (20 – 22in), bitches 45·7 – 50·8cm (18 – 20in). In AKC, dogs 53·3 – 60cm (21 – 23½in), bitches 48·2 – 53·3cm (19 – 21in). In FCI, dogs 53·3cm (21in) minimum, bitches 45·7cm (18in) minimum.
Weight: In FCI, dogs 19·9 – 29·9kg (44 – 66lb), bitches 16·9 – 24·9kg (37½ – 55lb).

Coat
Colour: Pure white, white and biscuit, cream.
Texture: A thick, close, soft and short undercoat, covered with an outer coat of straight harsh hair, which grows straight away from the body providing protection against extreme cold.

Schipperke

Origins
The general appearance of the Schipperke strongly suggests a Spitz breed. Indeed the breed was originally called Spitske. However, when the breed is allowed to retain its tail, the carriage seems to suggest a relationship with the other European herding breeds. The Schipperke is descended from the same herding dogs which produced the Belgian Shepherd Dog (Groenendael), the latter remaining as herders and Schipperkes becoming smaller watchdogs. Probably Schipperkes can be accredited with taking part in the first organized dog shows when, in 1690, a show was held at the Grand Palace of Brussels for dogs owned by Guild workmen. It was not until 1888 that their name was changed to Schipperke, which in Flemish means 'little captain', a reference as much to the breed's air of self-importance as to their association with the barges of the Flemish canals.

Characteristics
The general appearance is of a small, cobby animal with a sharp expression, intensely lively, presenting the appearance of being always on the alert. The head is distinctly foxy with small, rather oval, dark brown eyes and sharply pointed, stiffly erect ears. The neck is strong and rather short, the shoulders muscular and sloping with perfectly straight forelegs. Hindquarters are fine compared with the fore-parts, the rump tailless and rounded; the feet small and cat-like.

Samoyed

Schipperke

Standard Schnauzer

Giant Schnauzer

Group

Non-sporting. Utility (KC). Pet Dogs (FCI).

Size

Weight: 5·4 – 7·2kg (12 – 16lb). In AKC, up to 8kg (18lb). In FCI, large dogs 4·9 – 9kg (11 – 20lb), small dogs 2·9 – 4·9kg (6½ – 11lb), miniatures under 2·9kg (6½lb).

Coat

Colour: Black, but other whole colours are permissible in Britain, though not in America.

Texture: Abundant, dense and harsh, smooth on the head, ears and legs, but erect and thick round the neck, forming a mane and frill, and with a good culotte on the back of the thighs.

Schnauzer, Standard

Origins

The Standard Schnauzer may be regarded as the forerunner of the three Schnauzer breeds: Miniature, Standard and Giant. The Schnauzer is a German breed with a long history dating back to the 15th and 16th centuries. In its blood may run Poodle blood, some Spitz and some Pinscher blood, but the Schnauzer has long been a distinctive breed used in its various sizes as a vermin killer, a yard dog and a most effective guard. Larger types were much used as Army dogs and in all its roles the breed has shown itself to be adaptable, trainable and intelligent.

Characteristics

The Schnauzer is a powerfully built, robust, sinewy, nearly square dog with a temperament which combines high spirits, reliability, strength, endurance and vigour. The head is strong and elongated, moderately broad between the ears, the medium stop is accentuated by prominent eyebrows and the muzzle is powerful. The eyes are of medium size, dark, oval and set forward; ears are V-shaped, neat and dropping forward or cropped in countries where the operation is permitted. The neck is moderately long and slightly arched, set cleanly into flat and sloping shoulders. Forelegs are straight and elbows set close to the body under a moderately broad and deep chest with visible breast-bone and well-sprung ribs. The thighs are slanting, flat and well muscled. The tail is carried high and docked to three joints.

Group

Working. Utility (KC). Non-sporting (RASKC).

Size

Height: Dogs 45·7 – 50·8cm (18 – 20in); maximum height 1·2cm (½in) less in FCI, bitches 43 – 48·2cm (17 – 19in). In AKC, dogs 47 – 49·5cm (18½ – 19½in), bitches 44 – 47cm (17½ – 18½in). In RASKC, dogs 48·2cm (19in), bitches 45·7cm (18in).

Coat

Colour: All pepper and salt colours in even proportions and pure black.

Texture: Hard and wiry, with a good undercoat.

Schnauzer, Giant

The description for the Giant Schnauzer is similar to the Standard Schnauzer in Kennel Club standards except for the following:

Size

Height: Dogs 65 – 69·7cm (25½ – 27½in), bitches 60 – 65cm (23½ – 25½in).

Schnauzer, Miniature

The description for the Miniature Schnauzer is similar to the Standard Schnauzer in Kennel Club standards except for the following:

Group

Utility (KC). Terrier (AKC).

Size

Height: In KC, dogs 35·5cm (14in),

bitches 33cm (13in). In AKC, 30·4 – 35·5cm (12 – 14in).

Setter, English

Origins

Although it is likely that the setters originally sprang from imported spaniel stock, there is evidence that by the late 16th century the two groups of bird dogs were distinctly differentiated. The Setter, with its long head, curly coat and well-developed ability to find and point game,

Left Irish Setter, *top* English Setter, *above* Gordon Setter.

showed evidence of crosses with Pointers, the large Water Spaniel and the Springer Spaniel. The modern breed was largely developed from a strain kept pure for over 35 years by its breeder, Reverend A. Harrison. In 1825, Edward Laverack obtained stock from him, from which, by inbreeding, he produced the foundation stock for the modern breed in both Britain and North America. English Setters were among the select group of breeds to be scheduled at the Newcastle-on-Tyne show in 1859.

Characteristics

The English Setter is an intensely friendly and quiet-natured dog with a keen game sense. It is of medium height, clean in outline, and elegant both in appearance and movement. The head is long and rather lean with a well-defined stop. The skull is oval from ear to ear. The eyes should be bright, mild and intelligent and of a dark hazel colour, the darker the better. The ears are of moderate length, set low and hanging close to the cheek;

the tips are velvety, the upper parts clothed in fine silky hair. The neck is long, muscular and lean, the forequarters well set back, the chest deep in brisket and the body of moderate length and well ribbed-up. Hindquarters have well-bent stifles. The tail should be set almost in line with the back, the feather long, soft and silky.

Group

Gundog. Sporting (AKC). English Hunting Dogs (FCI).

Size

Height: Dogs 65–68·5cm (25½–27in), bitches 61–65cm (24–25½in). In AKC, dogs 63·5cm (25in), bitches 61cm (24in).

Weight: Dogs 27·2–29·9kg (60–66lb), bitches 25·4–28kg (56–62lb).

Coat

Colour: May be either black and white, lemon and white, liver and white or tricolour; flecked rather than heavy patching is preferred.

Texture: Slightly wavy, long and silky, the breeches and forelegs well feathered.

Setter, Gordon

Origins

As early as 1620 Markham, a contemporary writer, was able to remark that the 'black and fallow setting dog' was the 'hardest to endure labour'. But it was not until the end of the 18th century, when the fourth Duke of Gordon's kennel of Setters had made the breed famous, that the Gordon Castle Setters began to achieve fame outside Scotland and were described as being 'easy to break and naturally back well. They are not fast dogs, but they have good staying powers and can keep on steadily from morning until night. Their noses are first class and they seldom make a false point'. The Gordon Setter has never achieved the popularity of the Irish or English Setters and so, perhaps, has avoided some of the worst effects of popular demand and remains an honest, basically sensible gundog.

Characteristics

The breed is stylish, built on galloping lines, having a thoroughbred appearance consistent with its build, which is comparable to that of a weight-carrying hunter. The back is strong, fairly short and level, the tail shortish and the head fairly long, clearly lined and with an intelligent expression. The head is deep rather than broad, with a slightly rounded skull. Eyes are of a fair size, dark brown and bright, ears are medium sized and rather thin, set low and hanging

close to the head. The neck is long, lean and arched to the head, set into long shoulders, sloping well back. The body is deep in brisket with ribs well sprung, loins wide and slightly arched.

Group

Gundog. Sporting (AKC). English Hunting Dogs (FCI).

Size

Height: Dogs 66cm (26in), bitches 62cm (24½in). In AKC, dogs 61–68·5cm (24–27in), bitches 58·4–63·5cm (23–25in).

Weight: Dogs 29·4kg (65lb), bitches 25·4kg (56lb). In AKC, dogs 24·9–36·2kg (55–80lb), bitches 20·4–31·7kg (45–70lb).

Coat

Colour: Deep shining coal-black without any rustiness, with tan markings of a rich chestnut red.

Texture: Should be soft and shining, straight or slightly waved, but not curly. Long hair on ears, under stomach and on chest, back of fore and hind-legs and under the tail.

Setter, Irish

Origins

Ireland is the home of two breeds of setter, the Red and White and the Red. The former never achieved any sort of popular recognition and now survives only in the kennels of a few enthusiasts. The Red Setter however has achieved a degree of popularity which may not always have been to its benefit as it has led to the breed being carelessly bred. In the early 19th century the Earl of Enniskillen's kennel contained nothing but solid-coloured dogs which Stonehonge records as being of a 'blood red, or rich chestnut or mahogany colour' and it is from the kennels of such breeders that the modern uniformally coloured breed has emerged.

Characteristics

Irish Setters must be racy, full of quality and have a kindly expression. The head is long and lean, the skull oval from ear to ear, the stop well defined and the muzzle deep. The eyes are dark hazel or dark brown; the ears are of moderate size and fine texture and are set on low and hang close to the head. The neck is moderately long, very muscular and slightly arched. The shoulders are fine at the points, deep and sloping, the chest is rather narrow in front and as deep as possible. The straight sinewy forelegs have plenty of bone while the hindquarters are wide and powerful with well-bent stifles. The tail is set on moderately low, strong at the root and tapering.

Group

Gundog. Sporting (AKC). English Hunting Dogs (FCI).

Size

Height: In AKC, dogs 68·5cm (27in), bitches 63·5cm (28in).

Weight: In AKC, dogs 31·7kg (70lb), bitches 27·2kg (60lb).

Coat

Colour: Rich chestnut with no trace whatever of black.

Texture: Of moderate length, flat and as free as possible from curl or wave on body; long and silky on ears, brisket, legs and tail.

Shetland Sheepdog

Origins

The Shetland Sheepdog, in spite of a considerable degree of similarity to the larger Rough Collie, is not a miniature version of that breed, but is a distinctive breed produced in response to the peculiar demands made by the hard climate and terrain of the isolated northerly islands off Scotland. These islands have produced distinctive and hardy breeds of small sheep and ponies and the Shetland Sheepdog falls into the same category. The breed is undoubtably of ancient origin but, due to lack of records, we know little of its history before it achieved the distinction of being recognized as a breed by the Kennel Club in 1914.

Characteristics

The Shetland should be instantly appreciated as a dog of great beauty, intelligence and alertness. It should be affectionate and responsive towards its owner, but may be reserved in its attitude to strangers. The head is refined, a long blunt wedge tapering from ear to nose; the eyes, of medium size, almond-shaped and set obliquely, are dark brown in colour except in the case of merles where blue is permissible. The ears are small and carried semi-erect with the tips dropping forward. The neck is muscular and well arched, the shoulders well laid and the forelegs straight, muscular and clean with strong bone. The chest is deep, the ribs well sprung and the back level with a graceful sweep over the loins. The hindquarters should be broad and muscular. The tail is set on low and must reach the hock joint and never be carried above the level of the back.

Group

Working. Shepherd Dogs (FCI).

Size

Height: Dogs 36·7cm (14½in), bitches 35·5cm (14in); anything over

2·5cm (1in) above these heights would be disqualified. In AKC, 33 – 40·6cm (13 – 16in).

Coat
Colour: Tricolour, sable, blue merle, black and white or black and tan.
Texture: Must be double: the outer coat of long hair of harsh texture and straight, the undercoat short and close. The mane and frill should be abundant, the fore-legs well feathered and the hind-legs with profuse trouserings.

Shih Tzu

Origins
Records dating from AD 624 show that dogs were given as tribute to the Tang Emperor by K'iu T'ai; paintings and carvings show these dogs and others offered in later tributes to have been very like the modern Shih Tzu. Whether these dogs originated in Tibet or in some part of the Byzantine Empire is not known, but the centuries of careful breeding which the Chinese have devoted to the breed must be regarded as sufficient to regard the breed as Chinese. These self-important little dogs, favoured by the Court because of the close association between the Buddha and his pet dog, preceded their royal masters about the court and by their barking warned lesser mortals to avert their eyes from the personifications of the Sun and Sons of Heaven. Shih Tzu means lion dog, a reference more to the breed's courage than to its appearance.

Characteristics
The Shih Tzu is a very active, lively and alert dog with a distinctly arrogant carriage. The British Standard expressly says it is neither a terrier nor a toy dog. The head is broad and round, wide between the eyes with a short square muzzle. The eyes are large dark and round but not prominent. The ears have long leathers, are pendulous and heavily coated. Forequarters are short and muscular, the body is well coupled and sturdy, the chest broad and deep. Hind-quarters are short and muscular and the tail is heavily plumed and carried well over the back.

Group
Utility (KC). Toy (AKC). Pet Dogs (FCI). Non-sporting (RASKC).

Size
Height: Not more than 26·6cm (10½in). In AKC, 22·8 – 26·6cm (9 – 10½in), with 27·9cm (11in) as an upper limit.
Weight: 4·5 – 8kg (10 – 18lb), ideally not more than 7·2kg (16lb). In AKC, 5·4 – 6·8kg (12 – 15lb).

Shetland Sheepdog

Shih Tzu

Coat
Colour: All colours are permissible.
Texture: Long and dense but not curly, with a good undercoat.

Siberian Husky

Origins
This is a breed forged in the hardest imaginable environment among the Chukchi people who inhabited the frozen wastelands of north-eastern Asia. The Chukchi were nomadic hunters who depended for their survival on the strength, speed, courage, intelligence and toughness of the breed they had developed by rigorous selection. So well did they succeed that when the breed was matched in Alaska against the very much bigger native breed, they de-

monstrated a considerable superiority. They continue to give sterling service to man when he has need to venture into the hostile Arctic and Antarctic wastelands.

Characteristics
The general appearance is of a medium-sized working dog, quick and light on its feet and graceful in action. The moderately compact and well-furred body, erect ears and brash tail suggest its northern heritage. Its characteristic gait is smooth and seemingly effortless and its body proportions reflect its power, speed and endurance.

Group
Working.

Size
Height: Dogs 53·3 – 60cm (21 – 23½in),

bitches 50·8 – 56cm (20 – 22in).
Weight: Dogs 20·4 – 27·2kg (45 – 60lb),
bitches 15·8 – 22·6kg (35 – 50lb).

Coat

Colour: All colours, from black to pure white.

Texture: Double, of medium length; the undercoat dense and soft, the overcoat straight and smooth-lying, never harsh or standing straight away from the body.

Siberian Husky

Sloughi

Origins

Although the Arab races are not particularly fond of dogs, they treat the Sloughi as if it were one of the family. The nomadic tribes of North Africa value the Sloughi as a hunter and as a guard. Much of their hunting takes place at night to avoid the heat of the sun and when the quarry is active. As a consequence of this the breed has itself a tendency to be nocturnal in its habits.

Characteristics

The general appearance of the Sloughi is of a very racy dog, with a frame impressive for its muscular leanness and delicacy. In outline the breed closely resembles a racing Greyhound. The eyes are large dark and deep set. In Britain, the Sloughi is regarded as a smooth-coated Saluki.

Group

Hound (KC). Coursing (FCI).

Size

Height: In FCI, 60 – 70cm ($23\frac{1}{2}$ – $27\frac{1}{2}$in). In KC, 58·4 – 71cm (23 – 28in).

Coat

Colour: Sable or all shades of fawn with or without a black mask.

Texture: Smooth and close.

Spaniel, American Cocker

Origins

A distinctive and glamorous gundog which has been developed in America from Cocker Spaniels imported from England. It has now achieved a considerable degree of popularity on both sides of the Atlantic, both as a companion and as a show dog.

Sloughi

Characteristics

The breed is the smallest member of the gundog group. It is sturdy and compact with a cleanly chiselled and refined head with rounded skull and pronounced stop. The eyes are round, full and look directly forward, the ears long and lobular with fine leather and well feathered. The neck is long, muscular and free from throatiness, the shoulders well laid back. The body is short and compact, the back strong, the chest deep and the quarters wide and well muscled. The breed never appears long or low. The tail is well set on and docked short.

Group

Gundog. Sporting (AKC). English Hunting Dogs (FCI).

Size

Height: Dogs 36·7 – 39·2cm (14½ – 15½in), bitches 34·2 – 36·7cm (13½ – 14½in).

Coat

Colour: Various.
Texture: Silky, flat or slightly wavy and profuse.

Spaniel, Brittany

Origins

Oppian in AD 150 wrote of the uncivilized people of Britain and of their dogs. He, like other contemporary writers, used Bretagne to refer to Britain, whereas in a later period the word was used to refer to Brittany in France. Certainly the Welsh Springer and the Brittany Spaniel have much in common and may share a common heritage, though by the 18th century Dutch and French painters were depicting dogs which unquestionably are the forerunners of the modern breed of pointing spaniel. The breed shares many of the characteristics of the Setter in its manner of work and is in fact the only pointing spaniel. Some puppies are born without tails, others are docked short.

Characteristics

In appearance the breed has some resemblance to a very lightly built Springer: a compact, closely knit dog of medium size, with the agility and stamina to cover a lot of ground. The stern is of medium length, rounded and slightly wedge-shaped. The ears are dark and leafy, lying flat and close to the head. The neck is of medium length. The body square in outline, the shoulders sloping and muscular, the back short and straight, the chest deep with plenty of heart room. Hindquarters are broad, strong and muscular with powerful thighs and well-bent stifles.

Group

Sporting (AKC). Setters (FCI).

Size

Height: 44 – 52cm (17½ – 20½in). In FCI, dogs 49 – 50·8cm (19¼ – 20in), bitches 47·5 – 50cm (18¾ – 19¾in).
Weight: 13·6 – 18kg (30 – 40lb).

Coat

Colour: Dark orange and white or liver and white, roan. No black.
Texture: Dense, flat or wavy without excessive feathering.

Spaniel, Cavalier King Charles

Origins

The Cavalier King Charles Spaniel is a recreation of the toy dog favoured by King Charles II and which bears his name, but which over the years had departed from its original form. Impetus

American Cocker Spaniel

Brittany Spaniel

Cavalier King Charles Spaniel

to recreate this attractive toy Spaniel in its original form was given by a Mr Eldridge, an American, who, in 1920, offered prizes of £25 for Blenheim Spaniels possessing 'long faces, flat skulls, no inclination to be domes, no stop and a beauty spot in the centre of the forehead'. By 1928, a Club had formed and the breed was established.

Characteristics
The breed is active, graceful, has a sporting character and is free in action. The head is flat, the stop shallow, the muzzle tapered. The eyes are large, dark and set well apart, the ears are long and set high, the mouth should be level. The body is short-coupled with good spring of rib, the back level. The forelegs are straight with moderate bone. The tail is undocked.

Group
Toy (KC). Pet Dogs (FCI).
Size
Weight: In KC, 4·5 – 8kg (12 – 18lb).
Coat
Colour: Black and tan, ruby (rich red), Blenheim (chestnut and white), tricolour.
Texture: Long, silky and free from curl, with ample featherings.

Spaniel, Clumber

Origins
The Clumber is a very different animal from other spaniels – heavier, longer and lower to the ground – indicating that we should look for different origins. The body shape suggests some Bassett Hound blood, while the heavy head is suggestive of the old Alpine Spaniel. The

Clumber Spaniel puppy

breed itself seems to have been produced from imported spaniels kept by the Duke of Newcastle at his Clumber Park Estate in Nottinghamshire. As is so often the case when one kennel concentrates its attention on producing dogs for a particular purpose, a distinctive type soon emerges and is quickly appreciated by other sportsmen. By 1859 this breed was being shown and had achieved considerable popularity as a gundog particularly well adapted to a country with abundant game. In more recent years the breed has declined in popularity and is maintained in small numbers because of the enthusiasm of a few dedicated breeders.

Characteristics
The Clumber is nothing if not distinctive: it is a dog with a thoughtful expression, very massively built but active, and moves with a rolling gait which is characteristic of the breed. The head is large, square, and massive with pronounced occiput, heavy brows and deep stop, the muzzle is heavy with well-developed flew. The eyes are dark amber showing some haw, the ears large and vine-leaf shaped, well covered with straight hair. The neck is fairly long, thick and powerful. The shoulders are sloping and muscular, the chest deep, the legs straight, thick and strong. The body is long and heavy, close to the ground; the back is straight, broad and long. The hindquarters are very powerful and well developed. The tail is low set and carried level with the back.
Group
Gundog. Sporting (AKC). English Hunting Dogs (FCI).
Size
Weight: Dogs 24·9 – 31·7kg (55 – 70lb), bitches 20·4 – 27·2kg (45 – 60lb). In AKC, dogs 24·9 – 29·4kg (55 – 65lb), bitches 15·8 – 22·6kg (35 – 50lb).
Coat
Colour: Plain white with lemon markings, orange permissible.
Texture: Abundant, close, silky and straight. The legs are well feathered.

Spaniel, English Cocker

Origins
The name of the breed provides clues to both its original function and its origins. The Cocker Spaniel, like other spaniels, is a descendant of the dogs which, in Spain, were used to drive birds into nets. It is referred to in the prologue to Chaucer's *Wife of Bath's Tale* showing that 'Spaynels', even by the 14th century, had attained some degree of popularity in England. However, at this time the

distinctions between spaniels of different types had not been drawn, though by 1780, when Thomas Bewick wrote his *History of Quadrupeds*, he was able to say 'the Springer or Cocker is lively, active and pleasant, and an unwearied pursuer of its game and very expert in raising woodcocks and snipes from their haunts in woods and marshes'. Then the breed was called the cocking-spaniel. The dog used to flush out woodcock, and thus it came by its present name.

Characteristics

The general appearance of the Cocker is of a merry sporting dog, well balanced and compact. The head is well developed and cleanly chiselled, neither too fine nor too coarse. The eyes should be full but not prominent, the rims tight, with an expression of intelligence and gentleness; the ears are long and set low, well clothed with long silky straight hair. The neck is of moderate length and clean in throat, the shoulders sloping and fine, the chest well developed and the brisket deep. The legs are well boned, straight and feathered. The body should be immensely strong and compact for the size and weight of the dog. The hindquarters should be wide, well rounded and very muscular, with feathering above the hock. The tail should not be docked in such a way that its merry action is interfered with.

Group

Gundog (KC). Sporting (AKC). English Hunting Dogs (FCI).

Size

Height: Dogs 40·6 – 43cm (16 – 17in), bitches 38 – 40·6cm (15 – 16in). In KC, dogs 39·2 – 60·6cm (15½ – 16in), bitches 38 – 39·2cm (15 – 15½in).
Weight: Dogs 12·7 – 15·4kg (28 – 34lb), bitches 11·7 – 14·5kg (26 – 32lb). In KC, 12·7 – 14·5kg (28 – 32lb).

Coat

Colour: Various; in self colours no white is allowed except on the chest.
Texture: Flat, silky in texture, never wiry or wavy, with sufficient feather; not too profuse and never curly.

Spaniel, English Springer

Origins

Bewick did not differentiate between Springer and Cocker Spaniels, though there was in the early 17th century a tendency to refer to the larger spaniels, which were used to startle game so that they sprang into the air, as Starter or Springer Spaniels. With the advent of quick-firing guns which increased their popularity, these early Springers were divided into the lighter Welsh Springers and the heavier English. The latter, for a while, had a variety developed by a Duke of Norfolk, known as Norfolk Spaniels.

Cocker Spaniel

English Springer Spaniel

Characteristics

The general appearance of the modern Springer is that of a symmetrical, compact, strong, upstanding, merry and active dog, built for endurance and activity. He is highest on the leg and raciest of all the British land spaniels. The skull is of medium length and fairly broad, the foreface well chiselled below the eyes, fairly deep and square in flew. The dark hazel eyes should be neither too full nor too small, and the ears are lobular in shape, set close to the head, of good length and width but not exaggerated. The neck is long and muscular, well set into the shoulders. The forelegs are straight and nicely feathered. The body strong and neither too long nor too short, the chest deep with well-sprung ribs. The loins are muscular and strong with a slight arch. Thighs are broad, muscular and well developed, hocks moderately bent. The stern is set low, well feathered and has a lively action.

Group

Gundog. Sporting (AKC). English Hunting Dogs (FCI).

Size

Height: 50·8cm (20in). In AKC, dogs 50·8cm (20in), bitches 48·2cm (19in).
Weight: 22·6kg (50lb). In AKC, 22·2 – 24·9kg (49 – 55lb).

Coat

Colour: Any recognized land spaniel colour is acceptable, but liver and white and black and white are preferred.
Texture: Close, straight and weather-resistant, without being coarse.

Spaniel, Field

Origins

This is one of the members of the gundog group which popularity has unaccountably by-passed in favour of other breeds with less obvious attractions. This English breed was largely established as a type, much resembling the Sussex Spaniel, developed by Phineas Bullock. For some time during its early career in the show ring it was classified with Cocker Spaniels.

Characteristics

A well-balanced dog, noble, upstanding and sporting, built for activity and endurance and combining beauty with utility and unusual docility. The head is strongly characteristic of the breed, the skull has pronounced occiput, the muzzle is long and lean. The eyes are not full, receding or overhung; dark hazel in colour showing a grave expression but not hard. The neck is long, strong and muscular set into long and sloping shoul-

Field Spaniel

Irish Water Spaniel

ders which give great activity and speed. The forelegs should be of fairly good length and not too heavily boned. The body is of moderate length, well ribbed-up to a good strong loin, the chest deep, the back and loins strong and muscular. The tail is carried as an extension of the back, never elevated above it.

Group

Gundog. Sporting (AKC). English Hunting Dogs (FCI).

Size

Height: About 45·7cm (18in).
Weight: 15·8 – 22·6kg (35 – 50lb).

Coat

Colour: Black, liver, golden liver, mahogany red, roan, or any of these colours with tan over eyes, on feet.
Texture: Flat or slightly waved, never curled but is silky and appears glossy and refined.

Spaniel, Irish Water

Origins

The Irish Water Spaniel represents a very old type of dog whose remains have been found in archaeological sites throughout Europe and which had emerged in Ireland as a distinct breed probably as early as the 12th century. At this period and for some time afterwards they were called by various names, including Shannon Spaniels, Rat or Whiptail Spaniels and as the Southern Irish Water Spaniel. From the 12th century until the emergence in 1834 of Boatswain, who was to help establish the modern breed, there are records and descriptions of these very distinctive dogs leaving Ireland as gifts and tributes. Nowadays, the Irish Water Spaniel is a gundog bred to work in shooting.

King Charles Spaniel

Tibetan Spaniel

Sussex Spaniel

Characteristics

The head is of good size, the skull high, the muzzle long, strong and somewhat square, the face covered with characteristic curls and the topknot formed of longer curls. The eyes are small and dark, the ears very long and lobular, again covered with long curls. The neck is powerful, long and arched, set into sloping and powerful shoulders. The back is short, broad and level, strongly coupled in hindquarters. The forelegs are well boned and straight, the hindquarters powerful with long well-bent stifles. The tail is distinctive, short and straight, set low and partially covered with curls, partially with straight hair.

Group

Gundog (KC). Sporting (AKC). English Hunting Dogs (FCI).

Size

Height: Dogs 56 – 61cm (22 – 24in), bitches 53·3 – 58·4cm (21 – 23in). In KC, and RASKC, dogs 53·3 – 58·4cm (21 – 23in), bitches 50·8 – 56cm (20 – 22in).
Weight: Dogs 24·9 – 29·4kg (55 – 65lb), bitches 20·4 – 26·3kg (45 – 58lb).

Coat

Colour: A rich dark liver.
Texture: Should be composed of dense, tight, crisp ringlets free from woolliness and having a natural oiliness.

Spaniel, King Charles

Origins

A toy spaniel which derives its name from its popularity in the court of King Charles II, which was so great that few portraits of the period seem to be without the customary King Charles Spaniel reclining on milady's lap, or peeping from behind a chair. Though it was Charles II who gave his name to the breed, toy spaniels had been popular for some time before. Mary, Queen of Scots

was fond of them and one even accompanied her to her death.

Characteristics

The King Charles has a massive head with large dark eyes full of expression, a short snub muzzle and long, pendulous, well-feathered ears, set low and lying close to the cheeks. The body proportions should be those of a miniature spaniel.

Group

Toy. Pet Dogs (FCI).

Size

Weight: 3·6 – 6·3kg (8 – 14lb). In AKC, 4 – 5·4kg (9 – 12lb).

Coat

Colour: Black and tan, Prince Charles (tri-colour), Blenheim (red on white),

ruby (self-coloured chestnut red).
Texture: Long, silky and straight.

Spaniel, Sussex

Origins

A Mr Fuller, aided and abetted by Phineas Bullock, had a considerable hand in developing this distinctive spaniel. The breed was developed in days when breeding was organized in a very different way, utilizing large numbers of sturdy well-trained dogs. As conditions have now changed and spaniels with a greater turn of speed and able to cover more ground have become more popular, the breed now exists in dangerously low numbers, relying on the enthusiasm of a few admirers for survival.

Welsh Springer Spaniel

Characteristics

The Sussex Spaniel is massive and strongly built, with a characteristic rolling movement quite unlike that of any other spaniel. The skull is broad, with pronounced stop, the occiput decided but not pointed. Eyes are fairly large, hazel coloured with a soft expression not showing overmuch haw. Ears are thick, fairly large and lobular, set moderately low. The neck is long, strong and slightly arched, not carrying the head much above the level of the back. The shoulders are sloping, forelegs well boned and muscular. The chest is deep and wide, the back wide and fairly long. Hindquarters are strongly developed. The tail is set low and not carried above the level of the back.

Group

Gundog (KC). Sporting (AKC). English Hunting Dogs (FCI).

Size

Height: 38 – 40·6cm (15 – 16in).
Weight: Dogs 20·4kg (45lb), bitches 18kg (40lb). In AKC, 15·8 – 20·4kg (35 – 45lb).

Coat

Colour: Rich golden liver.
Texture: Abundant and flat, with no tendency to curl and with ample undercoat.

Spaniel, Tibetan

Origins

Throughout ancient history the rulers of China, Tibet and neighbouring countries showed great interest in the small breeds of dogs which inhabited their courts and which were their constant companions, serving as food tasters, status symbols and even having religious significance. These dogs were exchanged between the courts, dogs from Tibet moving to China with possibly the Happa becoming the ancestor of the Pekingese and the Carla becoming the ancestor of the Tibetan Spaniel. Other dogs very similar to the Tibetan Spaniel were also present in Japan and South Korea and these too might have contributed to the formation of the breed.

Characteristics

The breed is gay, intelligent and aloof with strangers. The head is small in proportion to the body and proudly carried, the skull domed, the muzzle short, the mouth slightly undershot. The ears are of medium size and pendulous. The neck is moderately short, the body fairly long and well ribbed-up. The forelegs are slightly bowed with moderate bone, the feet small and neat. The tail is set high, richly plumed and carried in a gay curl over the back when moving.

Group

Utility (KC). Pet Dogs (FCI). Non-sporting (RASKC).

Size

Height: 25·4cm (10in).
Weight: 4 – 6·8kg (9 – 15lb).

Coat

Colour: All colours are allowed.
Texture: Double coat, silky in texture and not overcoated. The males are encouraged to grow a profuse mane.

Spaniel, Welsh Springer

Origins

History does not record the advent of the Welsh Springer Spaniel as a distinctive breed, though it is certain that red and white spaniels very similar to the modern Welsh have existed for very many years since they are to be seen in many old sporting drawings and paintings. The standard for the breed confirms its ancient origin and refers to its old Welsh name of 'Starter'. The Welsh Springer is a first class gundog and makes an excellent companion as well as an eye catching show dog. The breed deserves more attention than it nowadays receives.

Characteristics

The head is of moderate length and slightly domed with a clearly defined stop. The eyes are hazel or dark, the ears set moderately low and comparatively small. The neck is long and muscular, clean in throat and neatly set into long, sloping shoulders. Forelegs are of medium length, straight, well boned and moderately feathered. The body is not long, is deep in brisket with well-sprung ribs and a slightly arched muscular loin, well coupled-up. Quarters are strong and muscular, hocks are well let-down and stifles moderately bent.

Group

Gundog. Sporting (AKC). English Hunting Dogs (FCI).

Size

Height: Dogs 48·2cm (19in) maximum, bitches 45·7cm (18in) maximum.
Weight: In FCI, 15·4 – 20·4kg (34 – 45lb).

Coat

Colour: Dark rich red and white.
Texture: Straight and thick, of a silky texture, never wiry or wavy.

Swedish Vallhund

Origins

Both the resemblance and the similar function in life argue some shared ancestor between the Västgötaspitz and the Corgi. The fact that both have distinct Spitz characteristics seems to indicate origins in Scandinavia. Like the Corgi however, this Swedish breed has only recently been recognized, in 1948.

Characteristics
The breed is low slung, long in the body, small and muscular. The carriage and expression indicate vigilance, courage and energy. The tail is naturally short, not docked, and should not exceed 10cm (4in) in length.

Group
Working (KC). Shepherd Dog (FCI).

Size
Height: 33 – 40·6cm (13 – 16in).
Weight: 9 – 14kg (20 – 31lb).

Coat
Colour: Preferably grey.
Texture: Of fair length, hard and dense, the undercoat fine and tight.

Swedish Vallhund

T

Terrier, Airedale

Origins
The Airedale is by far the largest of the terriers and for that reason is sometimes referred to as the King of Terriers. In fact, the breed's size makes him something of an oddity and probably, both in origin and function, owes much to the hound group as it does to the terriers. The breed was developed to combine some of the capabilities of both terrier and hound, terrier characteristics being inherited from the Old English Rough-Coated Black and Tan Terrier, and hound characteristics, including size, from the Otter Hound. The breed's size, courage and intelligence make the breed excel-

lent guard and police dogs. It has also been used as a hunting dog for exotic game in many lands.

Characteristics
The Airedale is keen of expression and quick of movement. His character is shown by the expression of the eyes and by the carriage of the ears and tail. The head is long and flat with stop hardly visible, the jaws deep, powerful, strong and muscular. The eyes are dark, small, full of terrier expression, keenness and intelligence, the neck clean and muscular set into long, well-laid-back shoulders. Forelegs are perfectly straight. The back is short, strong and level, the ribs well sprung, the loin muscular; the chest is deep but not broad. Hindquarters are powerful with well-bent stifles. The tail is set on high and carried gaily but it should not be curled.

Group
Terrier.

Size
Height: Dogs 58·4 – 61cm (23 – 24in), bitches, 56 – 58·4cm (22 – 23in). In AKC, dogs are 58·4cm (23in) and bitches slightly less.
Weight: In FCI, dogs 20·4kg (45lb), bitches slightly less.

Coat
Colour: Black or dark grizzle with tan markings.
Texture: Hard, dense and wiry.

Terrier, American Staffordshire

Origins
The American Staffordshire Terrier is one of a handful of breeds with origins in other countries, but which has developed in America into a breed with very different characteristics from that of its counterpart at home. The Stafford was registered in America in 1935, but it was only in 1972 that the changes which had taken place were officially recognized by a change of name to American Staffordshire Terrier. However, since the 19th century, a distinctive breed has been developing under the various names of Pit Dog, Pit Bull Terrier, Yankee Terrier or American Bull Terrier. The first two names give a clue to the breed's use: they were and are used for organized fights against each other in the 'pit', an activity which demands a rare sort of courage from a dog, a willingness to die rather than concede defeat. The breed, though a terror with other dogs, is gentle with people, impressive in appear-

Airedale Terrier

American Staffordshire Terrier

Australian Terrier

ance and, in the right hands, tractable. In recent years some have been imported into Britain, but since none were from stock registered with the AKC they have not been shown at recognized shows.

Characteristics

The breed gives an impression of great strength, muscularity, agility and considerable courage. It is stocky rather than long-legged or racy in outline. The shoulders are wide and slope into a fairly short back which slopes to the croup. The ribs are well sprung and deep, the tail low set and tapers to a fine point. The forelegs are straight with round bone, hindquarters are well muscled with hocks well let down. The ears are usually cropped in North America.

Group
Terrier.

Size
Height: Dogs 45·7 – 48·2cm (18 – 19in), bitches 43 – 45·7cm (17 – 18in).

Coat
Colour: Any colour, but all white, black and tan or liver not to be encouraged.
Texture: Short, glossy, close and stiff to the touch.

Terrier, Australian

Origins
One of very few terrier breeds which originated outside the British Isles, though undoubtedly bred from old British breeds, but precisely which ones it is not possible to say. The Australian's slightly old-fashioned appearance is probably closer to some of these old breeds than are their modern counterparts. Recognition of the breed came in 1892 with the formation of a club to look after its interests, since which time the breed has achieved a modest popularity throughout the world.

Characteristics
The Australian Terrier is a rather low-set dog, compact and active with a long head, flat skull, full between the eyes, with a soft top knot and a low powerful jaw. The eyes are small, keen and dark in colour; the ears are small, set high on the skull, pricked or dropped towards the front and fringed with long hair. The neck is inclined to be long in proportion to the body, with a frill of hair. The forelegs are perfectly straight, set well under the body, with a slight feather at the knee. The body is long in proportion to its height, well ribbed-up, and the back is straight. The hindquarters have good strong thighs with hocks slightly bent. The tail is docked.

Group
Terrier.

Size
Height: 25·4cm (10in).
Weight: 4·5 – 5kg (10 – 11lb). In AKC, 5·4 – 6·3kg (12 – 14lb). In FCI and RASKC, desirable weight is 6·3kg (14lb).

Coat
Colour: First, blue or silver-grey body, tan colour on legs and face, the richer the better, the top knot is blue or silver. Second, clear sandy or red.
Texture: Straight hair 5 – 6cm (2 – 2½in) long, of hard texture.

Terrier, Australian Silky

Origins
The Silky Terrier may be regarded as a second generation Australian since it is said to have originated from a cross between the Australian Terrier and imported Yorkshire Terriers. It is just as likely to be a smaller, silkier coated variation of the Australian, retained and bred for its attractive appearance and disposition, and valued by urban dwellers for its easy adaptation to city life. Only in 1955 did the breed come to be known by its present name, previously

Australian Silky Terrier

Bedlington Terrier

Border Terrier

having been called the Sydney Silky. In its homeland it has been recognized as a distinct breed since the early years of the century. It was first exhibited in 1907, had its original standard drawn up in 1909 and was recognized in America in 1959. In Britain the few imports have failed to find any popularity, perhaps because of the breed's similarity to the Yorkshire Terrier.

Characteristics

The Silky is a lightly built, moderately low-set toy dog of pronounced terrier character and spirited action. The head is strong, wedge-shaped and moderately long, the stop shallow. The ears, V-shaped and pricked, are set high and carried erect; the eyes are small and dark, with a piercingly keen expression. The neck is medium long, fine and to some degree crested, fitting into sloping shoulders. The body is low set and fairly long, the back line straight, the brisket extending to just below the elbows. The tail is set high and carried erect.

Group

Toy. Terrier (FCI).

Size

Height: Approximately 23cm (9in) at the withers.
Weight: 3·6 – 4·5kg (8 – 10lb). In FCI, 4 – 4·9kg (9 – 11lb).

Coat

Colour: Blue and tan, the topknot silver or fawn.
Texture: Flat, fine in texture, glossy and silky.

Terrier, Bedlington

Origins

This is one of the sporting terriers which have their origins among the valleys of north-east England. The Bedlington's present name and its original name of Rothbury Terrier indicate precisely its place of origin. As a breed it owes much

to the old rough-coated breeds which were kept as vermin killers by the sporting farmers and shepherds of Northumbria. Bedlingtons were developed with a longer leg, a longer, leaner head and a characteristic roached back, all of which suggest some Whippet blood, as does their ability to course a rabbit. The first club was formed in 1877, since which time the breed's original hardness and fighting qualities have been overlaid with a quiet gentle disposition, and its appearance in the hands of skilled trimmers has been transformed, and is very distinctive.

Characteristics

A graceful, lithe, muscular dog with no sign of either weakness or coarseness. The head should be pear or wedge-shaped and the expression in repose mild and gentle, though not shy or nervous. When roused, the eyes should sparkle and the dog look full of temper and courage. Bedlingtons are capable of galloping at great speed. Movement is distinctive: rather mincing, light and springy in the slower paces, and could have a slight roll when in full stride.

Group

Terrier.

Size

Height: 40·6cm (16in). In AKC, dogs 40·6 – 44cm (16 – 17½in) and bitches 38 – 41·8cm (15 – 16½in).
Weight: 8 – 10·4kg (18 – 23lb). In AKC, 7·7 – 10·4kg (17 – 23lb).

Coat

Colour: Blue, blue and tan, liver or sandy.
Texture: Very distinctive, thick and linty, standing out well from the body, but neither wiry nor straight.

Terrier, Border

Origins

Another breed with origins in Northumbria and which may retain a greater similarity to the ancient terrier stock than do its cousins, the Dandie Dinmont and the Bedlington. The Border Terrier was developed to run with hounds, and to be able to eject a fox from its earth, and so was an essential part of the system of fox control in the sheep-grazed hills of Northumbria. The name derives from the

Boston Terrier

breed's connection with the Border Fox-hounds, though neighbouring packs also contributed to its development, as have other packs of both Fox and other hounds since recognition in 1920. The breed probably retains very close contact with its original purpose and is still much valued as a genuine working terrier, though one which is also at home in the show ring or by the fireside.

Characteristics

The Border Terrier is essentially a working terrier able to follow a horse and must combine activity with gameness. The head is a distinctive feature of the breed, resembling that of an otter, moderately broad in skull, with a short strong muzzle. The eyes are dark with a keen expression, the ears V-shaped and dropping forward close to the cheek. The neck is of moderate length, forelegs straight and not too heavy in bone. The body is deep, narrow and fairly long, the ribs carried well back and not oversprung, the hind-quarters strong and racy. The tail is undocked, moderately short, and thick at the base.

Group

Terrier.

Size

Weight: Dogs 5·8 – 7kg (13 – 15½lb), bitches 5 – 6·3kg (11½ – 14lb).

Coat

Colour: Red, wheaten, grizzle and tan or blue and tan. White is permitted only on the chest.

Texture: Harsh and dense and not over-long with a close undercoat. The skin must be thick; the American standard asks for a loose-fitting skin.

Terrier, Boston

Origins

An American breed, the Boston Terrier was the result of crosses between imported English Bulldogs and terriers made in the 1870s by Robert C. Hooper and William O'Brien of Boston. They were first exhibited as Round Heads or Bull Terriers, but as a distinct and stable type developed the name was changed to Boston Terrier. In 1891 the first breed club was formed in America and in 1893 the breed was recognized by the AKC.

Characteristics

The breed has a characteristically gentle disposition and is eminently suitable as a companion and as a house pet. The Boston is smooth-coated, short-headed, compactly built and well balanced. The head is square, the muzzle short and the eyes large and round. The ears are carried erect and may be cropped. The neck is of fair length and the body deep, with a good width of chest. The shoulders are sloping, the back is short, the loins short and muscular with a slight cut up. Forelegs are set moderately wide apart, are straight in bone and well muscled; hind legs are short in hock, have a bend of stifle and are well muscled. The tail is short fine or tapering and may be straight or screw.

Group

Non-sporting. Utility (KC). Pet Dogs (FCI).

Size

Weight: Not exceeding 11·3kg (25lb). Divided into classes for under 6·8kg (15lb), 6·8 – 9kg (15 – 20lb), and 9 – 11·3kg (20 – 25lb).

Bull Terrier

Coat

Colour: Brindle with white markings; black with white is permissible, but not preferred.
Texture: Short, smooth, bright and fine.

Terrier, Bull

Origins

America differentiates between white and coloured Bull Terriers, but in England no such difference exists and they remain, white or coloured, the same breed. The breed is not of ancient origin, but was produced by crosses of the now extinct English White Terrier with the type of Bulldog which existed in the early 19th century. The breed owes its development to James Hinks, a Birmingham dog-dealer who, according to Rawdon Lee writing in 1894 (sixteen years after the death of James Hinks), was quite prepared to test the quality of his show dogs in fights against other dogs. Not for nothing is the breed known as the gladiator of the terrier group, though nowadays breeders have succeeded in producing a dog with all the old ability to fight, but with a much more sociable disposition.

Characteristics

The Bull Terrier must be strongly built, muscular, symmetrical and active, with a keen, determined and intelligent expression. It should be full of fire and courage, but of even temperament and amenable to discipline. The head is a characteristic of the breed being long, egg-shaped and free from hollows or indentations. The eyes are narrow, triangular and obliquely placed, black or as dark a brown as possible; the ears are small, thin and erect. The neck is long, arched and very muscular, fitting into strong and muscular shoulders. The body is well rounded, the back short and strong, the hindquarters powerfully muscled. The tail should be short.

Group

Terrier.

Coat

Colour: White or coloured.
Texture: Short, flat, even and harsh to the touch with a fine gloss. The skin should fit the dog tightly.

Terrier, Miniature Bull

Origins

This miniature version of the Bull Terrier only achieved recognition as a separate breed in 1943. However, because of small numbers available to breed from, the problems of miniaturization and a comparatively short history, the breed has not yet attained the standard achieved by the larger version.
The standard is as for the Bull Terrier, except:

Size

Height: Not more than 35·5cm (14in).
Weight: Not more than 9kg (20lb).

Terrier, Cairn

Origins

A descendant of the working terriers used in Scotland and the Isle of Skye and, though no longer in demand as a working terrier, the breed retains much of the appearance and some of the characteristics of the older breeds. The breed has had a variety of names and its history is not at all well documented, so that it is not possible to be certain to which of our modern breeds it is closest. Authorities in the past often saw the Cairn as a short-haired Skye Terrier, but after a protest by Skye Terrier breeders the name was changed to Cairn Terrier at the beginning of this century. As such the breed has achieved a considerable popularity.

Characteristics

This terrier should impress with its fearless and gay disposition, the general appearance of an active, game and shaggy little dog, strong though compactly built, very free in movement and with a general foxy appearance. The breed should stand well forward on forepaws, and have a compact straight back of medium length with deep well-sprung ribs. The hindquarters are very strong, the tail short and well furnished with hair.

Group

Terrier.

Size

Height: In AKC, dogs 25·4cm (10in), bitches 24cm (9½in).
Weight: 6·3kg (14lb). In AKC, dogs 6·3kg (14lb), bitches 5·8kg (13lb).

Coat

Colour: Red, sandy, grey, brindled or nearly black with dark points.
Texture: Must be double-coated with a profuse, hard but not coarse outer coat, and a short, soft, close undercoat. It must not have any open coat.

Cairn Terrier

English Toy Terrier

Dandie Dinmont Terrier

Terrier, Dandie Dinmont

Origins

A breed which owes its present name to the character in Walter Scott's *Guy Mannering*, but which was certainly in existence in the Cheviot Hills long before the book was written. The Dandie is a close relation of both the Border and Bedlington Terriers, and, although very different in overall appearance, the discerning eye can see some family resemblances. The breed has never achieved a great popularity either as a show dog or as a companion.

Characteristics

The Dandie is a very distinctive breed with a strong and rather large head. The dark eyes, set wide apart, are full and round, the ears pendulous, falling close to the cheek. The neck is very muscular and well set into strong shoulders. The forelegs are short with immense muscular development and bone, set wide apart. The body is long, strong and flexible, the ribs well sprung, the chest let well down between the forelegs. The topline is low over the shoulders and arched over the loins, forming a shallow 'S'. Hindquarters are set wide apart, the thighs well developed. The tail is rather short, carried a little above the level of the body.

Group

Terrier.

Size

Height: 20·3 – 27·9cm (8 – 11in).
Weight: 8kg (18lb). In AKC, 8 – 10·8kg (18 – 24lb).

Coat

Colour: Pepper or mustard.
Texture: A mixture of hardish and soft hair, giving a coat which feels crisp to the touch but not wiry.

Terrier, English Toy

Origins

The English Toy Terrier, formally called Toy Black and Tan Terriers or Toy Manchester Terriers, names which are perhaps more descriptive both of their origins and their appearance than is the present one. Dr Caius in 1570 recognized that small versions of the old Black and Tan existed, but it was in the rat pit that these small dogs made their reputation. Often weighing no more than 2·7kg (6lb), they were matched either to kill a certain number of rats against the clock, or in competition with another dog. Sadly the breed is now dangerously depleted in numbers and good specimens are hard to come by, though this small, hardy, clean and attractive little fellow with such a long history in Britain would make an excellent companion in any home and deserves a greater degree of popularity.

Characteristics

A well-balanced, elegant and compact Toy dog with a terrier temperament and characteristics. The head is long and narrow, the ears 'candle flame' shaped, thin and erect, and the eyes very dark, small and almond-shaped. The neck is long and graceful and slightly arched, the chest narrow and deep, the front straight with fine bone. Front movement is akin to the 'extended trot'; a hackney action is undesirable. The body is compact, the back slightly arched over the loin. Hindquarters are rounded and have a good turn of stifle. The tail is set low and reaches to the hock; it should not be carried above the level of the back.

Group

Toy.

Size

Height: 25·5 – 30·5cm (10 – 12in).
Weight: 2·7 – 3·6kg (6 – 8lb).

Coat

Colour: Black and tan; the standard is very precise about the distribution of tan.
Texture: Thick, close, smooth and glossy.

Terrier, Fox, Smooth

Origins

The Smooth Fox Terrier is undoubtedly the aristocrat of the terrier group, able to look back over a long history of work with hounds. At the beginning of the century, it was among the most popular of companions and show dogs. This early popularity has left a considerable literature devoted to the breed and a mass of carefully drawn illustrations which demonstrate that the breed has changed very little since, for example, the publication of Daniel's *Rural Sports* in 1801. So highly prized were Fox Terriers in the late 1800s that large kennels were maintained and prices ran into several hundreds of pounds.

Characteristics

The dog must present a gay and active appearance and is compactly built, though the Fox Terrier must not be cloddy or in any way coarse. The symmetry of the Foxhound may be taken as a model for the breed: he must stand like a cleverly made hunter, covering a lot of ground, yet with a short back.

Group

Terrier.

Size

Height: In AKC, dogs 39cm (15½in) maximum, bitches proportionately lower.
Weight: Dogs 7·2 – 8kg (16 – 18lb), bitches 6·8 – 7·7kg (15 – 17lb). In AKC, dogs 7·7 – 8·6kg (17 – 19lb), bitches 6·8 – 7·7kg (15 – 17lb).

Coat

Colour: White should predominate, brindle, red or liver markings are objectionable. Otherwise this point is of little importance.
Texture: Straight, flat, smooth, hard, dense and abundant.

Terrier, Fox, Wire

Origins

The early Fox Terrier breeders, just as working terrier breeders do today, did not differentiate between smooth and broken-coated dogs, the adage of 'handsome is as handsome does' being applicable here. Both coats appeared in the same litter but for companions and show dogs the smarter smooth coats were at first preferred. The wire coats followed them into the show ring about twenty-five years after their debut. Nowadays, with better skills in trimming and presentation, it is the Wire which takes the high prizes.

Characteristics

As for the Smooth, *except coat texture.*

Size

Height: Dogs 39cm (15½in) at withers, bitches proportionately lower.
Weight: Dogs 8kg (18lb), bitches 7·2kg (16lb).

Smooth Fox Terrier

Wire Fox Terrier

Coat

Colour: As for the Smooth.
Texture: Dense and wiry, like coconut matting.

Terrier, Glen of Imaal

Origins

Very few of this breed are seen in the show ring or as companions outside their native Wicklow Mountains where their unique qualities are highly prized among a select band of enthusiasts. The breed first appeared in the show ring in 1934, but has not taken to its new career with enthusiasm. The breed remains just as it has been described for many years, 'mostly blue and tan, with an occasional wheaten and black and tan, short of leg, long in body, and not straight in front but dead game'. Here is a breed which deserves more attention.

Characteristics

The Glen of Imaal Terrier is gentle and lovable with children, not destructive of fowl and generally abstains from fighting. Like all terriers of Ireland, it loves water, it

is silent in its work and about the house. The skull is strong, the ears pendulous, the eyes brown and placed well apart. The forelegs are short with great bone, bowed and splayed. The chest is wide and strong. The stern is thick at the base, well set and carried gaily.

Group

Terrier.

Size

Height: Not more than 35·5cm (14in).
Weight: Up to 15·8kg (35lb).

Coat

Colour: Blue and tan, wheaten.
Texture: Long and coarse.

Terrier, Irish

Origins

The Irish Terrier shares much of the same origins as the Kerry Blue, the other Irish terrier which has achieved distinction in the show ring. The breed made its debut in the show ring in 1879, but was known and admired by the sporting gentry of Ireland for very many years before. The breed is hardy and adaptable

Glen of Imaal Terrier

Irish Terrier

like so many of the terriers, it is loyal, and makes an excellent guard.

Characteristics

The Irish Terrier standard suggests that dogs which are very game are usually surly or snappish; people experienced with working terriers would argue that the opposite is true, surly or snappish dogs are usually cowardly. However this merely means that the temperament of the Irish Terrier is not quite so exceptional as the standard suggests. It is even-tempered especially with people, though sometimes fiery with other dogs, a nuisance in a working terrier. The dog is active, lively, lithe and wiry in appearance, free from clumsiness neither cloddy nor cobby. The head is long, the skull flat, the eyes dark, the ears small and V-shaped. The neck of fair length, the shoulders fine, long and sloping well into the back. The chest is deep and muscular, the body moderately long, the loins muscular and slightly arched. The hindquarters have powerful thighs and moderately bent stifles. The tail is generally docked.

Group

Terrier

Size

Height: 45·7cm (18in) at the shoulder.
Weight: Dogs 12·2kg (27lb), bitches 11·3kg (25lb).

Coat

Colour: Whole coloured bright red, red-wheaten or yellow-red.
Texture: Hard and wiry having a broken appearance.

Terrier, Kerry Blue

Origins

The Kerry Blue shares a common ancestry with the Soft-Coated Wheaten Terrier and shares, too, a common

Kerry Blue Terrier

birthplace among the mountains of Kerry, where it was developed to provide sport, security and companionship for the sporting farmers of that area. Nowadays, by careful breeding, skilful trimming and painstaking presentation, it has been transformed into a very successful show dog, to a far greater degree than other Irish Terriers. It is much more dandified than when it first appeared in the ring or lived the sporting life about the farms of Kerry.

Characteristics

The breed should exhibit a disciplined gameness. The Kerry Blue is a compact, powerful terrier showing gracefulness and an attitude of alert determination, with a definite terrier style and character throughout. Typically it should be upstanding, well knit and well proportioned, with a well-developed and muscular body. The head is long and lean, the jaw strong and deep, the eyes dark and the ears small and V-shaped. The neck is strong and reachy, running into sloping shoulders. The forelegs are straight and powerful, the hindquarters

large and well developed. The body is short, coupled with a good depth of brisket, the chest is deep with well-sprung ribs. The topline is level, the tail set high and carried erect.

Group

Terrier.

Size

Height: Dogs 45·7 – 48cm (18 – 19in) at shoulder, bitches slightly less. In AKC, dogs 45·7 – 49·5cm (18 – 19½in), bitches 44 – 48cm (17½ – 19in).
Weight: Dogs 14·9 – 16·7kg (33 – 37lb), bitches ideally 15·8kg (35lb). In AKC, dogs 14·9 – 18kg (33 – 40lb), bitches slightly less.

Coat

Colour: Any shade of blue.
Texture: Soft, silky, plentiful and wavy.

Terrier, Lakeland

Origins

The Lakeland was developed as a working terrier with the packs of hounds which hunt the rugged country in England's Lake District. He is to the North Western hunts of England what

Lakeland Terrier

Manchester Terrier

the Border Terrier is to the hunts of the North East and it is inevitable that during the development of both breeds there should be traffic between the two regions. Nowadays, unlike the Border, the breed has split to produce two distinct types: those which are still used for work and which are to be seen in some numbers at terrier shows organized by hunts, and a very much more refined and skilfully groomed type shown at Kennel Club shows where, in spite of its very small numbers, the breed achieves considerable success.

Characteristics
The breed has a smart, workmanlike appearance with a gay, fearless demeanour. The skull is flat and refined, the eyes dark and the ears moderately small, V-shaped, and carried alertly. The neck is reachy, the shoulders well laid back, forelegs are straight and well boned. The chest is narrow, the back strong and moderately short. The hindquarters are strong and muscular, with well-turned stifles and hocks low to the ground. The tail is well set or carried gaily, but not over the back.

Group
Terrier.

Size
Height: Not to exceed 36·7cm (14½in) at the shoulder. In AKC, 35·5 – 38cm (14 – 15in).
Weight: Dogs 7·7kg (17lb), bitches 6·8kg (15lb). In AKC, the standard for both is 7·7kg (17lb).

Coat
Colour: Black and tan, blue and tan, red, wheaten, red grizzle, liver, blue or black.
Texture: Dense and weather-resisting, harsh with good undercoat.

Terrier, Manchester

Origins
Old prints show that a great many of the old terriers of different types were black and tan. As far back as 1570, Dr Caius was able to describe a Black and Tan Terrier breed, though lower to ground and rougher coated than its modern counterpart, the Manchester Terrier. The Manchester Terrier was developed for sport by the working people of Lancashire, people who did not follow the sports which required a great deal of money, but who looked to a day's ratting or rabbiting with their terriers to provide recreation. The breed then needed, as well as all the instincts of other working terriers, a dash of speed which it might have lacked. It had to live with its owner, share his home, and today the Manchester Terrier still makes an ideal house dog, being clean, and a good guard. It is surprising that the breed has not achieved a greater degree of popularity, perhaps its humble origins are less attractive than the exotic histories to which some breeds lay claim.

Characteristics
The dog is compact, with a long head, narrow in skull, with small, dark, sparkling eyes, and small V-shaped ears carried above the top line of the head. The neck is fairly long and free from throatiness. The forequarters are clean and well sloped, the forelegs quite straight and set well under the body. The body is short with well-sprung ribs, the topline slightly roached and with a pronounced tuck-up. The hindquarters are well bent in stifle. The tail is naturally short.

Group
Terrier.

Size
Height: Dogs 40·6cm (16in), bitches 38cm (15in).
Weight: In AKC, over 5·4kg (12lb) and not exceeding 9·9kg (22lb). In FCI, dogs 8kg (18lb), bitches 7·7kg (17lb).

Coat
Colour: Black and tan, jet black and rich mahogany; the standard is precise in its description of the placement of tan markings.
Texture: Close, smooth, short and glossy of a firm texture.

Terrier, Norfolk

Origins
One of the smallest of the terriers, but one which retains all their sporting instincts. Until 1964, the breed could have either drop or prick ears, but at that time

Norfolk Terrier

Norwich Terrier

the two types were separated and the prick-eared variety became Norwich Terriers. (Both types are known as Norwich Terriers in the USA.) It is said that the breed was developed by Frank Jones, a horse-breaker from Cambridgeshire, who introduced his terriers to stables in the area where they earned their keep by killing rats. The breed was brought back almost from the point of extinction by Miss Macfie, a Sussex breeder, but even today the breed is not common.

Characteristics

The Norfolk Terrier has a lovable disposition, is not quarrelsome, has a hardy constitution and is alert and fearless. It is a small, low, keen dog, compact and strong with a short back, good substance and bone. The skull is wide and slightly rounded, the muzzle wedge shaped and strong, and the stop should be well defined. The eyes are oval, deep set and dark, giving an alert, keen and intelligent expression. The ears are V-shaped and drop forward, close to the cheek. The neck is of medium length and strong, fitting into clean and powerful shoulders with short powerful and straight legs. The body is compact with a short back, level topline and well-sprung ribs. Hindquarters are well muscled with a good turn of stifle. The tail is docked.

Group

Terrier.

Size

Height: Ideal height is 25·4cm (10in) at withers.

Weight: 4·5 – 5·4kg (10 – 12lb).

Coat

Colour: All shades of red, red-wheaten, black and tan and grizzle.

Texture: Hard, wiry and straight, lying close to the body.

Scottish Terrier

Terrier, Norwich

Origins

The breed dates from the early years of the century when it was known as the Jones Terrier and shares its short history up to 1964 with the Norfolk Terrier.

Group

Terrier.

The standard is as the Norfolk Terrier, except that it has pricked rather than dropped ears.

Terrier, Scottish

Origins

It is difficult to be precise about the history of the Scottish Terrier because the name has long and variously been used to describe any one of several terrier breeds which originate in Scotland. Certainly the terriers of Scotland have a long history dating back to the 14th century. Rawdon Lee writing at the end of the 19th century claimed that the Scottish Terrier was the original Skye Terrier. The original standard for the breed was drawn up in 1880 by J.B. Morrison and although the appearance of the breed has changed considerably since that time, this is to a very large extent a product of differing methods of presentation rather than significant changes to the dog itself. It is doubtful, however, that modern terriers could do the job among the rocks of the Scottish hills for which their forbears were justly famous.

Characteristics

The Scottish Terrier is a sturdy thick-set dog set on short legs, alert in carriage. The head gives the impression of being long for the size of dog, the almond-

Sealyham Terrier

Skye Terrier

Soft-Coated Wheaten

shaped eyes are dark brown, the ears neat, pointed and erect. The muscular neck is of moderate length set into long sloping shoulders. Forelegs are straight and well boned with strong pasterns. The chest is fairly broad and hung between the forelegs, with well-rounded ribs carried well back. The back is short and very muscular, the topline straight and level. Hindquarters are remarkably powerful with big and wide buttocks. The tail is of moderate length.

Group
Terrier.

Size
Height: 25·4 – 27·9cm (10 – 11in). In AKC, about 25·4cm (10in).
Weight: 8·6 – 10·4kg (19 – 23lb). In AKC, dogs 8·6 – 9·9kg (19 – 22lb), bitches 8 – 9·5kg (18 – 21lb).

Coat
Colour: Black, wheaten or brindle of any colour.
Texture: The undercoat is short, dense and soft, the outer coat harsh, dense and wiry.

Terrier, Sealyham

Origins
This is one of the very few breeds which owe their development to the work and inspiration of one man. Between 1850 and 1891 Captain John Edwardes of Sealyham in Haverfordwest, Wales, set out to develop a strain of terrier which would match up to his demanding standards in being able to hunt fox, otter or even badger. There is no doubt that he succeeded in his aim and produced a tough, game and strong strain of terrier which quickly became popular among those who shared Captain Edwardes' sporting interests. By 1910 the breed was appearing in the show ring and embarking on further development which has now made it a very different animal from

the one envisaged by Captain Edwardes, but one that makes a first class watchdog.

Characteristics
The general appearance should be of a free-moving dog, with a slightly domed skull and powerful long jaw. The eyes are dark and round, and the ears falling at the side of the cheeks are rounded. The neck is fairly long, thick and muscular, the forelegs short, strong and straight. The body is of medium length, level with well-sprung ribs. The hindquarters are powerful, with strong hocks and well-bent stifles. The tail is carried erect.

Group
Terrier.

Size
Height: Not to exceed 30·4cm (12in). In AKC, 26·6cm (10½in).

Weight: Dogs maximum 9kg (20lb), bitches maximum 8kg (18lb). In AKC, dogs 10·4 – 10·8kg (23 – 24lb), bitches slightly less.

Coat
Colour: Mostly all white or white with lemon, brown or badger pied marks on head and ears.
Texture: Long, hard and wiry.

Terrier, Skye

Origins
Some authorities argue that the Skye Terrier and the present Scottish Terrier share common origins and that the modern Skye, with its extraordinary appearance, is a fairly recent development. In fact Dr Caius was able to describe the breed from the 'barbarous borders fro'

the uttermost countryes northward' which 'by reason of the length of heare, makes show neither of face nor of body.'

Characteristics

The Skye Terrier is a one man dog, distrustful of strangers, but not vicious. The head is long with powerful jaws, the dark eyes are close set and full of expression. Ears may be prick or drop and should be fringed with hair. The neck is long and slightly crested, the shoulders are broad, the chest deep and the forelegs short and muscular. The body is long and low to the ground, the hindquarters well developed and muscular. The tail should not be carried over the back. The American standard is precise about measurements of various parts of the body, including coat length.

Group

Terrier.

Size

Height: 25·4cm (10in); total length 105·4cm (41½in).
Weight: 11·3kg (25lb).

Coat

Colour: Dark or light grey, fawn, cream, black, all with black points.
Texture: A soft, short, woolly, close undercoat is hidden by the long, hard, straight, flat topcoat which is such a characteristic feature of the breed.

Terrier, Soft-coated, Wheaten

Origins

The breed shares much the same origins and original purpose in life as the Kerry Blue Terrier; indeed it could almost be argued that the two are but colour varieties of the same breed, their different appearance owing more to the hairdresser's art than to any basic differences. Legend has it that terriers the colour of ripe wheat existed in Ireland before dogs from the wrecked ships of the Armada introduced the colour which produced the Kerry. Why the Armada's battleships were carrying dogs the legend omits to explain. It is a nice story and perhaps more suitable to the history of an Irish breed than a more pedantically documented one. Certainly the breed retains all the sporting instincts of its predecessors, whether hunting for rats, fox or badger, or being matched against a badger or some other dog.

Characteristics

The soft wheaten-coloured coat is the most obvious characteristic of the breed. In Ireland and in America the coat is trimmed, in Britain trimming is objected to by many breeders. The breed should be good tempered, spirited and game, full of confidence and humour and make delightful, affectionate companions when they have the correct temperament. Wheatens are of medium size, compact, short-coupled, strong and well built, standing four square with head and tail up. A good wheaten makes a very attractive sight.

Group

Terrier.

Size

Height: Dogs 45·7 – 49·5cm (18 – 19½in), bitches less.

Weight: Dogs 15·8 – 20·4kg (35 – 45lb); in FCI 15·8kg (35lb) only, bitches less.

Coat

Colour: A good clear wheaten.
Texture: Soft and silky, loosely waved or curled.

Terrier, Staffordshire Bull

Origins

One of the two gladiatorial members of the terrier group evolved to fight with other dogs or to bait bull, bear or badger. The old breeds used for these savage sports were mastiffs or Bulldogs which were too slow and ponderous for the 19th-century Corinthians who introduced a dash of terrier blood to give speed and agility and so laid the foundations of the 'Bull and Terrier' breed. By virtue of its association with the Black Country this breed was to become the Staffordshire; James Hinks crossed it with the Old English White Terrier to produce the Bull Terrier. Only in 1935 was the Staffordshire recognized as a breed, but it is now one of the most popular show terriers and one to which the showing ring has introduced no element of foppery. The breed still enjoys a good fight, but with people, particularly children, is a most faithful companion and an excellent and fearless guard.

Characteristics

The Staffordshire should have great strength for its size and, although very muscular, should be active and agile. The head is short, the skull broad with a pronounced stop, the cheek muscles are very pronounced, the fore-face short and powerful. The eyes are round and look straight ahead. Ears may be rose or half prick. The neck is short and muscular, set into wide, strong shoulders on straight, well-boned legs. The body is close coupled with a level topline, the ribs well sprung and the loins rather light. Hindquarters should be well muscled with well-bent stifles. The tail is low set and carried like an old-fashioned pump handle.

Group

Terrier.

Size

Height: 35·5 – 40·6cm (14 – 16in).
Weight: Dogs 12·7 – 17·2kg (28 – 38lb), bitches 10·8 – 15·4kg (24 – 34lb).

Coat

Colour: Red, fawn, white, black or blue, or any of these colours with white. Brindle or brindle and white. Black and tan is not encouraged.
Texture: Smooth, short and close to the skin.

Staffordshire Bull Terrier

Terrier, Tibetan

Origins

Legend places the breed's origins in the Lost Valley of Tibet and, with a breed whose history stretches back 2000 years, legend may be as reliable as supposed fact. The breed in Tibet was regarded as a companion which brought luck to its owner and which had religious significance. They are called in that country 'Luck Bringers' or 'Holy Dogs' and were kept purely as companions and symbols of status. Why in the West they are called terriers, with which group they have no affinity whatsoever, is difficult to say. The breed is healthy, tough and affectionate, an ideal companion.

Characteristics

The general appearance is rather like that of an Old English Sheepdog in miniature. The head is of medium length and slightly domed, the eyes are large and dark, the ears V-shaped and pendant and the mouth level by preference. The forelegs are straight and heavily furnished, the hind legs slightly longer and with well-bent stifles. The body is compact and powerful for its size, well ribbed-up and with a slightly arched loin. The tail is of medium length, set fairly high and carried in a gay curl over the back; it is very well feathered and often has a kink near the end.

Group

Non-sporting. Utility (UK).

Size

Height: Dogs 35·5 – 40·6cm (14 – 16in), bitches slightly smaller.
Weight: In AKC, average 9·9 – 10·4kg (22 – 23lb), but may be 8 – 13·6kg (18 – 30lb).

Coat

Colour: Any colour except chocolate or liver.
Texture: Double-coated, the undercoat of fine wool and the top coat profuse, but not silky or woolly, long and either straight or waved.

Terrier, Welsh

Origins

The Welsh Terrier is the counterpart of the Lakeland which in some ways it resembles. It was used to accompany the hunts in Wales in order to drive fox or otter from places of refuge. Until the turn of the century there appears to have been little distinction made between the Welsh and the Old English Black and Tan Terrier.

Characteristics

The Welsh Terrier has a gay, volatile

Tibetan Terrier

Welsh Terrier

West Highland White Terrier

Yorkshire Terrier

disposition and is only rarely shy. It is affectionate, obedient and biddable. The head is flat and rather wider between the ears than a Fox Terrier, the jaw is powerful, the stop not too defined. The eyes should be small and dark, well set in. The ears are V-shaped, set fairly high, and are carried forward and close to the cheek. The neck should be of moderate length, slightly arched and slope gracefully into long shoulders set well back.

The body is short and well ribbed-up, the loin strong. The forelegs are straight and muscular with ample bone, the hindquarters should be strong with muscular thighs, hocks well bent and let down. The tail is well set on, but not carried too gaily.

Group

Terrier.

Size

Height: 39·2cm (15½in).
Weight: 9 – 9·5kg (20 – 21lb).

Coat
Colour: Black and tan preferred.
Texture: Wiry, hard, very close and abundant, should be double.

Terrier, West Highland White

Origins
According to the Malcolm family, the breed has its origins in Poltallock, Scotland, where for three generations the family bred these white terriers. Certainly the breed was called the Poltallock Terrier and the Roseneath Terrier, but it is likely that these places only concentrated on developing and refining a white strain of the old Scottish Terriers. In so doing, they produced a smart, courageous and hardy little sporting dog, which is now much valued as a companion and has achieved considerable success in the show ring.

Characteristics
The general appearance is that of a small, game and hardy terrier, possessed of no small amount of self-esteem. The breed is strongly built, deep in the chest and back ribs, the back level and the quarters powerful. Movement is free, straight and easy all round. The head is slightly domed, the jaws strong without a snipey appearance. The eyes are set wide apart, are of medium size and dark in colour giving a sharp and intelligent look. The ears are small and carried erect. The neck is set into nicely sloping shoulders. The tail is 12·7–15cm (5 – 6in) long, not docked and is carried jauntily but not over the back.

Group
Terrier.

Size
Height: Dogs 27·9cm (11in), bitches may be about 2·5cm (1in) less.

Coat
Colour: Pure white.
Texture: Outer coat hard and free from curl, undercoat short, soft and close.

Terrier, Yorkshire

Origins
Although by Victoria's reign the Yorkshire Terrier, because of its diminutive size and glamorous coat, had been taken up as a fashionable pet, its origins are much more humble. Originating among the Scottish Terriers, the breed was taken up in the 1840s by Yorkshire weavers who wanted a sporting little terrier for ratting expeditions or for competition in the rat pits. It was popular with the weavers, perhaps because of its attractive coat, which owed something in texture to the Skye Terrier and in colour

to the now extinct Waterside Terrier. The breed in those days weighed anything up to 9kg (20lb) with 4·5kg (10lb) being regarded as an ideal but, when killing rats ceased to be part of the breed's purpose in life, the size was even further reduced.

Characteristics
The general appearance should be that of a long-coated terrier, very compact and neat, the carriage conveying an air of importance. The head is rather small and flat, not too prominent or round in skull, the eyes dark and sparkling and the ears small, V-shaped and carried erect or semi-erect. The forelegs are straight, the body very compact with a good loin and level topline. The tail is cut to a medium length and carried a little higher than the level of the back. The coat is the important characteristic of the breed and the standard lays down precise requirements as to length and shading on different parts of the body.

Group
Toy. Pet Dogs (FCI).

Size
Weight: Up to 3kg (7lb).

Coat
Colour: A dark steel blue, not silver blue, with rich bright tan markings.
Texture: Long and perfectly straight, not wavy, glossy and of a fine silky texture.

Vizsla, Short-haired Hungarian

Origins
The breed is sometimes called the Hungarian Pointer, which gives more obvious clues to its origins and use than the less familiar name of Vizsla. Drawings dating from the Magyar invasions 1000 years ago show Vizsla-like dogs being used in conjunction with falcons, and manuscripts of the 14th century make it clear that the Vizsla's role in falconry was well defined and that care was taken to ensure the purity of the breed. World War I threatened the future of the breed, but it was brought back almost from the point of extinction to become a first class dual-purpose gundog and to embark on a very successful show career in both Britain and America.

Characteristics
The breed is robust yet lightly built, showing power and drive in the field, but with a tractable and affectionate nature in the home. The head is lean and

Short-haired Hungarian Vizsla

muscular, moderately wide between the ears and with a moderate stop; the ears are thin and silky with rounded leathers hanging close to the cheeks. The eyes are of medium size. The neck is strong, smooth and muscular, moderately long and arched, set into shoulders well laid back. The back is short, the withers high and the top line slightly rounded with a chest moderately broad and deep. Forelegs are straight, strong and muscular, hind legs with moderate angulation of stifles and hocks. The tail is docked and set just below the level of the back. The gait is far reaching, light footed, graceful and smooth.

Group
Gundog. Sporting (AKC). Setters (FCI).

Size
Height: Dogs, 56 – 61cm (22 – 24in), bitches 53·8 – 58·4cm (21 – 23in). In KC, dogs 57 – 63·5cm (22½ – 25in), bitches 53·3 – 59·6cm (21 – 23½in). *Weight:* In KC, 22 – 29·9kg (48½ – 66lb).

Coat
Colour: Solid, rusty gold or dark sandy yellow in different shades.
Texture: Short, smooth, dense and close-lying, without evidence of a woolly undercoat.

Vizsla, Wire-haired Hungarian

The standard is as the Short-haired Vizsla except:

Coat
Texture: Wiry.

Weimaraner

Origins
The breed has a history which only goes back to the beginning of the 19th century when it was produced by crossing Bloodhounds with native German hunting breeds, such as the Red Schweisshund, and became known simply as the Weimar Pointer. The Weimaraner is, therefore, yet another of the breeds which talented German breeders produced in order to fulfil some particular purpose or need. In its early days the Weimaraner was used to hunt Europe's larger game, boar and deer, but is now very much at home fulfilling the duties of a gundog accompanying modern sportsmen. The Weimaraner is not a kennel

dog, being happier and working better when living as part of the family. The breed's distinctive grey colour, silent and effortless movement have earned him the popular name of 'Grey Ghost'.

Characteristics
The breed must be fearless, friendly, protective and obedient. The Weimaraner is a medium-sized grey dog with considerable presence. Its head is moderately long and aristocratic with moderate stop; the eyes are unusually light, amber or blue-grey, and the ears long and lobular, slightly folded and set high. The forelegs are straight and strong, the hindquarters powerful and moderately angulated. The body is square in outline with a level topline and sloping croup, deep chest and moderate tuck-up. The tail is docked.

Group
Gundog. Sporting (AKC). Setters (FCI).

Size
Height: Dogs 61 – 69cm (24 – 27in), bitches 56 – 64cm (22 – 25in). In AKC, dogs 63·5 – 68·5cm (25 – 27in), bitches 58·4 – 63·5cm (23 – 25in). In FCI, dogs 59 – 70cm (25 – 27in), bitches 57 – 65cm (23 – 25in).

Coat
Colour: Preferably silver grey, shades of mouse or roe grey.
Texture: Short, smooth and sleek. In the long-haired Weimaraner the coat is 2·5 – 5·8cm (1 – 2in) long on the body and the limbs are feathered.

Welsh Corgi, Cardigan

Origins
The breed shares a common heritage with its more popular cousin from Pembrokeshire.

Characteristics
Apart from the fact that Pembrokes are without tails and Cardigans have good full ones, the two share considerable and obvious similarities. The tail in the Cardigan is moderately long and set in line with the body, closely resembling the brush of a fox. The Cardigan is also slightly larger, with not such a sharp head, and larger ears.

Group
Working. Shepherd Dogs (FCI).

Size
Height: As near 30·4cm (12in) as possible at the shoulder.
Weight: Dogs 9·9 – 11·7kg (22 – 26lb), bitches 9 – 10·8kg (20 – 24lb).

Coat
Colour: Any colour except white. Blue merles may be wall-eyed.
Texture: Short or medium, and of hard texture.

Welsh Corgi, Pembroke

Origins
The breed is universally familiar because of its present association with the British Royal Family with whom it shares a long heritage. The two breeds of Corgi, the Pembroke and the Cardigan, and the as

Weimaraner

Welsh Corgi, Cardigan

Welsh Corgi, Pembroke

Whippet

yet unrecognized Lancashire Heeler, were developed as specialist cattle dogs sometime during the 12th century. The Corgi is said to have been brought over from Holland by Flemish weavers who settled around Haverfordwest, Little England in west Wales. Certainly such a history would do much to explain the distinct Spitz characteristics carried by the Corgi and which may have produced, crossed with the Old Black and Tan Terriers, the lighter built Black and Tan Heelers. However, whatever may have been its distant origins there can be no doubt but that the breed in recent times has become firmly established as a housedog and showdog.

Characteristics

The Corgi is low set, strong, sturdily built and active, giving an impression of substance and stamina in small space. It is, in fact, not a small breed but a medium-sized breed on short legs. The head in all respects is foxy, the neck and body fairly long. A deep rib cage, a firm level topline and a short loin add to the impression of strength. The legs are short, fore-arms slightly turned inwards and hind-quarters moderately angulated. The tail is docked as short as possible, though some puppies are born without a tail, a trend which breeders may encourage.

Group
Working. Shepherd Dogs (FCI).

Size
Height: 25·4 – 30·4cm (10 – 12in).
Weight: Dogs 9 – 10·8kg (20 – 24lb), bitches 8 – 9·9kg (18 – 22lb). In AKC, dogs 13·6kg (30lb); bitches 12·7kg (28lb).

Coat
Colour: Red, sable, fawn, black and tan or with white markings on legs, chest and neck.
Texture: Short or medium length and of hard texture.

Whippet

Origins
The Whippet is not, in spite of obvious and undeniable similarities, a miniature Greyhound. It is the working man's sight hound, intended for coursing small ground game and for racing against its fellows. The breed came into existence in the early 19th century when punitive laws which prevented working people from keeping sporting dogs had been relaxed, at least to the extent that small ground game and vermin could legitimately be hunted. In its early days the breed was known as a snap-dog, the term often being ascribed to the breed's ability to snap up rabbits though it is possible that 'snap', a English dialect word meaning 'food', also refers to the breed's ability as a provider. The breed's speed over a furlong also made exciting racing, a sport which predates the more commercially organized Greyhound races and which still flourishes in England.

Characteristics
The breed should convey an impression of balanced muscular power and strength allied to elegance; the dog is built for speed and should possess great freedom of action. The skull is long and lean, the expression bright and alert, the ears fine and rose-shaped. The neck is long, muscular and slightly arched, set into oblique shoulders. The chest is very deep, the back broad and firm showing a definite arch over the loin. Forelegs are straight and quarters strong with well-bent stifles. The tail is long and tapering.

Group
Hound. Greyhounds (FCI).

Size
Height: Dogs 47cm (18½in), bitches 44cm (17½in). In AKC, dogs 48·2 – 56cm (19 – 22in), bitches 45·7 – 53·3cm (18 – 21in), 1·2cm (½in) above or below these limits to disqualify.

Coat
Colour: Any colour or mixture of colours.
Texture: Fine, short, as close as possible.

5 | Shows and Trials

Each year hundreds of shows and trials around the world test a wide range of dogs' physical attributes and abilities, from their obedience to conformity to standards.

Below: Last minute grooming in the show ring.

Britain leads the world in the size of show events, in part because the distances that have to be travelled by entrants are relatively short. Ten thousand dogs are regularly entered in six or seven British shows each year. The total number of events and the total number of entrants are much greater in the United States, although the numbers attending each event are smaller. In the United States and Australia 3,000 to 4,000 entrants is a figure often attained, as it is in European countries such as Sweden and Belgium.

Every country has separate classes for dogs and bitches. Additionally, the classes for each sex are subdivided to make competition more equal. Britain has by far the largest number of these divisions, which also serve to prevent classes becoming unwieldy through growth in the number of entries. The following is the Kennel Club definition of classes at championship and open shows held in Britain.

Minor Puppy For dogs of six and not more than nine months old on the first day of the show

Puppy For dogs of six and not more than 12 months on the first day of the show

Junior For dogs of six and not more than 18 months of age

Maiden For dogs that have not won a Challenge Certificate or a first prize at an open or championship show (exceptions include Puppy and Minor Puppy classes)

Novice For dogs that have not won a Challenge Certificate or three or more first prizes at a championship or open show (some classes excepted)

Tyro For dogs that have not won a Challenge Certificate or five or more first prizes at open or championship shows (some classes excepted)

Debutante For dogs that have not won a Challenge Certificate or a first prize at a championship show (some classes excepted)

Undergraduate For dogs that have not won a Challenge Certificate or three or more first prizes at championship shows (with exceptions)

Graduate For dogs that have not won a Challenge Certificate or four or more first prizes at championship shows in graduate, post-graduate, minor limit, mid limit, limit and open classes

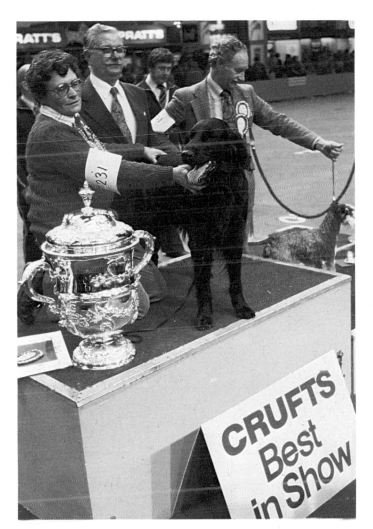

Post-graduate For dogs that have not won a Challenge Certificate or five or more first prizes at championship shows in post-graduate, minor limit, mid limit, limit and open classes

Minor Limit For dogs that have not won two Challenge Certificates or three or more first prizes in all at championship shows in minor limit, mid limit, limit and open classes, confined to the breed, at shows where Challenge Certificates were offered for the breed

Mid Limit For dogs that have not won three Challenge Certificates or five or more first prizes in all at championship shows in mid limit, limit and open classes, confined to the breed, where Challenge Certificates were offered for the breed

Limit For dogs that have not won three Challenge Certificates under three different judges or seven or

Opposite: A Saluki is Veteran Winner alongside the Reserve Winner, a Beagle. Above left: Best in Show at Crufts, 1980 was Ch. Shargleam Blackcap, a Flat-coated Retriever. Above: An old English Sheepdog judged Best of Breed and Reserve Best Working Dog. Left: An Irish Wolfhound and young handler in the Junior Showman class.

more first prizes in all, at championship shows in limit and open classes, confined to the breed, where Challenge Certificates were offered for the breed

Open For all dogs of the breeds for which the class is provided and eligible for entry at the show

Veteran For dogs of an age specified in the schedule but at least five years old on the first day of the show

The Commonwealth system follows this pattern quite closely, although classes are fewer. The American system is much simpler and is usually restricted to minor puppy, puppy, bred-by-exhibitor, American-bred, open and champion classes. At shows organized under FCI rules the subdivisions usually comprise puppy, junior, open, working and champion.

For many the highlight of a show is the choosing of overall best dog. First the individual class winners parade before the judge. The best of all the males is chosen and then the best female. This dog and bitch then meet and one is adjudged to be Best of Breed. The Best of Breeds are then all judged in their relevant groups (Hound, Gundog, Terrier, Utility, Working and Toy). One will be chosen Best of Group. The six group winners file back into the ring and the judge makes his choice for the Best in Show. It is always an exciting moment.

Judging is definitely an art, and because of this judges can reflect widely differing shades of opinion. It is also a thankless task and a lonely one. The judge, like the referee, may be thought by losers to have made a bad choice, but his decision cannot be disputed.

The principles of judging a breed are quite easily understood. When showing first began the societies of particular breeds drew up breed standards. These are, in effect, word pictures of a breed. Enthusiasts knew what the dog was required for, they knew what its historical characteristics were and they did not want them to alter substantially in the future. The breed standards became the 'blueprints' for both breeders and judges, and they remain so today.

A judge has fixed in his mind a picture of the ideal dog for the breed. He examines the individuals presented to him and compares them with his conception of this ideal configuration. But why do dogs have to conform to a certain shape, and why should humans lay down what this shape should be? The answer is found in history. Most

dogs are basically working dogs. They were evolved to perform certain tasks. They have in their make-up the breed characteristics that fit them for their work.

The Cocker Spaniel, for example, is bred for rough shooting and the recovery of small game. Although small enough to go into close cover, where space is limited, this dog must have sufficient strength to force its way through dense undergrowth. Hence the thick, short body. A Cocker Spaniel is required to have well laid-back shoulders, otherwise a day's activity would tax him beyond endurance. Its head must be held high, because it carries game which can be quite heavy. This also means that the neck should be fairly long and elegant. The fore-face needs strength for the same reason. So we have a general picture of a Cocker Spaniel that is well suited to perform its traditional role.

If every effort had not been made down the years to retain these breeds of a uniform style and shape it would now be almost impossible to distinguish a Cocker Spaniel from a Labrador Retriever, or even from a Welsh Terrier.

The breeds would have become inextricably mixed, and few people would think that desirable. Part of the attraction of any animal is the variety of breeds or species, and no dog lover would forego that delight.

The reverse of a mixture of breeds is what is known as type. It is a term that is difficult to define, although in general type is a characteristic peculiar to one breed. All breeds have it. Round eyes, for example, might look similar but they are very different in, say, the Pekingese and the Griffon. And the curly tail of the Pug bears little resemblance to that of the Basenji. The prick ears of the Corgi and the German Shepherd are equally dissimilar. And some dogs, for example the Jack Russell Terrier, are not a registered breed but rather are considered a type. So type is that curious difference, and is unmistakable to the true connoisseur.

It follows that a judge who specializes in a particular breed may be more likely to recognize type than one who assesses a number of different breeds. But all judges look for sound animals and those that move correctly and with-out signs of weakness or distortion catch the judge's eye.

Judging dogs according to group involves comparing the entries with the ideal for each breed. A Peke is not compared with a Great Dane as such, but rather with the judge's idea of the ideal for each breed. For example, if there were just two animals in the class it would be easy to assess the dogs. The Great Dane might be, let us say, a fine, strong and elegant specimen, sound in movement with a look of dash and daring about it. It might have a good head, a small, dark eye, a well-arched neck and strong, muscular hind quarters. On the other hand the Pekingese might have a serious fault such as a 'weak' head and a protruding nose. As the standard demands a small, compact dog, if this Peke, in addition to its head-faults had a very long and oversized body and carried its tail between its legs, then even the most casual observer would not hesitate in placing the Great Dane above it. As for two, so it is possible for a skilled judge to rank 20 dogs in order. The winner will be the animal that most closely approximates the judge's idea of the ideal for that breed.

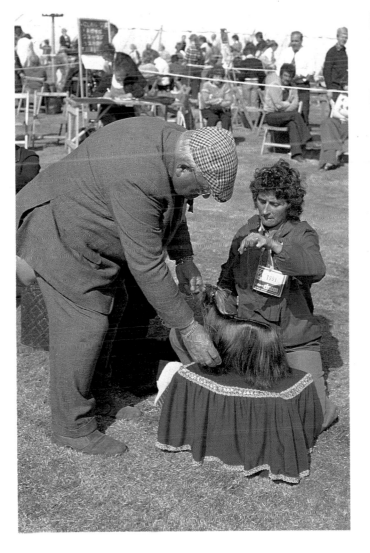

At shows, judges look for the entrant that most closely approximates the standard for that particular breed. Left: At a major venue in the United States, Spaniels are shown before the judge. Above: A judge uses his hands as well as his eyes. This Yorkshire Terrier is being assessed for conformation. Right: Handlers make final adjustments to their dogs in an Afghan Hound class before the judging begins. Long-coated dogs such as Afghans need a great deal of show grooming if they are to compete successfully.

Different countries have different systems by which a champion is decided. In some, such as Britain, it is particularly difficult for certain breeds to win this coveted title. In others, including a number of European countries, it is possible for a dog to become a champion without ever being assessed against another dog of the same breed. Some countries have very few dogs of certain breeds, while competition is always toughest in the more popular breeds. There are four different procedures for awarding the title of champion in dog shows throughout the world. They are systems that are followed in either Britain, the Commonwealth, the United States or Europe.

A judge at a British championship show may award a Challenge Certificate to the best of each sex in a breed. It is never automatic, for if he does decide to make such an award the judge must certify in writing that the animal is, in his opinion, worthy of the title of champion. When three Challenge Certificates have been awarded to the one dog by three different judges (one must be gained after the animal is 12 months old), the dog gains the permanent title of champion. It is a much-prized accolade because of the few Challenge Certificates awarded. There is an annual limit of 30 for the numerically strongest breeds. For breeds with smaller numbers of entries the most that can be given in a year may be as low as six. It is more difficult to achieve champion status under the British system than under any other.

A modified form of the British procedure occurs in Commonwealth countries, with the exception of Canada. South Africa also follows this system. In most countries the allocation of Challenge Certificates is more liberal than in Britain.

A points system is used in the United States. To become a champion a dog must accumulate 15 points. Points are awarded to the best of each sex (champions excluded) in accordance with the number of dogs of the breed competing at each show. The numbers that determine the points value of a show vary in different parts of the country. The lowest point rating is 1 and the highest is 5. Two of the shows at which a champion has succeeded must be major shows carrying 3, 4 or 5 points. Less popular breeds can have difficulty meeting this requirement because it is often hard to find a show with sufficient entries for certain breeds to enable the entry to merit 'major' status.

The Canadian Kennel Club runs a similar arrangement to the American one, although at least 10 points must be awarded by not less than three different judges.

All Scandinavian and western European Kennel Clubs, plus some in South America and eastern Europe, operate under the auspices of the Federation Cynologique Internationale, the International Canine Federation (FCI). This body was founded in 1911 by the French, German, Belgian, Dutch and Austrian Kennel Clubs to control and organize dog shows. The FCI creates champions by awarding what are cumbersomely known as Certificates of Aptitude, Championship International, Beauty (CACIB). Four of these must be won in at least three different countries under three different judges. CACIBs are given in all breeds at international shows regardless of the number of dogs competing. It is possible for a dog to win a CACIB without meeting another member of the same breed.

Judging time for Standard Poodles. This breed, so closely identified nowadays with shows, was originally used extensively as a gundog. It proved particularly adept at retrieving birds from lakes and streams and its coat was clipped around the legs to make swimming easier. Bands of hair were retained around the joints to keep them warm. This style of presentation is known as the Lion clip (in the United States it is referred to as the Continental clip). Grooming Poodles is a job for the experts but breeders who show their dogs regularly can make a fine art of clipping.

The routine of judging, although varied slightly by different practitioners, is broadly similar. It involves looking, feeling and the study of a dog's movement. When the entrants come into the ring the judge will glance at each of them and then proceed to go through a detailed physical examination, one dog at a time. He will use his hands quite a lot. This may appear to be 'theatre' but it is not; the combination of eye and hand tells a good judge all he needs to know about a dog.

Then comes movement, sometimes the most searching assessment of all. It is possible for a skilled handler to pose his dog in such a way that its blemishes will be minimized, if not entirely hidden from view. Toes with a tendency to turn out can be place in the correct position; and a dog with hind legs tucked underneath can be trained to stand with them placed well out behind. Loose elbows, a badly carried head, cow hocks – all these and many other faults may not be detected when the dog is stationary. But when the animal moves everything is plain to see. The dog's gait can be assessed as can the carriage of the tail and the way in which the head is held.

Below: While the dog stands quietly, a judge uses her hands to assess bone structure. Finer points of conformation may be invisible to the eye and so require gentle handling. Bottom: The manner in which an entrant moves is a further category of assessment. A dog may look good when standing still but fail to display the same degree of excellence when moving. Deportment and gait are both important factors in the overall picture that a judge forms of each entrant. Limbs that appear good when stationary may not live up to expectations when in motion and show faults not immediately apparent.

Field trials are competitions for working gundogs, and in some countries for hounds, in which judges assess the ability of the dogs to carry out the purpose for which they have been bred and trained. Dogs have worked with men for centuries in the pursuit of game, originally for the sole purpose of providing food but in more recent times as an adjunct to field sports.

The traditional style of shooting in Britain has been dictated by the type of country in which game is to be found and which requires the dog-handler and gun-bearer to be on foot. Gundogs have been developed for specialist purposes and thus the majority of field trials are for the specialist breeds. Four categories of field trial are licensed by the Kennel Club. The most popular are those for Retrievers and Spaniels. A number of trials are held for Pointers and Setters, breeds which although of different origin perform the same function, and a smaller but increasing number of trials are organized for what are classified as the breeds which hunt, point and retrieve. These are the dual purpose breeds first developed in Europe to fulfil all roles expected of a gundog.

The term 'field trial' is used to denote the meeting for the purpose of holding competitions between dogs, and the individual competitions are designated 'stakes'. Generally two stakes are held at each trial – an open or all-aged stake, which as the names suggest are open for entry by dogs of any age or experience, and a further stake in which younger dogs compete. This latter stake is described variously as puppy, derby, novice or non-winner according to the definition of the eligibility for entry laid down by the organizing society. The number of dogs which may compete on any one day is limited. In stakes lasting one day, it is usual to allow no more than 12 dogs to run, while two day stakes are normally confined to a maximum of 24 dogs.

All field trials are run as nearly as possible to an ordinary day's shooting and the planting of game to be found or retrieved is positively discouraged. The object of a field trial is to test dogs on live game and it is not unknown for trials to be declared null and void due to a shortage of the necessary game.

Retriever trials are most frequently run on fields of sugar beet, kale or turnips and are held between October 1 and February 1. The growing tendency is for one day trials to be held consisting of an open or all-aged stake (for older dogs) or a novice or puppy and non-winner stake (for young dogs). Stakes may be confined to one breed or include all breeds of Retriever. The most common breeds are the Labrador and the Golden. The Flat-coated Retriever is also popular.

A draw is made before the trial to determine the order in which dogs will come under the judges. In the field, the usual procedure is for the judges, handlers and dogs, guns and beaters to walk the ground in line abreast, four or six dogs being in the line at any one time, depending on the number of judges decided by the organizers of the trial. When a bird is flushed and shot, the judges decide which dog shall be sent to retrieve it. Dogs are assessed for their steadiness, ability to mark the fall of game, their drive and style while retrieving, and their nose work. Note is also taken of their quickness in gathering game, the degree of control required by the handler and the way in which game is retrieved and delivered back to the handler. Each

dog is run twice under the judges unless it disqualifies itself, most commonly by being out of control or failing to retrieve a bird which is then found by another dog. The decision on the order of prize winners is made after a final walk up or by arranging a drive.

The Retriever championship each year is organized by the International Gundog League (Retriever Society), entry for which is earned by gaining points in certain open or all-aged stakes. In addition, the first prize winner in these specified stakes is awarded a field trial certificate. Two such certificates qualify a dog for the title of field trial champion.

The two most common breeds of working Spaniel used in Britain are English Springers and Cockers, the former being predominant. Stakes at trials may be scheduled for one breed only or may be open to any variety of Spaniel. They are run under two judges, with a referee standing by to adjudicate if required. Each dog is run in turn under the judges, odd numbers under one judge and even numbers under the other. In the second round this sequence is reversed so that both judges see all dogs. A third run for the best dogs may also be held.

The ground for Spaniel trials must contain plenty of cover for game as dogs are assessed for their questing and quartering, game finding and flushing in addition to their ability to retrieve and deliver.

Pointer and Setter trials are traditionally run in the spring and early summer, when no game is actually shot, or at the beginning of the grouse season in August and September. Breeds which take part are Pointers, English Setters, Irish Setters and Gordon Setters. It is necessary for

Field trials are a judge of a gundog's working abilities. Above right: The handler takes aim before his dog sets out to retrieve the shot game. Below: By means of a whistle and voiced commands a handler directs his dog in its tasks. Right: Mission accomplished – a dog approaches its handler with the game held gently between its teeth. Far right: The judges compare notes after the trial and an enjoyable day of tests and achievements is considered.

the ground to be open with plenty of space for the dogs to quarter yet to contain enough depth of cover to prevent the game from being flushed too early. The dogs are run in pairs under two judges.

Judges assess the pace and control of dogs while quartering, their game-finding ability and their style on point when they have scented game. Credit points are given for natural backing, that is to say the recognition that the fellow dog in the pair is on point and turning to stand and face towards it. At trials where game is not shot, dogs are expected to drop to a shot fired into the air as the pointed game is flushed. Normally each dog will have two runs under the judges, with a third or even fourth run to decide the final order of the best dogs.

Trials for breeds which hunt, point and retrieve are held for the general purpose gundogs and may include German Pointers, Large Munsterlanders, Weimaraners, Hungarian Vizslas and other European breeds which are not specialized in one functional aspect of shooting dogs. Stakes are confined to 12 dogs and are held on one day. The dogs are run singly under two judges and are required to quarter ground in search of game, to point game, to be steady to flush, shot and fall, and to retrieve on command. Great emphasis is placed on the work of these dogs in water and their inclination to enter it.

The title of field trial champion is accorded to those Retrievers, Spaniels, Pointers and Setters which win the championships of their respective categories or gain two first prizes in open or all-aged stakes which qualify for the championships. There is no championship stake for the breeds which hunt, point and retrieve; the title of field trial champion for them is gained by winning two open stakes.

More than 1,000 field trials are held in the United States each year. They are divided into four categories, those for pointing dogs, retrieving dogs, flushing dogs and for trailing hounds.

The American Kennel Club does not confine the licensing of field trials to affiliated societies. Field trials are of three types. A member field trial is one at which championship points may be awarded and is held by a club or association which is a member of the AKC. A licensed field trial is given by a club or association which is not a member of the AKC but which has been specially licensed to hold the trial. Championship points may be awarded at such a trial. Informal events at which championship points are not awarded can also be held by clubs whether or not they are members of the AKC. These are termed sanctioned field trials, for which AKC approval must be obtained.

Judges are not licensed in the United States for field trials in the same way as show judges. Any reputable person who is in good standing with the American Kennel Club may be approved to judge a field trial. Nevertheless, all dogs which run in licensed or member field trials must be registered with the AKC.

The American Kennel Club licenses nearly 400 pointing breed trials each year. They are organized by specialty clubs and the following breeds are recognized for entry in these trials: Brittany Spaniels, Pointers, German short-haired Pointers, German Wirehaired Pointers, English Setters, Gordon Setters, Irish Setters, Vizslas, Weimaraners and wirehaired pointing Griffons. Trials may contain puppy stakes (for dogs of 6-15 months), derby stakes (6-24 months), open or all-aged stakes (for dogs of any age over 6 months) and limited stakes (confined to non-winners of any age over 6 months). In addition some stakes may be entered only by dogs which are owned and handled by *bona fide* amateurs.

The qualities required of dogs of the pointing breeds in the United States are similar to those sought in Britain, but the larger tracts of land available mean the dogs quarter more widely and range further, with judges and frequently

handlers on horseback. Birdfields may be designated in which game placed previously is available for the dogs to seek and point. Dogs may have to retrieve fallen game.

Championship points are gained by the dogs placed first, the number of points being determined by the number of starters in the trial. A maximum of five points can be gained at any one trial. A dog which wins 10 points in at least three trials is recorded as a field champion with the reservation that in some breeds points must also have been gained in certain specified stakes. The title of amateur field champion can be gained by winning 10 points in amateur stakes. Parent breed clubs – there is one for each breed – also run one national championship stake per year for which dogs must qualify for entry.

Retriever trials are run as closely as possible to an ordinary day's shooting. They are open to the various breeds of Retriever and/or Irish Water Spaniels. Only amateurs may judge licensed or member retriever trials. Procedures are generally similar to those in Britain.

Interest in Spaniel trials is relatively small in the United States, but the AKC does set out regulations for them. The specialized ability of the Spaniel has apparently not been generally needed, hence the breeds are not popular for work. A number of trials for Springer Spaniels are held each year but the working Cocker may be discounted.

Hound trials are popular in the United States, Beagle trials running second in number to those of the pointing breeds. The hounds are run as braces on rabbit, as small packs on rabbit or hare, or as large packs on hare only. Dogs are entered in classes according to their height and are run in series of packs as decided by the organizers. Hounds are marked by the judges according to their performance and gain points for the title of field champion depending on their placing, the points being multiples of the number of starters. In addition, trials are held for Basset Hounds and to a lesser degree for Dachshunds.

The kennel authorities of continental Europe operate under the auspices of the *Fédération Cynologique Internationale* (FCI), the central controlling body based in Belgium. General regulations are set out for the various types of field trials for gundogs, hounds and the terrier breeds, but differences in hunting customs and laws concerning the protection of animals in the member countries make it impossible for compulsory regulations to be laid down covering all countries. There is considerable interest in the work of dogs in the field and the species of game available vary a great deal.

Fewer trials are held in Australia than in the United States and Western Europe. There are, of course, fewer clubs and organizations and the wildlife pattern varies considerably throughout the country. Nevertheless, the interest in working the sporting breeds exists and continues to be encouraged.

Left: Beagle trials are hugely popular in the United States, where the main quarry is the cottontail rabbit and the hare. The dogs are divided by sex and size, up to 33cm (13in) and up to 38cm (15in). Below: The badges on this man's coat indicate a seasoned enthusiast.

Regardless of its beauty, conformation or purpose, it is necessary that a dog should be an acceptable member of the society in which it lives, and this in turn means that it must be trained and it must be obedient. A considerable amount of ringcraft training has always been essential for the show dog and a high degree of specialized training is vital for field trial competition. The encouragement of obedience training generally, however, and the setting up of formalized competition in obedience since the 1920s has been enthusiastically received in all parts of the world. It has led to the establishment of qualifications which can be gained by achieving set standards rather than purely by winning over other dogs. It is not necessary for a dog to be better than others for it to gain a recognized title but simply for it to demonstrate that it has reached the necessary standard of training and has a degree of agility. At the same time, the competitive element has been maintained by the award of prizes and titles.

Standards are graded, the initial emphasis being on the basically obedient dog which will walk at heel and sit as instructed – in effect, the companion dog. At more advanced levels, exercises become more difficult, and at the highest level the natural abilities of the dog are also tested in scent discrimination and tracking exercises.

In all obedience training and competition the aim is for the dog to work in a happy, natural manner. Although the performance of both dog and handler is judged in relation to closely defined criteria, great emphasis is placed on the dog's willingness and enjoyment of its work and on the smoothness and naturalness of the control of its handler.

The judging of obedience is based on the actual performance of the team of dog and handler. Sloppy work can be seen and noted by all and a movement of one or two inches by a dog can make all the difference between success and failure.

In Britain more than 500 dog training clubs are registered with the Kennel Club. In addition a large number of specialist breed societies, principally in the working breeds, take great interest in obedience training. Hundreds of shows licensed by the Kennel Club are held annually.

The Kennel Club licenses working trials and obedience classes separately. It is not necessary for a dog to be pure-bred for it to take part in these events. A special register for crossbred dogs, known as the Working Trials and Obedience Register, is maintained.

The first working trial was held in 1924 and was confined to German Shepherd Dogs. There are three trial categories: championship, at which Kennel Chub working trial certificates are offered; open, which are open to all dogs but which may limit the number of competitors; and members, which are restricted to dogs owned by members of the club promoting the trials.

Five types of stake may be scheduled. The lowest grade is the Companion Dog (CD) stake, which includes control exercises such as heel on leash, heel free and sending the dog away, stay exercises, agility tests including clear jump, long jump and scaling a vertical wooden wall, retrieving a dumbbell and an elementary search test. The Utility Dog (UD) stake comprises many of the foregoing and includes search and tracking exercises and a test for steadiness to gunshot. Working Dog (WD) and Tracking Dog (TD) stakes include similar tests requiring greater application. The fifth type of stake, in addition to control, nosework and agility, requires the style of work normally associated with police and other security operations, including the

The photographs show some of the features of working trials. Below: The dog's acute sense of smell is tested in following a trail. Above right: In areas such as police work a dog is trained to hold a person without inflicting injury. Right: Sheepdog trials are among the most interesting for spectators. Instructed by its handler, the dog guides a group of sheep over a marked course. The dog is also required to separate some sheep from the herd of five or so sheep, and then shepherds all of them into a pen which the shepherd then closes.

pursuit and detection of a 'criminal' and the search and escort of a suspected person. This is the Police Dog (PD) stake.

In championship working trials the winners of PD and TD stakes are awarded working trial certificates, two of which, if awarded by different judges, qualify a dog for the title of Working Trial Champion. In all stakes certification is given to those dogs which obtain 70 per cent in each group of exercises. The letter CD, UD, etc may then be added after the dog's name. An overall total of 80 per cent of marks available permits the accolade of Excellent to be added, CD Ex, UD Ex, and so on. A rather complicated system of qualification enables dogs to progress through the grades of stake at working trials.

Obedience trials were developed from working trials. In Britain they do not involve tests of agility or other aspects of physical dog work. They are concerned almost entirely with response to the command of the handler. Only in the scent discrimination test and the temperament test is the dog not under direct instruction. Classes are graded as Beginners, Novice, A, B, and C. Dogs graduate through the classes by virtue of wins in the lower grades.

Obedience shows are classified as championship, open, limited or sanction in the same way as beauty shows. Limited and sanction shows are confined to members of the organizing club, while open shows have no such restriction. All classes may be included in any show, dogs and bitches being scheduled separately, but the qualification for entry in Championship Class C is very stringent. It is in this class that the first prize winner is awarded an obedience certificate. Some 40 sets of obedience certificate (dog and bitch) are allocated by the Kennel Club each year, and a dog which gains three

obedience certificates under three different judges is entitled to be described as Obedience Champion.

Each year at Crufts dog show, the Kennel Club schedules the Obedience Championships, open to all dogs which in the previous year have won obedience certificates. This is an event which holds nationwide interest, and the winner in each sex is automatically elevated to the title of Obedience Champion.

Although working trials and obedience classes are closely allied, the actual events have an entirely different ambience. Working trials are held on open land but obedience classes are conducted within the precincts of a show venue.

American arrangements for the testing of dogs in obedience differ from those in Britain but the tests themselves are very similar. There are no working trials as such but almost all of the exercises involved are grouped in obedience trials, as they are known. Tracking tests, which equate with the tracking element of British working trials, are conducted separately.

Obedience competition began to develop in the United States in the late 1920s and early 1930s. It was felt that man-work – involving dogs being trained to attack even a protected man – was not appropriate, and to this day no American Kennel Club obedience title requires this activity. The American Kennel Club encourages not only clubs formed for the express purpose of obedience training but also many specialty clubs which are members of the AKC.

Whereas in Britain obedience competition is largely confined to Border Collies, German Shepherd Dogs and working sheepdogs (crossbreds normally with a predominance of Collie ancestry), only purebred registered dogs are permitted to compete in obedience trials, tracking tests or sanctioned matches in the United States. Some relaxation is allowed in that spayed bitches and neutered dogs may be entered in obedience competition, as may dogs which might be disqualified from the show ring for non-compliance with the breed standard. As in Britain, bitches in season are not permitted to compete in obedience trials.

The regulations for obedience trials provide for three main classes or standards – novice, open and utility.

Novice class A is for dogs which are not less than six months of age and have not won the title CD. The handler of a dog in this class must be the owner or immediate family of the owner. In Novice B class, the handler may be the owner or any other person. Simple exercises are involved: heel on leash, stand for examination, heel free, recall, long sit and long down. A qualifying score is obtained by gaining 170 points out of a possible 200 provided that more than half marks are obtained in each separate exercise. Three qualifying scores in Novice classes earn the title CD and a Companion Dog certificate is issued by the American Kennel Club. The test of standing for examination by the judge is a crucial one since it is easy for a dog to lose all points by showing shyness or resentment.

The photographs show some of the features of obedience trials. Below: This Pointer incurs penalties for having broken from a line. Right: Obedience trials also serve to display the athletic abilities of entrants. The Pointer has successfully cleared a high hurdle, and the Collie is shown in the middle of a lower but longer jump. Collies have a worldwide reputation and are often chosen for these trials because of their ability to learn and obey.

The second grade is Open class. Dogs which have won CD may be entered in Open A, handling being confined to owner or immediate family. The title CDX is granted after a dog has gained 170 points at three different trials in Open class under three different judges when the total entry in each class was at least six. Open B class is for dogs which have won CD or CDX, and dogs may continue in this class even after they have won the next grade of UD.

The exercises in Open class are more demanding and include a retrieve on the flat and over a high jump. The height of the jump demanded varies, one and a half times the height of the dog being the standard. Dispensation is given in some breeds, requiring them to jump only their actual height. The heavier breeds such as Mastiffs and St Bernards are permitted this relaxation as are some of the smaller breeds such as Dachshunds, Skye Terriers and Bulldogs. The maximum height for the high jump in any event is 914mm (36in), the minimum being 203mm (8in).

A broad jump is also included in Open class, the distance set to twice the size of the high jump for any particular dog.

Utility class is the next and highest grade, Utility A being for those dogs which have won the title CDX. The UD title is won in the same way as other titles with the stipulation that there must have been at least three dogs competing in each qualifying class. Utility B class is confined to dogs which have won the UD title. Tests in Utility class include control by signal, scent discrimination and directed retrieve and jumping.

It is possible for a dog to gain the title Obedience Trial Champion by gaining points in Open B or Utility classes by virtue of first or second prize wins. The number of points gained on each occasion is related to the number of competing dogs. A set number of first prize wins is also mandatory before the title is awarded.

Tracking dog tests are licensed by the American Kennel Club which enable dogs to gain an additional title of TD.

The *Fédération Cynologique Internationale* encourages obedience training in member countries, the emphasis lying on working and herding breeds. The tests are similar to those of working trials in Britain. It is recognized that the working dog should be useful as well as goodlooking and in order to obtain the title of FCI International Beauty Champion, working dogs must qualify in a working trial in addition to gaining the requisite show awards.

There is great and growing interest in obedience competition in Australia, where the American system of grading has been adopted. As in some other countries, it is common to find 'encouragement classes' scheduled at obedience trials, these being very simple tests intended to introduce the newcomer to competitive obedience.

Work and Sport

Although they are often thought of simply as objects of pleasure, dogs are still highly valued for the special services they perform in town and country. They may be found on the farm, aiding the police, hauling loads, guiding the blind – and leading the chase in the hunt.

Below: A Beagle pack.

One of the oldest functions of a dog is herding. Dogs that herd show great variation of type, which is only to be expected, for herding animals are found the world over.

Training demands individual attention. Formal sheepdog training usually starts at about six months with normal heel and sit commands. The young sheepdog will be taught to get used to sheep before actually working with them. Over a period of time, commands – mostly by whistle – will reinforce the dog's understanding of what is required.

The best known of all sheepdogs is the German Shepherd or Alsatian, though it is rarely used nowadays for herding. Other functions have taken over, and it is much more often found working with the armed services, the police and in guard work. Indeed, the Collie is now the most commonly used shepherding dog. The Border Collie is probably the best for the job, though it was only recognized by the British Kennel Club as recently as the late 1970s. Apart from herding, the Border Collie has proved most popular for obedience tasks and does exceptionally well in both sheepdog and obedience trials.

Before the growth in popularity of the Border Collie, the Rough Collie (or Scottish Collie as it is often called) was extremely popular. Millions of people have seen the Lassie films, which immortalized the Rough Collie as an intelligent and affectionate animal, hero of many desperate situations. There is a close cousin, the Smooth Collie, and a fourth type greatly different from the others, the Bearded Collie. This could be likened to a miniature Old English.

It is probable that the Bearded Collie was crossed with the Old English Sheepdog in the latter part of the 19th century to increase its rather small numbers. The Old English (or Bobtail as it is sometimes called) was well established in a number of English counties, particularly Hampshire and Dorset, and in Wales. It is believed to have developed from the old herders' dogs. Today it is mostly a show dog and rarely works.

Also of the Collie type, but not known as a Collie, is the Shetland Sheepdog or Sheltie. This dog, as its name suggests, originated in the Shetland Isles, where it was developed by crofters for the tough conditions that prevail there.

Other popular herding dogs are the two types of Welsh Corgi. These are more likely to be found as pets, particularly the tailless Pembroke Corgi as opposed to the more rare Cardigan, which has a long brush-like tail. Although the Corgi has, for very many years, been used

for herding cattle and then sheep, and driving them to the markets of England, the breed achieved little recognition until the 1920s. The popularity of the Pembroke Corgi has grown tremendously since the breed became a favourite with the British Royal Family.

Closely resembling the Welsh Corgi is the Swedish Vallhund. This breed was not officially recognized in its native land until the early 1940s, although it is a cattle and sheep dog of many years' standing. In looks it is very similar to the Corgi.

Almost every country where cattle or sheep are reared has its own particular type of herding dog, and the majority have been adapted to suit local conditions. Most European breeds are bigger than those found in Britain. This is because, until quite recently, they were called on to act not only as herding animals but also as guard dogs, protecting the flocks from wild animals, especially wolves. Dogs of this category include the Appenzell and Entlebuch Mountain Dogs of Switzerland. They are used for herding and droving and are well known as extremely alert watch dogs.

In neighbouring Italy, the best known of that country's breeds is the Maremma, a large white dog not dissimilar to the Pyrenean at first glance. It makes an excellent guard, especially of flocks of sheep. The origin of the breed goes back to the Kuvasz from Hungary, the watch dog of the ancient Magyars with a history of being a first-rate herding dog. Again in Italy there is the Bergamaschi which, although not so well known as the Maremma, is widely used in Lombardy.

The Bergamaschi has affinities with the Komondor, which succeeded the Kuvasz. The Kuvasz is also renowned as a guard dog of exceptional ferocity. Until recently the Komondor was rarely seen outside its native Hungary but now it is becoming quite well known in the British show-ring, commanding attention because of its unique thickly matted coat. Its origins go back 1,000 years and more. It is the best known of the Hungarian herding dogs, the others being the Puli and the Pumi.

The Komondor and Puli may share a common ancestry with the Briard, which is France's best-known shepherd dog. Again the Briard is versatile, being used as both a pack dog and a general army dog, displaying the ability of many working dogs to do more than one job. Second only to the Briard is the Beauceron.

Across the border in Belgium are the Groenendaels, Malinois and Tervuerens which also double as guard dogs and herding animals. The Groenendael (or Belgian Shepherd Dog) is often called a cousin of the German Shepherd.

The German Shepherd is an outstanding dog, known throughout the world. Basically it is a sheepdog but it has been trained to do many things, from police duty to guiding the blind. While this dog is often called an Alsatian, purists insist that it is properly known as the German Shepherd Dog. It is popular in many activities, not least with those who specialize in obedience. The breed responds well to any form of training and can thus also become a spectacular show animal. Unfortunately, many dogs of this type are incorrectly trained, and often not trained at all. They can therefore become a public nuisance if their natural instincts are not properly harnessed.

Australia has banned the import of German Shepherd Dogs but it is a country that has a spectacular dog of its own, well equipped to cope with cattle and sheep in an often difficult environment. The Kelpie is probably the world's most energetic working dog. It is the best-known Australian sheepdog.

Another tough Australian is the Heeler, or Australian Cattle Dog, which is popular in New South Wales and Victoria. It owes its ancestry in part to the old blue merle type of Collie that was introduced into Australia by Scottish immigrants.

In Holland there are three varieties of the Dutch Herder, which has both Giant Schnauzer and German Shepherd Dog in its make-up. Among other pastoral dogs is the Russian Owtcharka, a herder and guard dog; the Estrela or Portuguese Sheepdog, another heavily built and valuable protector of flocks that has hauled carts; and the Pyrenean Mountain Dog, originally a herder but now more a fashionable pet than a worker, having handed over its duties to the smaller Pyrenean Sheepdog.

Butchers in southern Germany used the Rottweiler, named after the town where it originated, as a droving dog to take cattle to market. It was nearly extinct in 1900 but has increased in number since then.

On farms the world over, dogs are to be found at work, helping farmers to control their sheep and cattle, and moving animals from field to field. **Left:** A sheepdog keeps a vigilant eye on its charges. **Above left:** The energetic Kelpie is kept busy on Australia's large sheep farms, rounding up sheep for shearing. The breed is descended from Scottish sheepdogs. **Right:** A forrester is accompanied on his rounds by two hounds.

Dogs that draw carts or sleds may be divided into two main categories: those found in countries with cold climates, which are mainly of the Spitz family, and those of warmer countries, which are generally of the Mastiff type. Many dogs have been active as draught animals for centuries, but the advent of motorized transport has reduced the number now used for this purpose. Spitz are still used for such tasks as pulling sleds over snow and ice during winter and carrying packs in the warmer weather. The Mastiff types have been associated with hauling dairy or bakery carts in provincial towns in Europe for very many years.

Not all Spitz are employed as sled dogs, but it is to this family that the Husky belongs. There are many types of Husky. Probably the most famous of all is the Alaskan Malamute, originally found throughout Alaska, but since the gold rush days of the 19th century the breed has deteriorated as other breeds have been introduced to the strain. The Alaskan Malamute is no longer confined to cold areas, and has acclimatized successfully to temperate and warm climates in North America and elsewhere. The Siberian Husky is a sled dog also used for racing.

Versatile is probably the most appropriate description of the Samoyed, a general purpose dog found in northern Siberia. For centuries this breed was used for herding as well as for sled work, but today it is almost exclusively used as a sled dog. It has been trained for hunting animals for their fur and supplying its owners with wool and hide.

The Eskimo and Indian races of North America rely heavily on their sled dogs, as indeed do trappers, policemen and traders in the frozen north. A true sled dog is easily recognized by a sharp, pointed muzzle and broad skull, sharp and pointed ears, a powerful body and a coat of rough hair standing out from the body.

Mastiff haulage dogs generally have rounded heads, deep muzzles with a pronounced 'stop,' and mostly pointed ears. They have powerful bodies and the tail is usually low set. Two such are the Large Swiss Mountain Dog and the Bernese. Coming from the canton of Berne, it was widely used for hauling carts to market.

Another type is the Newfoundland. In the fishing season these dogs haul the fishermen's carts loaded with cod and in the winter they haul fuel for fires. In addition, the Newfoundland works well in water. It is a prodigious swimmer and as a result is extremely useful as a sea and river rescue-dog.

The famous St Bernard is, regrettably, no longer a true working dog and its rescue work is negligible. For some 300 years, however, these animals were used by the monks of the Hospice of the Great St Bernard Pass in their native Switzerland when travellers became lost in the snowy uplands. It is estimated that they rescued some 2,000 people. Today, however, the greatest achievement of the St Bernard is attained in the show-ring.

Above: In the frozen vastness of Alaska the Husky and sled make an unbeatable team for hauling goods over land.
Opposite top: Inside the Arctic Circle a dog team passes a seal hunter's camp, often a source of food. **Right:** A team of Huskies run hard during a long-distance race in Alaska.

Throughout the world the Bloodhound has been used for hunting criminals and escaped convicts, and in the old days in the United States it was used to track down runaway slaves. The scenting ability of the breed is of the highest order. The Bloodhound is tenacious in following a trail, and one such event involved a total of 104 hours of tracking. A feature of this animal's appearance is the abundance of skin that wrinkles over its forehead, which gives it a rather superior look. Though the head is large the long ears reduce the impression.

The Dobermann Pinscher has also proved itself as a first-class police dog, a guard dog and a cattle dog. In Europe and North America, the breed has cropped ears but in Britain the ears hang by the side of the head. Its greatest impact is probably made as a patrol dog in police or armed service.

The Dalmatian or Carriage Dog has outlived its usefulness to man as a working animal. Its duty was to run under the carriages of wealthy folk and if a stop was made by the roadside, to protect the travellers and their belongings. The black-spotted white coat enabled the dog to merge with the shadows at night, which meant it often could not be seen by highwaymen and other criminals.

No amount of technological innovation has displaced the role of dogs as working members of the armed forces throughout the world. They are especially useful as patrol animals, particularly on airfields where much open ground has to be covered. They run faster than man, attack efficiently and command great respect from anyone who has to face them. They are agile enough to squeeze into places where men cannot, and their powers of scent and hearing are superior to man's. Correctly trained, a dog can be invaluable to policemen, prison officers, service personnel and all who have to protect human beings and property, or enforce the law and control crowds.

German Shepherds can be trained to track, guard, attack and 'arrest' as well as perform at shows. Apart from this breed there is the Dobermann Pinscher, Weimaraner, the Belgian Shepherd Dogs, Schnauzer and even Airedale and Labrador that are regularly used in service. For scenting and tracking the German Shepherd may be useful but there are probably few better than the Bloodhound or the Labrador Retriever. Labradors have proved ideal for sniffing out drugs and secret caches of arms and ammunition. They are widely used around docks, where exceptionally heavy demands are made on checking passengers, vehicles and freight.

German Shepherds demand careful training. They can

In security and detective work, trained dogs have an important role to play. Opposite top: Checking a truck for drugs. Opposite bottom: A White House security officer and his patrol dog pose in the grounds of the presidential mansion. Above: This dog is being trained to protect a case of valuables from a would-be thief. Left: A keen-nosed animal uncovers a cache of drugs which its training has enabled it to detect.

be used only if they genuinely wish to please the handler. Anything less than total dedication to the task may result in a dog uncertain in temperament and unpredictable in action. One major difference between police and army dogs in Britain is that army dogs are not trained to attack in anything but a thorough way. Nor are they trained to retrieve, for in the field of battle they may well fetch an explosive device.

Dogs have also served as messengers. Work of this nature was regularly performed by dogs for the French army in World War I and has been continued since, though on a diminished scale. Today much messenger work has been taken over by radio and motorized transport. Another little recognized duty is the scenting out of wounded people. Red Cross dogs are among those trained specifically to find injured soldiers and civilians. The usual practice is that when a dog has located an injured person it will return to its handler and guide him to the place where the person was found.

Of all social work done by the dog, the one that most readily comes to mind is that of the guide dog for the blind. This was, strangely, a role that developed from World War I. At the end of hostilities blinded German soldiers were each given a trained guide dog to help them return to normal civilian life. The success of the venture soon encouraged other European countries to adopt the scheme. In the United States the Master Eye Institute was formed in 1926 and the British equivalent, the Guide Dog for the Blind Association, in the 1930s.

Training a guide dog takes at least six months. The British association uses in the main Labrador Retrievers, both black and yellow. Also used for the purpose are quite a number of Golden Retrievers and German Shepherd Dogs, and crosses of these breeds are also accepted. About 70 per cent of dogs used are bitches, being neither so dominant nor so easily distracted as the male. All are either spayed or castrated before starting their training.

No dog is kept in the training programme unless it clearly enjoys the tasks it is taught. The average working life of a guide dog is eight to nine years, during which time it is the friend, companion and the 'eyes' of its owner. All dogs are medically checked regularly during service.

Guide dogs give blind people independence, but both have to be trained if the partnership is to succeed. **Right: A blind lady grooms her Labrador. Below: A trainer accompanies a blind man and his dog as they cross the street. Opposite: A guide dog undergoes training by a handler at a busy pedestrian crossing in an English town.**

Hounds that rely on scent possess deep muzzles indicating a wide area of olfactory nerves, while those with greater visual powers have narrow fore-faces, giving greater length and breadth of vision from a keener eye. As for terminology in this area, Britain refers to work by scent as hunting, by sight as coursing and with the gun as shooting. In the United States the term hunting is usually applied to all three.

The prime object of hunting by scent is to demonstrate hound work – the close following of the line of quarry, or the line to which the scent may have drifted. Scent is the essential element left by any quarry, which enables the dogs to follow it. It varies greatly according to terrain, climatic conditions and the quarry itself.

The huntsman controls his pack by horn, voice and whip. Each hunt has standard hunting calls to instruct the hounds. The calls also tell followers what is happening. The voice is used in a special manner to praise, indicate or rebuke.

Hounds used include Staghounds, Foxhounds, Harriers, Draghounds, Otterhounds, Bloodhounds, Beagles, Basset Hounds and a multitude of crosses and variations. The first four are followed on horseback; the Bloodhound on foot or horse, and the rest on foot. It is customary for each pack to have officers and a committee. A pack consists of from two to 80 or more couples.

Staghound packs are few and hunt to control and cull red deer. Foxhounds, developed by centuries of careful and skilful breeding, are the only really effective means of controlling the number of foxes. There are about 230 registered packs in Britain and Ireland and scores of unregistered packs. Britain uses one type of Foxhound but Americans hunt with the English, the American, the Penn-Marydel and the cross-bred Foxhound.

The Harrier, a smaller version of the Foxhound, hunts the European hare. It is strongly supported in Britain.

All over the world, breeds related to Foxhounds and Harriers hunt suitable live game. The Beagle is the most numerous of those that hunt hare, cottontail, jack rabbit and occasionally fox. It is widely used in Europe and is followed as well as used to drive game to the guns. In the United States and Canada this variety has greatest prominence as a field trial hound. There are well over 400 events licensed annually by the American Kennel Club to carry points towards the title of field trial champion. Hundreds of clubs flourish, many having their own grounds where the quarry, the cottontail, is carefully bred and scientifically reared. This quarry, which does not go to ground, is never killed but instead left as soon as it takes cover under brushwood or something similar.

Left: Bloodhounds hunting wild boar in Belgium. The Bloodhound has the most highly developed sense of smell of any domestic animal. It delights in following a trail. Top: A Pointer pack hunting in the United States. Pointers are especially suited to open country. Above: The sight of a huntsman in his pink hunting jacket has become a symbol of the English hunt.

In addition to the field trialers, the Americans have about 25 registered packs and Britain and Ireland more than 100. American registered packs hunt the European hare, the cottontail, jack rabbit and snowshoe. In northern Europe only the native hare is hunted. The rabbit is not a suitable quarry for European hunting as it goes to ground too quickly. No field trials are held for British packs but the Americans have competitive trials.

Basset Hounds hunt as Beagles do but they come in a greater variety of type, including many French varieties. The most popular are the Bassets recognized by the English and American Kennel Clubs, together with the 'English Basset,' a breed formulated with outcrossing. Packs of this type have found their way around the world.

Drag hunting is when rags soaked in methylindole, a mixture of linseed oil and turpentine, a bag of offal and blood, or a combination of all these is dragged over the ground and the animals are released to locate the scent and trace it to the finishing point. It may not stir the pulse quite as much as following live quarry but it does have practical advantages. The drag can be taken over fields and obstacles and terrain and jumps that can all be chosen to suit either experienced riders or novices on ponies.

Hound trailing is largely a British sport, although variations occur throughout the world. The hounds used are of a distinct type with a basis of Foxhound and a mixture of other breeds. They are 457–610mm (18–24in) at the shoulder and are registered in the stud books of the societies that govern the sport.

For puppies the trail is 8km (5 miles) and for adults it is 16km (10 miles). The longer distance is covered in 28–30 minutes, which is extremely fast as competing hounds have to negotiate high stone walls, gates, steep slopes, rough and rocky terrain. The method of laying the trail or drag is carefully defined. It is laid by two people. One leaves from the starting point and the other from the finishing line. The drag is laid by woollen rags that have been soaked in a mixture of paraffin, turpentine and aniseed.

Bloodhounds, which have the greatest scenting power and the finest voice of all, are used for hunting in the same way in packs, but on the 'clean boot.' A runner lays the trail and wears ordinary footwear which has no additional or artificial scent. The Bloodhound and its close variants are used by the police in some American states. Working trials with Bloodhounds are regularly held under the auspices of the American and British Kennel Clubs.

Coonhounds are a solely American hunter. They work at night as their usual quarry, the racoon, is nocturnal. The most specialized hound for following scent in water is the Otterhound. But because its quarry is almost extinct it is now legally forbidden to hunt it.

Left: The Deerhound is a large and aristocratic animal with a rough coat. It was widely used in the Scottish Highlands and had many influential supporters in Victorian times. Above: Afghans are often raced although the breed, which originated in the Middle East, was formerly a hunter of wolves and foxes. It is one of the fastest of all dogs. It has a distinctive appearance, with a pointed face and long coat. Right: Greyhounds pursue a dummy hare at a racetrack in the United States. Greyhound racing is a popular sport on both sides of the Atlantic. Stakes are much lower than for horse racing, but then the cost of purchase, upkeep and training is comparatively modest. Greyhounds are the fastest breed of dog in the world.

The sight, or gaze, hound is differently built from the one that hunts by scent. It is made for great speed and for rapid and balanced changes of direction. Of the domestic coursing breeds, those such as Saluki and Greyhound follow the type of their forebears most closely. The cross-bred variety of coursing dog, the Lurcher, is of mixed hound crossed with working dog, and the true long-dog is a cross of two coursing breeds. 'Lurcher' is also commonly used to describe Greyhounds, Deerhounds and the like; other terms are the Norfolk and the Smithfield Lurcher. This variety is a fashionable working companion that is useful for sport and a deterrent to foxes. It is not recognized as a breed by any canine governing body.

Coursing dogs usually work singly or in couples, but in some countries they are used in packs. Kangaroo, coyote, wild bear, sambur and other varieties of deer, elk, fox and types of hare are worked, but packs can suffer heavy casualties when hunting jackal or wild cat.

The recognized purebreds are Greyhound, Saluki, Sloughi, Whippet, Deerhound, Wolfhound, Borzoi, Afghan, Pharaoh, Ibizan and other lesser-known varieties.

Most numerous are Greyhounds, which course live hare and also race on tracks where they are fitted with wire muzzles and pursue an electrically operated dummy hare. Greyhound racing is a very popular sport. In Britain about 50 tracks are licensed by the governing body, the Greyhound Racing Association; there are also some 80 unlicensed tracks. Large sums of money are placed in bets, and authorities insist on strict security and veterinary inspection. Greyhound racing is also popular in such widely different countries as the United States, Mexico, Canada, Spain, Hong Kong and Australia, in addition to European nations. The live hare is coursed with couples of Greyhounds that wear differently coloured collars. They can be released only when the hare is at least 73 metres (80 yards) away. As with the hunting of other game, there is a close season.

The Whippet, being 9–11kg (20–25lb) in weight, runs more slowly at 48km/h (30mph) than the 64km/h (40mph) attained by the heavier Greyhound, which weighs 23–34kg (50–75lb). It is coursed and raced in the same way as the Greyhound, although in a straight line and not on an oval track.

Hounds of the Middle and Far East are still used for their original purpose in their native lands. They include the Afghan, Saluki, Sloughi, Ibizan and Pharaoh. Else-where, organized coursing of live game is participated in by owners who like to preserve the original working qualities of their dogs. Saluki owners are especially active in this regard but Afghan owners appear to prefer track racing. The Afghan runs at 48km/h (30mph); the Saluki is somewhat faster, although slower than the Greyhound.

Of the three main large gaze hounds, the quarry of the Deerhound and the Wolfhound is clear from the breed name. The Borzoi originally worked the wolf but is also used, as are others, on hare, coyote, deer and other quarry.

There are numerous lesser-known breeds. The Spitz breeds hunt game in Scandinavia. Icelandic and Nordic breeds serve as draught dogs and also provide sport. Siberian Huskies and Malamutes, the sled dogs, also race. The Cape Hunting Dog is the most efficient and ruthless canine hunter of all. It lives in packs and has a strict family hierarchy and hunts for survival without human aid.

Glossary

AKC American Kennel Club
Almond eyes Surrounding tissue of the eye forming an almond shape
Angulation Angles formed at joints; mainly between shoulder and forearm, stifle and hock
Apple/Dome skull Topskull rounded at centre
Arch Of loins, cut high at hip

Back Dorsal surface of body between hip and withers
Barrel chest Rounded in cross-section
Bat ear Erect, broad at base, rounded at tip, with opening facing forwards, normally rather trim
Blaze White stripe on centre of face, between the eyes and running down the nose
Blue Merle Blue and grey mixed with black
Breed Group of dogs with same appearance; in North America it is used to refer to the act of mating
Brindle Fine even mixture of black hairs with others of lighter colour
Brisket Forepart of body below chest and between forelegs
Brush tail Heavily haired, bushy tail

CACIB Certificate of Aptitude, Championship International, Beauty; awarded by FCI
Canidae The family of animals including dogs, wolves, foxes and jackals
Carpus Wrist-joint of forelimb
Castration Operation to sterilize dog by removal of testicles
Cat-foot Short, round compact foot
CD Certificate Companion Dog Certificate; awarded to competent dogs in AKC Obedience Trials, Novice Class
CDX Companion Dog Excellent Certificate; awarded to competent dogs in AKC Obedience Trials, Open Class
Challenge Certificate May be awarded at judge's discretion to best dog of its sex in a breed at a championship show and certifies that the dog is of sufficient merit to be worthy of the title of champion
Cheek Side of head, below ear
Chiselled Head clean-cut, particularly under the eyes; detailed modelling of head
Clip Style of trimming of the coat, as for Poodles
Cloddy Low, thickset and heavy, lacking in quality
Close-coupled Body short from last rib to hip; short loin
Close-season Period during which a particular game animal may not be hunted
Cobby Short bodied and compact
Collar Marking around neck; usually white
Coupling The body between ribs and pelvis; the loin
Coursing Pursuit of game by dog or dogs using sight (Britain)
Crest Arched, upper portion of neck
Crooked Normally of bones of the forelimbs
Cropped ear One with leather cut so that ear stands erect
Cross-breeding Mating of two different types of breeds or varieties
Croup Hind-end of back, just in front of tail
Culotte Longer hair on back of thighs
Cut-up Highly arched under belly

Dam Female parent
Dewclaw Rudimentary fifth digit, borne on inside of leg, usually forelimbs only but some breeds produce them on hind limbs and in some breeds they are required to do so
Dewlap Loose hanging skin under throat
Digits Toes, fore and hind
Docked Tail shortened by surgery
Dog show Competitive event at which prizes are awarded to best examples of each breed or variety; a means of recognizing and rewarding excellence

Domed Topskull evenly rounded; convex
Drag hunting When hounds and handlers follow an artificially laid scent trail over selected terrain
Drop ear Ear with ends folded or drooping forwards

Elbow Joint between humerus, ulna and radius
Erect ears Standing upright

FCI Fédération Cynologique Internationale (France)
Feathering Fringe of longer hairs on ears, legs, tail or body
Field trial Outdoors event at which gundogs and hounds are judged on their working abilities
Field Trial Certificate Awarded to winner of a Field Trial Stake
Field Trial Champion Winner of two Field Trial Certificates
Flat skull Not domed
Flews Pendulous upper lips, particularly at corners
Forearm Foreleg between elbow and pastern; the ulna and radius
Foreface Front of head between eyes; upper part of muzzle
Frill Longer hair on chest and sides of neck
Furnishings Longer hair

Gait Manner in which dog walks or runs
Gay tail Carried-up over the back, not drooping
Gazehound Hound that hunts by sight
Grizzle Bluish-grey colour
Guard coat Longer, smoother, stiffer hairs forming the top coat

Half-prick ear Erect, but for tips which fall forwards
Hare-foot Elongated, the middle digits longest
Harlequin Small splashes of colour usually black on white and usually confined to Great Danes
Haw Third eyelid at inside corner of eye
Hip Joint between hindlimb and pelvis
Hock True heel or tarsus
Hound glove Grooming brush with short bristles made in the form of a mitten or glove
Hound trailing Racing in which hounds follow an artificial trail over varied terrain
Hunting Pursuit of game by dog using scent (Britain), or by any means (USA)

In-breeding Mating of dogs with a recent common ancestor
International Beauty Champion Award made to working dogs by FCI

KC Kennel Club (of Great Britain)

Layback The angle of the shoulder blade relative to the vertical
Leafy Thin texture of the ears
Leather Flap of the ear
Let-down (hocks) Hocks close to the ground
Level bite When incisors of upper and lower jaw meet exactly edge to edge
Line breeding Mating of a dog to a relative in its own family, eg a dog to its grand-dam
Linty Soft and close coat
Liver Deep, reddish brown colour
Loin Side of body between last rib and hind quarters
Looped tail Tail carried over the back in an arch
Lumber Superfluous flesh

Mane Long hair on top and sides of neck
Mask Dark shading on foreface
Metacarpus True foot bones of foreleg; the pastern
Metatarsus True foot bones of hindleg
Molero Incomplete or abnormal ossification of skull, found in all young animals
Muzzle The head in front of the eyes; the upper and lower jaws

Obedience Certificate Awarded in various classes at Obedience Trials

Obedience Trials Event at which dogs judged on ability to follow commands
Obedience Trial Champion The highest award in AKC Obedience Trials
Occiput Upper, central ridge of skull
Otter tail Thick at root, flat in section and tapering, with hair parted on underside
Overhung Pronounced or heavy brow

Pack hound Hound which hunts as one of a group
Parent breed club In USA, national club, one for each breed
Parti-coloured Having patches of two or more colours
Pastern Foreleg between carpus and digits
Pendant ear Hanging ears, also called pendulous
Pepper and salt Evenly distributed mixture of white or light hairs with brown
Pied Having large patches of two or more colours
Plume Long fringe of hair on tail
Point of rump Rump at top of hind leg
Point of shoulder Shoulder at top of foreleg
Points The ears, face, legs and tail of a contrasting colour, usually white, black, or tan; also refers more generally to any desirable characteristics as in breed points
Prick ear Erect, usually with pointed tip; bat ear if it is erect and rounded
Puppy A dog less than 12 months old
Purebred A dog whose parents are known, of like breed and themselves of unmixed descent

RASKC Royal Agricultural Society for Kennel Control
Reachy Long and graceful
Receding Eyes set deep in their sockets
Ring tail Tail curving up and around almost in a circle
Roached Having the back curving convexly above the loin
Roan Unevenly distributed fine mixture of coloured and white hairs
Root of tail Base of the tail
Rose ear A small drop ear folded over and back, revealing inside of ear
Ruff Longer thick hair around the neck

Sable Having a lacing of black hairs over a lighter ground colour
Scissors bite Where outer side of lower incisors bears on inner side of upper incisors
Screw tail Short and twisted in a spiral
Selective breeding Successive mating of selected animals to produce offspring having desired characteristics
Self colour Of one colour
Semi-erect ear See Half-prick ear
Short-coupled See Close-coupled
Shoulder Top of forelimb
Sight hound See Gazehound
Sire Male parent
Snipey Muzzle pointed and weak
Solid Whole colour
Spaying Operation to sterilize bitch by removal of ovaries
Spitz Dog usually of Arctic origin with pointed face, prick ears and bushy, usually curled, tail
Splay foot Flat with spreading toes
Spring (of ribs) Fullness of curvature
Stake Individual competition at a Field Trial, either open or for younger dogs only, or competition at a show with enhanced prizes
Stern Tail of a sporting dog or hound (usually pronounced 'starn')
Stifle True knee joint, between femur and tibia and fibula
Stilted gait Up-and-down gait of a straight-hocked dog
Stop Step up in profile from muzzle to top of skull at the eyes
Stud Male used for breeding

TD Tracking Dog Certificate – awarded to competent dogs in AKC Tracking Tests
Throatiness Excess of loose skin beneath the throat

Topknot Tuft of long, usually soft hair on top of head
Topline Profile of the spine
Toy Small or miniature dog
Trace Dark stripe down back of Pug
Tracking Tests Events in USA at which dogs judged on tracking ability; equivalent to similar parts of British Working Trials
Triangular eye One set in tissue in such a way that eye appears three-cornered
Tricolour Having 3 colours: black, white and tan
Tucked-up Where depth of body is markedly shallow at loin; small waisted; see Cut-up

Type Characteristic qualities that distinguish a breed or family group

UD Utility Dog Certificate, awarded to competent dogs in AKC Obedience Trials, Utility Class
Undercoat Fine coat closest to the skin
Underjaw Lower jaw
Undershot Where lower incisors lie in front of upper ones when jaw closed

Wall eye Eye with a whitish iris, usually with blue

Wheaten Pale yellow or fawn colour, as wheat
Whole colour Of one colour only
Wiry Coat hard and wire-like
Withers Highest point of shoulders
Working Certificate Awarded in various classes at Working Trials and elsewhere
Working Trial Event in which dogs tested on agility, nosework, and ability to follow commands. In USA it is incorporated in Obedience Trials
Wrinkled Having loose, folded skin on forehead and face
Wrist The carpus

Index

Italicised page numbers refer to illustrations

Acknowledgements

The Publishers would like to thank the following individuals and organisations for their kind permission to reproduce the photographs in this book:–

J. Allan Cash: 186 above; Alton Anderson: 89 above, 103 bottom right, 145 above; Animal Graphics: 22, 38–39, 48 above, 65 above; Animal Photography: 17 centre, 18–19, 29 above, 35 above, 71 above, 82 centre left, 82 bottom left, 82 bottom right, (K. Barkleigh-Shute) 84 above, 84 bottom, 85 above, 85 bottom, 86–87 below, (Vloo) 87 above, 87 bottom right, 88 above, 89 bottom, 90, 91 bottom left, 92 bottom, 92–93 above, 94 above right, 97 bottom, 98 above, 98 bottom, 99, 100 above, 100 bottom left, (Vloo) 100 bottom right, 101, 103 bottom left, 105 above, 105 bottom, 107 bottom, 108 above, 108 bottom, 109 bottom, 110 bottom right, 110–111 above, 112, 113 bottom, 114 above left, 115 right, 116 bottom, 118 above, 118 bottom, 119, 120 above left, 120 bottom, 123 above left, 123 above right, 124 left, 125 bottom, 127, 128 centre, 128 bottom, 130 left, 130 right, 131 above, 131 bottom, 133 above left, 133 above right, 134 above, 134 bottom, 136 bottom, 138 above, 138 bottom left, 139, 140 above, 140 bottom, 141 above, 142 above right, 142 bottom, 144 right, 146 above left, 146 above right, 147, 149 above left, 149 bottom, 150 above, 150 below, 151 below, 152 above, 152 below, 153 above left, 153 below, 154 above left, 154 below, 155, 156 above, 156 centre, 156 below left, 156 below right, 157, 158, 159 above left, 159 above right, 159 below, 183 above, 187 below; Animals Unlimited: 2–3, 74 above, 75 below, 102 below left, 144 left; Ardea Ltd: (Ferrero) 137 below, (Ferrero) 178 above; Art Directors' Photo Library: 188 left; Aspect Picture Library: 188 right; K. Barkleigh-Shute: 52, 111 right, 145 below; British Airways: 79 inset; M. Buzzini: 93 below left, 106 below; Hanson Carroll: 4, 176–177, 187 above; Bruce Coleman Ltd: (Hirsch) 13, 21 above, (Reinhard) 104, 113 above, (Reinhard) 132, 172–173 below; Cooper Bridgeman Library: (Kenwood House) 16; Anne Cumbers: 50, 53 below, 96 below, 102–103, 109 above; A. Hamilton Rowan: 9, 170–171, 171;   Robert Harding Picture Library: 26–27; Michael Holford: 16–17 above; Alan Hutchison Library: 10–11; Jacana: (Labat) 7, (Varin-Visage) 25, (Labat) 63, (Mero Jacana) 94 above left, (Mero Jacana) 110 below left; Jayne Langdon: 164; Steve McCutcheon: 26, 180 left, 181 above, 181–182; John Moss: 1, 33, 45 above, 45 below, 46, 47, 60–61, 125 above, 141 below, 178 below; Diane Pearce: 133 below; Courtesy of Pedigree Petfoods: 24 above right, 24 bottom right, 24 below left; Philadelphia Museum of Art (purchased with funds from the American Museum of Photography): 15; Anne Roslin-Williams: 86 above left, 91 below right, 93 below left, 94 below, 95, 107 above, 114 above right, 121, 124 right, 126 above, 128 above left, 136 above, 142 above left, 143, 146 bottom, 148, 153 above right, 154 above right; Spectrum Colour Library: 65, 126 below; Michael Serlick: 30–31, 189; Guy Trouillet: 62, 67 below right; Courtesy of U.S. Treasury Customs Dept: 183 below; Mireille Vautier: 72 above; Zefa Picture Library: (Lemoine) Endpapers, (S. McKenna) 82–83, 91 above, 179.

Special Photography: Ray Block: 67 above, 71 below; Laurie Franklin Callahan: 21 below, 54 above, 56, 56–57, 58 above, 58 below, 59, 64, 69, 72 below, 75 above right, 76 left, 76–77 (inset), 182 above, 182 below; Jim Meads: 168, 169 above, 169 below left, 169 below right; John Moss: 54–55, 66–67, 68 left, 68 right, 73 above, 73 below, 78, 79, 88 below, 160–161, 162, 163 above left, 163 below left, 163 right, 165 left, 165 right, 166–167, 167 above, 167 below, 172, 173 above, 174, 175 above, 175 below, 184 above, 184 below, 185; Dick Polak: 44, 53 above, 75 above, left; Anne Roslin-Williams: 96 above, 97 above, 98 centre, 106 above, 114–115, 116 above, 117, 120 above right, 122–123 below, 128 above right, 134 centre, 137 above, 138 below right, 149 above right, 151 above left, 151 above right; Clive Sawyer: 20–21, 40, 42, 43, 43 (inset).

ILLUSTRATORS
Chris Blow: 49.
Frank Kennard: 23 below, 28, 29, 30, 31, 32/33, 33, 34/35, 37.
Studio Briggs: 12/13, 39.
Technical Art Services: 14, 23 top, 36, 41.